BTEC Level 3 National

Public Services

.3 1

Margaret Cronin
Marilyn Breeze
and Alan Spafford

DYNAMIC LEARNING

HODDER
EDUCATION
AN HACHETTE UK COMPANY

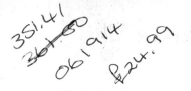

Orders: please contact Bookpoint Ltd, 130 Milton Park, Abingdon, Oxon OX14 4SB. Telephone: (44) 01235 827720. Fax: (44) 01235400454. Lines are open from 9.00–5.00, Monday to Saturday, with a 24 hour message answering service. You can also order through our website www.hoddereducation.co.uk.

British Library Cataloguing in Publication Data
A catalogue record for this title is available from the British Library

ISBN: 978 1 444 11550 5

First Published 2010
Impression number   10 9 8 7 6 5 4 3 2 1
Year   2012 2011 2010

Copyright © 2010 Marilyn Breeze, Alan Spafford, Margaret Cronin

Hachette UK's policy is to use papers that are natural, renewable and recyclable products and made from wood grown in sustainable forests. The logging and manufacturing processes are expected to conform to the environmental regulations of the country of origin.

Cover photo © Flying Colours Ltd.
Typeset by Fakenham Photosetting, Fakenham, Norfolk
Printed in Italy

Contents

Walkthrough

Prepare for what you are going to cover in this unit, and what you'll know by the end of it.

Learning outcomes:

By the end of this unit, you should:
1. Know the purpose and importance of public services skills

Helps you understand and remember key concepts and information.

Think about it!

Would you describe your class as a team? Or is it just a group of people in the same place at the same time?

Reinforce concepts with hands-on learning and generate evidence for assignments.

Activity 1

How many other qualities of a good instructor can you think of? Make a table and write the quality in one column and a description in the other.

A little question to help you evaluate and link key points.

Ask Yourself!

Should police community support officers have powers to arrest people?

Revise all those new words and what they mean.

Key terms

SMART stands for specific, measurable, achievable, relevant and time constrained.

Reminds you what you need to do to meet a grading requirement.

g Grading Tip!

To achieve a pass grade the evidence must show that you are able to:

P3 For P3, you need to identify the different skills required by public service workers, as discussed above, and explain a little about them.

Understand how your learning fits into real life and working environments.

Case Study

Firms fined over Hatfield crash
Two firms have been fined a total of £13.5 million for breaching health and safety regulations over the Hatfield train crash in 2000, in which four people died.

The comprehensive guide to what assessors will be looking for in your work.

Grading criteria

To achieve a pass grade the evidence must show that the you are able to:	To achieve a merit grade the evidence must show that, in addition to the pass criteria, you are able to:	To achieve a distinction grade the evidence must show that, in addition to the pass and merit criteria, you are able to:
P1 Outline the main purpose and roles of contrasting uniformed public services.	**M1** Explain in detail the role, purpose and responsibilities of contrasting uniformed public services.	**D1** Evaluate the role, purpose and responsibilities of a chosen uniformed public service.

This is your checklist for what you should know by the end of the unit!

End of Unit Knowledge check

1. List five ways in which public service employees can ensure they are in a fit state to carry out their duties.

Author biographies and Photo credits

About the authors

Marilyn Breeze had a long career in the public service sector, including working for the Police Service, the Education sector and Social Services before retraining as a lecturer in 1994. Marilyn is currently the Public Services Curriculum Co-Ordinator and lecturer at the Buxton College of Further Education, which is part of the University of Derby. She has also worked as an external verifer for a major awarding body for several years, has been involved with the writing of new specifications and has recently been appointed as a Standards Verifer and Centre Quality Reviewer. Marilyn has also recently been appointed and trained as a magistrate for her local area.

Margaret Cronin began working life as a police officer. She qualified as a teacher in 1992 and taught in English and Welsh schools, and achieved Master of Arts in Education in 1996. Margaret has also worked as a Registered Nursery Inspector carrying out inspections in pre-schools, day nurseries and independent schools. In 1997, she began lecturing in further education and was Programme Co-ordinator for Public Services. She is now an external verifier for a major awarding body and is involved in writing new specifications, from Level 1 to Level 5. Margaret is currently Director of her own training company.

Alan Spafford presently works with a major awarding body as an external verifier and has recently been appointed a Standards Verifier for Public Services and a Centre Quality Reviewer for the Midlands. He has been involved with sport and outdoor education all his working life for both private and Local Authority providers and is a former Departmental Head of Sport and Public Services at a Nottingham Further Education College. Alan has lectured on all levels of sport and public services courses for the last 18 years and presently lectures part-time at a FE college in Nottingham. Alan was recently involved in specification development for several major qualifications and is also a Peripatetic Internal Verifier for League Football Education on their Apprenticeship in Sporting Excellence course. His inspiration for writing this book comes from his two sons Jack and William.

Photo credits

The author and publishers would like to thank the following for permission to reproduce material in this book:

p. 2 © Canadian Press / Rex Features; p. 7 © Gregory Wrona / Alamy; p. 19 © PA Archive/Press Association Images; p. 25 © Brian J. Ritchie / Rex Features; p. 26 © Rex Features; p. 35 © Monkey Business Images / Rex Features; p. 54 © David Hartley / Rex Features; p. 58 Courtesy of Victim Support Cymru and Stonewall Cymru; p. 61 © INS News Agency Ltd. / Rex Features; p. 66 © Jeremy Selwyn / Evening Standard / Rex Features; p. 71 © Tim Rooke / Rex Features; p. 77 © Gregory Wrona / Alamy; p. 83 (top left) © Ingram Publishing Ltd; (top right) © Ingram Publishing Ltd; (bottom left) © Ingram Publishing Ltd; (bottom right) © Ingram Publishing Ltd; p. 88 © Ingram Publishing Ltd; p. 90 (left) © Ingram Publishing Ltd; (right) © Ingram Publishing Ltd; p. 91 © Ingram Publishing Ltd; p. 92 © Ingram Publishing Ltd; p. 93 © Ingram Publishing Ltd; p. 100 © 2003 Adam Pretty/Getty Images; p. 112 © Topical Press Agency/Getty Images; p. 120 © Extreme Sports Photo / Alamy; p. 158 © PA Archive/ Press Association Images; p. 162 © Heathcliff O'Malley / Rex Features; p. 179 © Atlantico/Press Association Images; p. 189 © SHOUT / Alamy; p. 192 © UPPA/Photoshot; p. 193 © Shout / Rex Features; p. 195 © Sally and Richard Greenhill / Alamy; p. 203 © pressmaster – Fotolia.com; p. 220 © Photofusion Picture Library / Alamy; p. 251 © PA Archive/ Press Association Images; p. 256 © 2006 Malte Christians/ Bongarts/Getty Images; p. 267 © Rex Features; p. 270 © John Birdsall/Press Association Images; p. 276 © Simon Price / Alamy; p. 276 © Per-Anders Pettersson/AFP/Getty Images; p. 278 Photo of Elibinayi Nzaylsenga, DA Events management, University of Greenwich; p. 281 © Margaret Cronin; p. 285 © Alex Segre / Rex Features; p. 292 © AP/ Press Association Images; p. 295 © Rex Features; p. 300 © Greater Manchester Police; p. 301 © Justin Williams / Rex Features; p. 304 © Ciaran McCrickard / Rex Features

Every effort has been made to obtain necessary permission with reference to copyright material. The publishers apologise if inadvertently any sources remain unacknowledged and will be glad to make the necessary arrangements at the earliest opportunity.

Unit 1
Government, policies and the public services

Introduction

This is a mandatory unit within all BTEC Level 3 National Public Services programmes. By studying this unit you will increase your knowledge and understanding of the government in the United Kingdom (UK), the democratic election process, how the government implements its policies and how these policies impact on UK public services.

Everyone in the UK is affected by the decisions made in government, whether they agree with these decisions or not.

Following the results of the General Election on 6th May 2010, no single party won sufficient seats to rule alone. The Conservative Party had the highest number of seats and now rule in a **coalition** government with the support of the Liberal Democrats. The Prime Minister and Leader of the Conservative Party is David Cameron. It is your responsibility to ensure that the information you provide for assessment is current.

Key term

Coalition – a **coalition** government is a cabinet of a parliamentary government in which two or more parties cooperate

Learning outcomes:

By the end of this unit, you should:

1. Know the different levels of government in the UK.

2. Understand the democratic election process for each level of government in the UK.

3. Know the impact of UK government policies on the public services.

4. Be able to demonstrate how government policies are developed.

Central government (also known as Parliament) in the UK is made up of (comprises) three elements:

- the House of Commons
- the House of Lords
- the Monarchy.

In a monarchy the king or queen is head of state. The UK is a 'constitutional monarchy', which means that the king or queen reigns, with limits to their power, alongside a governing body, Parliament.

Although the monarch is still symbolically the head of this type of constitution, in reality most of the powers have been transferred to ministers within government. In the UK the monarch performs a range of important duties, including giving 'Royal Assent' to laws passed by the UK and Scottish parliaments, the National Assembly in Wales and the Northern Ireland Assembly. The monarch also formally appoints the Prime Minister, other government ministers, judges, officers in the Armed Forces and other people.

Figure 1.1 The Palace of Westminster

Activity

Working in pairs, carry out research into the people who are appointed by the monarch in the UK.

Make a poster to display in your teaching room.

Activity

Carry out research into other countries that operate under a constitutional monarchy. Here are some to get you started:

- Belgium
- Spain
- Norway.

Make a list of the similarities and differences that exist in the countries you have investigated.

1.1 Know the different levels of government in the UK

P1 M1 P2 D1

The main levels of government that exist in the UK are central (national), regional and local. Government is paid for by the taxpayer, and is the main employer within the **public sector**. The UK is also one of 27 member states of the European Union (EU) and, as such, is subject to EU legislation.

Activity

Investigate the membership of the European Union. On a world map, identify the 27 member states and provide a brief history of the EU and its aims and purposes.

Central government

The UK central government is based at the Palace of Westminster, in London. This building is also referred to as the Houses of Parliament and comprises the House of Commons and the House of Lords. Central government is responsible for managing many different organisations that administer the ways in which policy and laws are carried out.

House of Commons

The four countries of the UK are divided into 650 areas of roughly the same population; these are known as constituencies. Each constituency elects a Member of Parliament (MP) to the House of Commons at each general election. On certain occasions there will also be a **by-election** in some areas, for example when an MP dies or resigns (or is removed) from office. The electoral system used in the UK, which will be explained in the next section, means that there are two parties that are traditionally stronger than all others. One of the political parties usually holds a majority in Parliament, which means

Key terms

By-election – an election that occurs when a Member of Parliament resigns, dies, or is disqualified or expelled
Public sector – a part of the state that deals with either the production, delivery and allocation of goods and services by and for the government or its citizens

that party has more MPs than all the others. If no party holds an outright majority, the party with the highest number of members might approach a smaller party to work with it in a coalition (as in the current situation with Conservative and Liberal Democrat parties).

House of Lords

Key terms

Hereditary peer – a title conferred on an individual and which, on their death, is passed on to the oldest son
Life peer – a title conferred on an individual but which is not passed on, and ends with the death of the holder

The House of Lords dates back to the fourteenth century and traditionally comprised those whose title was given because of their place in the Church of England, or who held a hereditary peerage (a title that passes automatically from one generation to the next). Not surprisingly the membership of the House of Lords was male-dominated but, with the appointment of more **life peers** and titles being awarded to both men and women, this pattern is changing. There are currently 26 'Lords Spiritual' (including 21 senior bishops) and almost 100 **hereditary peers**, alongside the appointed members.

The House of Lords reviews draft laws that have begun in the Commons. The Lords have the authority to recommend changes and may even prevent it from being passed into legislation by delaying their approval of the law. Sometimes the government will accept changes advised by the House of Lords to avoid unnecessary delays.

In addition to this legislative role, the House of Lords was, until recently, the highest court in the UK. If an appeal failed in other courts, people were able, in certain circumstances, to take their case to the Lords. This judicial function ceased when the Supreme

Court of the United Kingdom was introduced on 1 October 2009, as a result of the Constitutional Reform Act 2005.

Devolved national administrations

Devolved parliaments are the governments of Scotland, Wales and Northern Ireland. They carry out their roles in a similar way to the UK parliament, although they have fewer powers and responsibilities.

Scottish Government

The Scottish Government came about as a result of the Scotland Act 1998. It is responsible for devolved matters that include health, education and housing. The leader of the approximately 130 Members of the Scottish Parliament (MSPs) is called the First Minister (currently Alex Salmond). He is assisted by other MSPs. All these office holders are known as Scottish Ministers.

Welsh Assembly Government

The powers of the Welsh Assembly Government and the National Assembly for Wales are more limited than those given to Scotland. However, since the passing of the Government of Wales Act 2006, the Welsh Assembly can pass laws in some areas. The Welsh Assembly Government in power at the beginning of 2010 was formed soon after the 2007 (Welsh Assembly) election. Following a brief period of minority administration, Plaid Cymru joined Labour in a coalition government, currently under the leadership of Carwyn Jones.

Northern Ireland Executive

The Northern Ireland Executive and Assembly has powers similar to those in place in Scotland. At the time of writing, the Executive was led jointly by First Minister Peter Robinson (Democratic Unionist Party) and deputy First Minister Martin McGuinness (Sinn Fein).

Activity

The Regional Development Agencies Act 1998 (RDA) created eight regional assemblies in England, and another regional system in London. Identify the regions created by the RDA, then carry out research into the roles of each. This information could be presented on a map of England and displayed in the classroom for further reference.

Personnel within government

The leader of the party in power is known as the prime minister. At the time of writing this post is held by David Cameron, leader of the Conservative party. As you would expect from the title, the prime minister is the most senior member in the cabinet. He or she chairs cabinet meetings and selects ministers. The prime minister is also responsible for putting together government policy. In the past, the British monarch personally carried out these duties, but the day-to-day duties have now been passed to the prime minister. Although the prime minister is seen as being in charge, he or she is bound (in theory at least) to make decisions that have the support of the entire **cabinet**. While Parliament is 'in session', the cabinet usually meets twice a week.

Parliament is an integral part of the politics of the United Kingdom. Its main functions

Key term

Cabinet – the main government body that controls policy and co-ordinates the activities of governmental departments

are to examine and scrutinise the work of the government, debate and pass all new legislation and amendments to existing laws, and it also enables government to raise taxes. Part of this is done through the Customs and Excise Department. Within the UK government there are many departments, each led by a government minister whose title is often Secretary of State (e.g. Secretary of State for Education). This minister may be supported by a number of junior ministers. Several government departments cover the entire UK (for example, the Home Office and the Ministry of Defence), while others operate in England only, with devolved powers in Wales, Scotland and Northern Ireland.

An organisation known as the civil service carries out the decisions of government. This is a permanent body that is politically neutral, whose staff remain in post when the government changes – if it were determined by party loyalties there would be changes made at every election, and the work would not get done! Most government departments have their headquarters in and around the former Royal Palace in Whitehall, London, and because of this the centre of the civil service is often referred to as Whitehall.

National policy is dealt with by central government departments that include the Department for Education; the Department for Culture, Media and Sport; the Department of Health; the Department for Environment, Food and Rural Affairs; the Department for Transport.

In Wales, Northern Ireland and Scotland, the devolved governments work chiefly with the local authorities. The main link between local authorities and central government is the Communities and Local Government Department, which is responsible for national policy on how local government is set up, what it does, how well it works and how it is funded.

Branches of government

The making, approving and passing of laws in the UK is undertaken by three powers that work together to guarantee that the business of democracy is carried out in a straightforward manner, with as little disruption as possible.

The first branch is *legislative*, which has the power to make laws. This power is held by Parliament, comprising the House of Commons, the House of Lords and a number of parliamentary committees. As well as making new laws, Parliament has the power to reform old laws, if they need updating.

The *executive* branch has the power to suggest new laws, implement new laws and put the government's policy into practice. This work is undertaken by various government departments, the civil service and public services.

Finally, the *judicial* branch interprets the meaning of the law and decides if and where any laws have been broken. The responsibility for this is given to judges across all the courts of the land.

These three branches provide the separation of powers that protects the people of the UK against government actions that might be seen as unreasonable or extreme.

Local government

Local governments are arranged into one- or two-tier systems. Most of England and Wales adopt a two-tier system, having a county council and a district council. County councils are responsible for large areas and provide most public services, including schools, social services and public transport. Within each county there are smaller districts. The councils in these areas provide local services, such as housing, leisure and recycling. District councils are sometimes known as borough councils.

In most large towns and cities – and also in some small counties – there is just one level of local government that is responsible for all the services. This is called a unitary authority. In April 2009 unitary authorities were introduced into seven areas in England, replacing 44 local authorities.

Activity

Research the following types of local government:

- metropolitan district council
- borough council
- city council
- county council
- district council.

Work with the rest of the class to present your findings as a classroom display.

In Scotland there is a unitary system, with just one level of local government. Northern Ireland has local councils, but most services are carried out by other organisations. In some parts of England there are also town and parish councils, covering a smaller area. In Wales these are called community councils. These are sometimes described as the third tier of local government.

Some local authorities share services that cover a wider area, for example, police, fire service and public transport. England and Wales have a total of 43 police forces, while each of the 59 fire authorities across the whole of the UK is responsible for providing a firefighting service. The day-to-day operations of each fire service are the responsibility of the Chief Fire Officer (Firemaster in Scotland).

Local authorities are one of the biggest employers in the UK, totalling in excess of 2 million people. These include school teachers, social services, police, firefighters and many more who work in administrative roles within local authority organisations. The example in the case study demonstrates how a local authority has used its resources for the benefit of the local residents.

Case Study

Hammersmith and Fulham council in London has spent millions of pounds on its parks, and three of these have been awarded Green Flags. The Green Flag scheme encourages and rewards attainment in the management and maintenance of green spaces and promotes the enhancement of environmental protection, safety, cleanliness and accessibility.

The leader of the council, Stephen Greenhalgh, explained that the council has also opened the first new library in London for 40 years, the library at Shepherd's Bush (see Figure 1.2, opposite), which was built at no cost to the taxpayer, because major funding had been secured from the local Westfield shopping centre.

Many of the council staff have been relocated, meaning that all social care and support services are now available at the same place. This means that in excess of £350,000 has been saved on rents, council tax and other outgoings, and – most importantly – residents can access all services together.

Figure 1.2 The new Shepherd's Bush library

 Grading Tip!

To achieve P1 you will demonstrate that you understand the various levels of government and can provide an outline of responsibilities of each body. You might wish to use a diagram for this.

For M1 you will need to *explain* the responsibilities of each body at the different levels of government.

Government departments and public services

As outlined earlier in the chapter, there are many departments within central government. We will now examine some of these and investigate their roles. We will also consider how these departments affect UK public services.

Ministry of Justice

This department is responsible for strategy in the criminal and civil justice system. It sets policy on sentencing of offenders and includes the administration of the courts, tribunals and **constitutional reform**. When a suspect has been charged with a criminal offence, the way in which they are dealt

with – including court appearances and, if necessary, prison and probation – are the responsibility of the Ministry of Justice.

> **Key term**
>
> **Constitutional reform** – a major change to the constitution of a nation or state

Department for Education

This department, created in May 2010, was formerly known as the Department for Children, Schools and Families (DCSF). The stated aim of the DCSF was 'to make this [the UK] the best place in the world for children and young people to grow up.' (**www.dcsf.gov.uk**)

At the time of writing, the Department for Education is responsible for all aspects of teaching and otherwise supporting children and young people, and their families. It also seeks to ensure that children and young people achieve well and are provided with opportunities to pursue appropriate career choices. The Children's Plan seeks to accomplish the following five goals:

● to secure the wellbeing and health of children and young people
● to safeguard the young and the vulnerable
● to ensure an excellent education for all children and young people
● to keep them on the path to success
● to provide more places for children to play safely.

Department for Business, Innovation and Skills

This is one of the newest departments within the UK parliament and it was formed by merging the former Department for Business, Enterprise and Regulatory Reform and the Department for Innovation, Universities and Skills. The main role of this new department is to improve the means by which the UK can compete in a global economy and to build the UK's future economic strengths and create the jobs needed by the UK in the future.

Home Office

The Home Office is the department responsible for the Police Service. It also aims to reduce and prevent crime. It deals with passports and immigration and is also actively involved in counter-terrorism and drugs policies that affect the UK. Through these areas the Home Office seeks to ensure the safety of the UK and its citizens. The title of the person in charge of the Home Office is the Home Secretary.

Ministry of Defence

The MoD is the government department responsible for the Armed Forces in the UK: the Army, Royal Navy and Royal Air Force. The MoD decides how much money needs to be spent on defence, and also what equipment is needed by Armed Forces personnel.

Accountability of public services

In order that the public services carry out their roles and responsibilities in a way that should command the respect and trust of the public, there are a number of bodies which oversee their work and monitor their performance. It is, after all, the public that pays for the public services so they have a right to know that their investment is being used wisely. The major exception to this

arrangement is the Armed Forces, which inspect themselves. This was the case with the Police Service before the introduction in 2004 of the Independent Police Complaints Commission. Although it is funded by the Home Office, the IPCC is an independent body and remains free of government influence.

Table 1.1 provides information about some of the organisations that monitor the work of the public services in the UK. Additionally, local organisations exist to ensure that the day-to-day running of the services is carried out in an appropriate manner, and to act accordingly if complaints are made against the service. Examples of these local bodies include the Police Authority, the Strategic Health Authority and the Fire and Rescue Authority.

Every public service also needs to show that it is able to be accountable by the information it provides. They are required to produce a number of official documents which are then available for public scrutiny. These documents include a mission statement (which you will research when you begin your application in earnest) and an annual report, which provides information on how well the service has met its financial and performance targets.

As stated earlier, complaints made against the Police Service are investigated by the Independent Police Complaints Commission. The following case study describes how the IPCC investigated such a complaint, and the eventual outcome of the case.

Table 1.1 Roles of public services inspectorates

Body	Public service	Role
Inspectorate of Prisons, Probation, Police	Prison Service, Probation, Police	Inspection of organisations to ensure that aims are carried out
Defence Vetting Agency	Armed Forces Ministry of Defence	Carry out national security checks on personnel

Case Study

On Monday 8 February 2010, Ali Dizaei, a serving officer in the Metropolitan Police, was convicted of 'misconduct in public office' and 'perverting the course of justice'. The jury at Southwark Crown Court took less than three hours to find Mr Dizaei guilty of attacking Mr Waad al-Baghdadi outside a restaurant, then arresting him and falsely accusing him of assault.

In evidence Mr al-Baghdadi stated that many people were afraid of Mr Dizaei because of his influence in the local community. The jury was also told that the officer regularly left his police car on yellow lines while he ate at the restaurant, and that he did not pay for his meals.

In passing sentence, the judge, Mr Justice Simon, described the four-year sentence as a clear message that police officers are not above the law. He added that this applied regardless of an officer's rank, and that Mr Dizaei had shown a grave abuse of public trust.

Mr al-Baghdadi was praised by the Crown Prosecution Service (CPS) for having the courage to give evidence in court. A CPS spokesman described the corruption as deplorable, especially as the offender was a high ranking police officer at the time of the crime.

The IPCC described Mr Dizaei as 'a criminal in uniform' and added that he was 'a threat to the reputation of the Police Service'. It is the IPCC that will decide on any other punishment of Mr Dizaei; it has the power to remove him from office and to force him to give up any right to the pension he had accrued during his 24 years' service.

Update:

In March 2010, Mr Dizaei was removed from his position with the Metropolitan Police, following a tribunal hearing for misconduct. This means that, in addition to losing his £90,000 a year salary, he is likely to lose his pension, estimated to be in the region of £60,000 annually.

Think about it!

Do you believe that a member of the public services, convicted of a serious criminal charge, should lose everything they have worked towards during their career? Provide reasons for your answers.

(g) Grading Tip!

To achieve P2 you will need to identify *at least two* government departments and give an explanation of their responsibilities for a particular public service.

D1 requires an *evaluation* of these responsibilities. You might wish to consider the case study provided or investigate what is going on in your local area, and evaluate whether the body has in fact provided a satisfactory service.

1.2 Know the democratic election process for each level of government in the UK

Direct democracy refers to the right of every citizen over a certain age to attend political meetings and vote on the issue being discussed. There is also an assumption that the result of that vote will be accepted by all. It gives all people the right to take part, and does not take account of religious beliefs, gender, sexual orientation or physical wellbeing. In the UK only those serving a term of imprisonment are excluded from being directly involved in the democratic process; when they are released their democratic rights are restored.

The electoral process

The electoral process in the UK is known as representative democracy. This means the citizens elect representatives to make decisions on their behalf.

General elections

An elected government may preside for a maximum of five years. However, sometimes the prime minister will decide to call a general election before the entire term has been served. All those eligible to do so have the opportunity to vote into power those they wish to be their spokesperson in Parliament. The candidate with the highest number of votes is declared the Member of Parliament for that area. This method of voting is known as 'first past the post' and the party with the most members forms the next government. Each elected person (MP) represents an area called a constituency.

The MPs are accountable to the people they represent. If they fail to perform satisfactorily they can be removed by their constituents (the voters in their constituency). In practice the MP will either take into account the wishes of the citizens who have voted them into office, or they will take matters into their own hands and make decisions according to their own conscience.

Think about it!

Is it realistic for elected MPs to do what the voters wish *all the time* – or should they be able to exercise their own thoughts and beliefs?

When we remember that an MP generally received votes from only a majority of voters in the constituency, should they also take into account the wishes of those who voted for other candidates?

What about the citizens who did not vote – should they be represented?

Local elections

The rules that govern the timing of local elections are extremely complicated, and mean that voters in some areas of the UK vote at different times from others.

All councillors in English county councils, London borough councils and most of the non-metropolitan district councils must be elected every four years. In each of the three years when county council elections are not held, all other district councils and the metropolitan districts hold elections, when one-third of the total number of councillors are elected. A small number of district councils hold elections every two years – half of the councillors in these districts are elected on each occasion.

In Scotland, Wales and Northern Ireland all councillors are elected every four years.

European elections

The European Parliament is selected every five years. The most recent election was in 2009. There are 72 Members of the European Parliament (MEP) who represent the UK in Strasbourg. The UK is divided into just 12 regions, and each region has between three and ten MEPs.

The system of voting for MEPs differs from that for MPs. MEPs are elected by means of proportional representation. Each party publishes a list of candidates and voters choose one of these, or they may choose an independent candidate (one who holds no allegiance to any of the parties). The parties are then allocated a certain number of MEPs in relation to their share of the overall vote.

The home of the European Parliament is in Strasbourg, France. It meets in full session for one week in every month. For the remainder of the time the MEPs meet with specialist committees in Brussels, Belgium. The European Parliament shares a great deal of power with the Council of Ministers.

Voting

British citizens over the age of 18 who are on the electoral register (roll) are eligible to vote in elections. Currently there are approximately 2.5 million UK citizens living in other countries who are eligible to vote in UK elections. However, the vast majority of these citizens are not on the electoral register, so are not eligible. Many Commonwealth citizens living in the UK, and citizens of the Irish Republic and European Union are eligible to vote, as long as they reside in the UK and are registered on the electoral roll in their local area.

Key term

By proxy – if you vote by proxy you appoint another person to vote on your behalf

There are three ways in which citizens can cast their vote in the UK, and each individual decides which method is most suitable for their situation. Most people choose to cast their vote in person, while others select a postal vote, or can apply to vote **by proxy** – this means appointing someone to vote for them.

Those who wish to vote in person will receive a polling card that gives information on when and where they should vote – often a school, church or village hall is used for this purpose. Below is a step-by-step guide on how to vote in person at a polling station.

On election day you will:

- go to your local polling station (opening hours 7 a.m. to 10 p.m.)
- tell the staff your name and address
- take the ballot paper from a member of staff (this paper lists all candidates)
- take this paper into a polling booth
- read the paper carefully
- put a cross alongside the name of the candidate you want to select
- fold the paper in half and put it into the ballot box.

You should not let anyone else see who you have chosen. However, if you need assistance for any part of the process the staff at the polling station will be able to advise you.

Some people choose to register their vote in a postal ballot. An application for a postal vote can be made by anyone over 18 years old who is on the electoral register. If approved, the vote will be sent to the address identified on the form, about a week before the date of the election, to allow time for its return.

To apply for a postal vote:

- complete and sign an application form
- return the form to the relevant address
- when you receive your vote, complete and return it by the date stated.

If your vote arrives after the polling stations have closed it will not be counted.

The remaining method of voting is by proxy. This can be very useful for someone who wishes to vote but is unable to get to the polling station themselves. Examples of this could be if you are physically unable to vote in person, or if you will be away on holiday on the date of the election. Many proxy votes are granted to members of the Armed Forces, deployed overseas at election time.

Process for voting by proxy:

- complete and sign an application form
- return the form to the electoral registration office in your constituency.

Usually you must apply for a by proxy vote at least six days before the date of an election but, in the event of a medical emergency, you might be able to apply later than this.

You may appoint anyone to vote on your behalf provided that they too are eligible to vote in the election and are willing to cast your vote – you will probably wish to appoint someone who holds the same political views as you do! You cannot be a proxy for more than two people at any election.

(g) Grading Tip!

To achieve P3 you will need to provide evidence that you fully understand the process for at least one type of election (remember to say which level of government you are describing). Remember, you should describe the entire process from beginning to end and explain what type of voting system is used.

For M2 you will need to compare the election process for *at least two* levels of government (e.g. local and European).

1.3 Know the impact of UK government policies on the public services

P4 P5 M3 D2

Policies affecting public services

The UK government regularly publishes its policies, many of which will have an effect on the way in which public services operate. Some of these policies will affect all public services, for example those surrounding the need to operate within the law, such as laws related to human rights and equal opportunities. As with all UK employers, the public services are duty bound to incorporate the requirements of the legislation into their organisation. This could mean they have to employ extra staff or make adjustments for staff with a physical disability. These arrangements often result in extra costs to the organisation.

Grading Tip!

To achieve P4 you will need to provide a description of two government policies and explain how each policy has impacted on two public services.

Think about it!

In the example of the 'Building Britain's Recovery' policy, which public services do you believe will be affected by the scheme? Discuss this as a class, and remember to look beyond the obvious service, Job Centre Plus.

One of the measures of how well a government is performing at any given time is the 'unemployment register'. This is information published about the number of people who are not in work or education, and are eligible to receive financial benefits. In a bid to reduce the number of unemployed people in the UK, the government has announced its policy 'Building Britain's Recovery: Achieving Full Employment'. In December 2009 Yvette Cooper, Work and Pensions Secretary, announced that everyone under 25 years of age who had been unemployed for six months would be 'guaranteed a job, training or work experience'. This would amount to more than 100,000 people being removed from the unemployment figures. The cost of this initiative was estimated to be

£400 million, over a period of 18 months. Plans were also announced to provide assistance for unemployed older people, lone parents and carers.

Environmental policies

Environmental issues are widespread; we are always being warned about the need to save energy so that there will be enough to meet the needs of a growing population. The Sustainable Development Commission is an independent adviser, reporting to the government on environmental issues.

In November 2009, the Sustainable Development Commission (SDC) and the National Health Service (NHS) launched an interactive website, for use by health professionals, to demonstrate how health professionals can help to save money while at the same time making the NHS more sustainable. The model demonstrates how reducing energy consumption and waste, and also helping to prevent illness, can help the NHS to make big savings and provide benefits to patients, communities and the environment.

At the launch of the initiative, the NHS Chief Executive David Nicholson recognised that the NHS has a massive carbon footprint and called upon all those involved to adopt the model to 'attack the issue and make a difference on climate change'. The NHS is one of the biggest energy users in the UK.

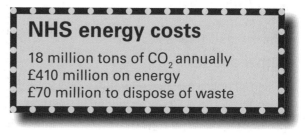

NHS energy costs

18 million tons of CO_2 annually
£410 million on energy
£70 million to dispose of waste

Living within environmental limits Respecting the limits of the planet's environment, resources and biodiversity – to improve our environment and ensure that the natural resources needed for life are unimpaired and remain so for future generations.	**Ensuring a strong, healthy and just society** Meeting the diverse needs of all people in existing and future communities, promoting personal wellbeing, social cohesion and inclusion, and creating equal opportunity.

Achieving a sustainable economy Building a strong, stable and sustainable economy which provides prosperity and opportunities for all, and in which environmental and social costs fall on those who impose them (polluter pays), and efficient resource use is incentivised.	**Using sound science responsibly** Ensuring policy is developed and implemented on the basis of strong scientific evidence, whilst taking into account scientific uncertainty (through the precautionary principle) as well as public attitudes and values.	**Promoting good governance** Actively promoting effective, participative systems of governance in all levels of society – engaging people's creativity, energy and diversity.

Figure 1.3 Sustainable development principles

Source: www.sd-commission.org.uk

Case Study

By redirecting waste from landfill and increasing domestic waste recycling (from just 4% to over 60%), an NHS trust in England was able save over £150,000. Another trust, in Wales, is expecting to save over half a million pounds and cut its carbon (CO_2) emissions by over 2,000 tons every year by adopting a combined heat and power system.

Activity

Carry out research into how your school or college manages any scheme that will encourage staff and students to be involved in saving energy, recycling materials or donating items for others to use.

Visit the website www.reducereuserecycle.co.uk for ideas on how you might begin a campaign at your place of study.

Other policies

Another policy that has affected public services was the Labour Government's Declaration of War on Iraq, on 20 March 2003. This led to the UK's Armed Forces being deployed in that country until 2009, alongside American and NATO personnel – a period longer than the Second World War. By the end of the conflict no fewer than 179 British service personnel had been killed, with many more injured and needing long-term care.

Possibly one of the widest-ranging government policies is that of the announcement, in April 2009, by the Department for Innovation in Universities and Skills that there would be drastic cuts in the amount of finance for universities. It was feared that this could lead to the loss of over 15,000 jobs in higher education, many of which could be in teaching staff, leading to the cancellation of a number of courses. In the worst-case scenario there were fears that some university campuses would have to close as a result of these economic cuts. In his pre-budget speech on 9 December 2009, the Chancellor (Alastair Darling) said that £600 million would be saved from across higher education. This figure would include amounts set aside for science and research, as well as support for students. At the same time, 2010 saw a very high increase in the number of applications from those wishing to begin university courses.

Initially this policy would seem to affect only the education sector but, when you consider that many staff at these establishments could lose their jobs, it would also put a strain on employment services. Also consider that there could be a great number of people unable to secure a place at a university – the knock-on effect could be that there are not enough suitably trained people to take up positions within organisations that demand highly skilled personnel.

ⓖ Grading Tip!

For P5 you may extend this information to include a discussion on how society has been affected by the policies you have described.

When attempting M3 you will need to *explain* how the policies have had an effect on each of the public services. You will need to include information on how government policies can be influenced by different groups, or social factors.

Finally, to be awarded D2, you must *evaluate* the impact of each of the government policies on all of the public services you have identified, and also on the communities that they serve.

Activity

Research some other policies that were announced by the Labour Government. Some examples are provided here, to get you started:

- **funding home care for the elderly and disabled**

- **introduction of body scanners at UK airports**

- **identity cards for UK citizens.**

Have all of these (and others you have identified yourself) become operational, or have they now been taken off the agenda?

1.4 Be able to demonstrate how government policies are developed

P6 **M4**

Government policies arise in response to a range of situations that occur outside Parliament. These might include promises that the parties made in their **manifesto** at the election, or a heightened threat of terrorism which means the government needs to change some of its operations. The major newspapers regularly publish **opinion polls** and, as a result, the government

Stages in the passage of a Public Bill

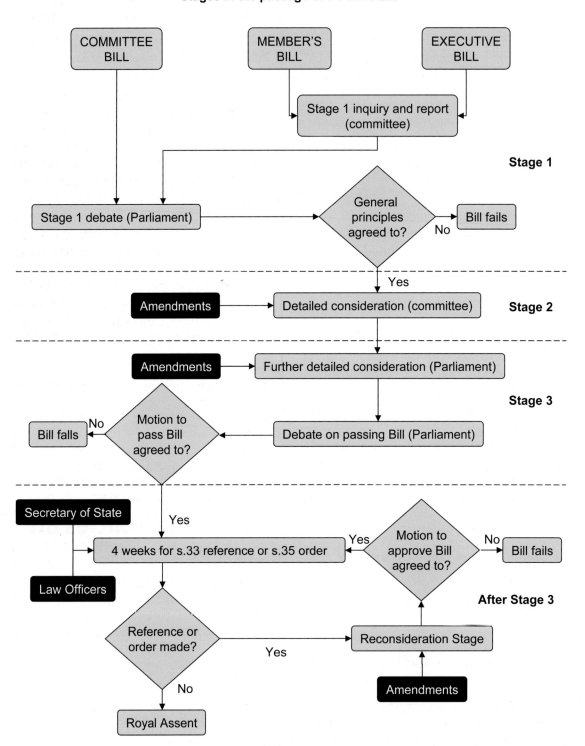

Figure 1.4 A Bill's journey through Parliament

Key terms

Green paper – a consultation document, to find out if there is sufficient interest in the suggested policy

Manifesto – a document that sets out what a political party will do, if they get into power

Opinion poll – an examination of the popularity of the major parties at anytime, based upon the responses given by a portion of the electorate

Royal Assent – the final stage of an Act becoming law, when it receives official approval from the monarch

White paper – a proposal for the new law, follows on after initial consultation is over

it becomes a more formal proposal and is written into a document known as a **white paper**. Within a relatively short period of time this proposal (now known as a Bill) will be put before Parliament to begin its journey through both Houses.

Before an Act of Parliament can become law it must pass through seven different stages, as outlined in Figure 1.4. When approval has been granted for the legislation, and any necessary alterations made, a date will be decided for its introduction. Sometimes this will be the same date as it receives **Royal Assent**; in other cases the bodies responsible for implementing the law need time to train their workforce, so the date on which the law comes into force is later than the date of the Act. Examples of this delay include the Police and Criminal Evidence Act (PACE), which was passed in 1984 but did not apply until 1986. Similarly, the Human Rights Act (1998) came into force on 2 October 2000.

might decide that a change to existing policy is necessary in order to increase their popularity in these polls.

When the government decides to implement a new policy there will be a series of meetings, attended by the cabinet and some other ministers. If the idea is met with a positive response, the process becomes formal and the idea is put into a **green paper**. The aim of a green paper is to ascertain the views of any interested person or organisation on the introduction of the proposed law. Public meetings could be held, focus groups might be set up and MPs will take the issue to their constituencies; people may respond by letter or email.

Once the general consultation period is over, if there is still support for the policy

⑨ Grading Tip!

To achieve P6 you need to *demonstrate* how government policies are developed. This could be carried out as a class activity to ensure that everyone has shown that they have fully understood the ways in which policies begin, and has participated in discussion and debate.

If you are attempting M4 you will need to provide an *analysis* of the developmental process.

End-of-unit knowledge check

1. Explain how the elements in the UK parliament provide a constitutional democracy.
2. Name the leaders of the main political parties in the United Kingdom.
3. Describe the role of the IPCC and the role of the Home Office.
4. Explain what is meant by Royal Assent.
5. Identify three factors that can affect government policy.

Grading criteria

In order to pass this unit, the evidence you present for assessment needs to demonstrate that you can meet all the learning outcomes for the unit. The criteria for a pass grade describe the level of achievement required to pass this unit.

To achieve a pass grade the evidence must show that you are able to:	To achieve a merit grade the evidence must show that, in addition to the pass criteria, you are able to:	To achieve a distinction grade the evidence must show that, in addition to the pass and merit criteria, you are able to:
P1 Outline the responsibilities of the levels of government in the UK	**M1** Explain in detail the responsibilities of the different levels of government in the UK	**D1** Evaluate the responsibilities of the different levels of government in the UK
P2 Describe the role of government departments in relation to public services including their responsibilities		
P3 Explain the electoral processes used in UK elections	**M2** Compare the electoral processes used at different levels of government in the UK	
P4 Describe, with examples, the impact of government policies on different public services	**M3** Explain the impact of different government policies on a range of public services	**D2** Evaluate the impact of government policies on public services and the communities they serve [IE4]
P5 Identify how society is affected by government policies		
P6 Demonstrate how government policies are developed [SM3]	**M4** Analyse how government policies are developed	

Unit 2
Leadership and teamwork in the public services

Introduction

Together

Everyone

Achieves

More

Good leadership and teamwork are at the heart of every public service. Public services employees regularly work in teams and rely on each other to carry out their individual roles effectively. This unit aims to explain the importance of good leadership and teamwork in the context of the public services. The consequences of a team not operating effectively could mean the difference between life and death in some services.

This unit will provide you with the theories relating to leadership and teamwork in a public services context, and will then help you to put the theory into practice, while developing your own teamwork and leadership skills. These skills include communication skills, time management skills, personal organisation skills and others which any public service employer will value. You will also learn about the different leadership styles and team roles.

Figure 2.1 Royal Marines working as a team

Learning outcomes:

By the end of this unit, you should:

1. Understand the styles of leadership and the role of a team leader.

2. Be able to communicate effectively to brief and debrief teams.

3. Be able to use appropriate skills and qualities to lead a team.

4. Be able to participate in teamwork activities within the public services.

5. Understand team development.

2.1 Understand the styles of leadership and the role of a team leader

Different styles of leadership used in public services

There are several different styles of leadership used in the public services – we are going to look at the main ones.

Democratic

This is a style of leadership where all members of the team are consulted and encouraged to be fully involved. Team members are allowed to use and develop their individual skills and expertise, which gives them a sense of value and raises morale. They feel valued and will develop a sense of ownership and responsibility for the success of the operation or project. The team leader still maintains control of the team and will make final decisions after drawing on input from the team.

Democratic leadership is not entirely suitable in some public services, as consulting all team members can be a lengthy process.

Case Study

A six-year-old girl has been reported missing to the police after disappearing from a playground near her home. A man had been seen acting suspiciously near the playground. The Police Superintendent has called all his officers to a briefing. He has asked all the officers for their opinions and views on what action should be taken. He has also asked the officers to think about their own individual skills and then to say which tasks they would prefer to carry out in the investigation.

1. Which style of leadership is the Police Superintendent using?
2. Do you think this leadership style is appropriate in the circumstances?
3. Give reasons for your answer.

Laissez-faire

The *laissez-faire* leadership approach can also be known as the 'hands-off' approach or the delegative approach. With this style of leadership the leader relinquishes control of the team and '**delegates**' control to the

Advantages of democratic leadership

- Team members feel in control.
- Team morale is raised.
- Sharing of skills and expertise leads to improved team performance.
- There is less of a 'power gap' between the team leader and team members.

Disadvantages of democratic leadership

- Process of consultation and discussion can be time-consuming and lengthy.
- Could lead to some confusion among team members about who is in control.

Key term

Delegate – to give authority, or hand over a task, to someone else

rest of the group. This means that the group is given power and freedom to establish their own roles and responsibilities and to make decisions for themselves. It requires trust on the part of the leader, who may find it difficult to hand over authority to others. This style can work well when the team is highly motivated and well trained, but can cause problems if the team members are not experienced enough to take on a leadership role.

This approach would be useful to use when different projects or exercises require specialist knowledge and expertise. One leader is not likely to have expert knowledge of all subjects and in this case control may be handed over to a team who do have the necessary skills and subject knowledge.

The *laissez-faire* style of leadership would not be appropriate where team members are lacking in experience, as they may require strong leadership and direction. It should not be used by leaders to delegate responsibility in order to cover up their own incompetence or lack of leadership skills.

Authoritarian or autocratic

Authoritarian or autocratic leadership is generally considered to be a traditional type of leadership where a leader wants to retain as much power as possible. This type of leader will make decisions and give orders to group members on what should be done, when it should be completed, and how it should be accomplished without any consultation with other group members. Although this is not always thought to be the best form of leadership, it is well suited to use in certain environments such as the armed forces, Police Service and Prison Service – settings where the lives of people depend on others following orders strictly to the letter. Appropriate use of the authoritarian style of leadership includes situations where the leader has all the information and knowledge to resolve a problem, or where there is insufficient time to consult others. Abuse of this style, however, can create a 'bullying' environment.

Bureaucratic

This style of leadership exists in organisations which are governed by rules, policies and procedures. It is based on extensive use of paperwork, administration, record-keeping and 'ticking boxes'. Large organisations such as local authorities may use this approach.

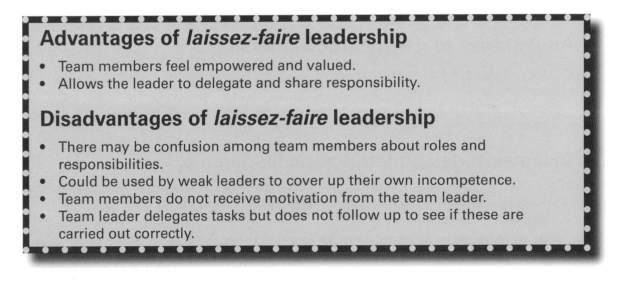

Advantages of *laissez-faire* leadership

- Team members feel empowered and valued.
- Allows the leader to delegate and share responsibility.

Disadvantages of *laissez-faire* leadership

- There may be confusion among team members about roles and responsibilities.
- Could be used by weak leaders to cover up their own incompetence.
- Team members do not receive motivation from the team leader.
- Team leader delegates tasks but does not follow up to see if these are carried out correctly.

Advantages of authoritarian leadership

- Should ensure that decisions are made by people with the appropriate knowledge.
- Order and discipline are maintained.
- Enables decisions to be made very quickly.
- Public services can be deployed quickly.
- Inexperienced trainees receive clear direction.

Disadvantages of authoritarian leadership

- Does not allow other team members to take responsibility and initiative.
- Motivation is often through fear.
- Respect of the team may be for the ranks of the leaders rather than for their qualities.
- May cause resentment among the team.
- Other team members may feel devalued.
- Could lead to low morale and poor performance by the team.

Case Study

The Chief Constable has called a meeting of his Chief Superintendents to discuss the targets which the service has been given by the Police Authority.

The aim is to reduce the number of incidents the police need to attend caused by young people drinking alcohol in the neighbouring towns. The largest number of complaints is from local residents experiencing minor damage to their property, littering of cans, bottles, etc. and noise nuisance.

Two Chief Superintendents return to their respective divisions and call a meeting of their Chief Inspectors and Inspectors.

One Chief Superintendent reports the problem and asks his staff to think about how it should be tackled. He asks them to go away, tackle the problems and report back in two months' time.

The other Chief Superintendent calls a meeting where he allocates tasks to each member of staff. He instructs one officer to arrange for all local public houses to be visited to warn them about serving alcohol to those under 18 years of age. He then instructs another officer to visit local off-licences and another to organise a series of meetings with local youth groups. A further officer is instructed to arrange for visits to be made to local schools and colleges. He tells all the officers that he wants a report from each of them in three weeks' time to let him know how they are progressing.

1. What two styles of leadership are being used above?
2. Which of the two styles do you think would be most effective in this situation? Why?

However, many other public services, both uniformed and non-uniformed, could use this leadership style, which is only suitable in organisations that are very structured. This is considered to be a classic style of leadership which does not generally promote creativity or innovative thinking. If this style is overused there could be a danger that team/staff members can become inflexible in their working practices and lacking in initiative and motivation.

Advantages of bureaucratic leadership

- Policies and practices are adhered to.
- Ensures order and routine.
- There is a clear structure.

Disadvantages of bureaucratic leadership

- Team members can become demotivated.
- There is a lack of creativity and innovation.
- Procedures and systems can be very rigid.
- Can be very labour intensive and unproductive.

Activity

Think of three leaders, either past or present. Think about their leadership style, and make a note of these.

Transactional

This is a leadership style which uses rewards or penalties as a means of leading a team. It could be classed as similar to the autocratic style of leadership in that the team leader tends to be fairly dominating, using rewards and penalties as a means of power and control. Some private organisations will pay large bonuses as an incentive to those who perform well, but this can be demotivating for those people who are not motivated purely by financial rewards.

Advantages of trans-actional leadership

- The work of team members is constantly monitored by the team leader.
- All tasks, including mundane, routine tasks, are completed and monitored.
- There is a clear command structure.

Disadvantages of trans-actional leadership

- Team members do not get job satisfaction as they are more focussed on the rewards and penalties.
- Team members have to do whatever their leader tells them to do, or face penalties.

Transformational

Transformational leaders are inspirational leaders who are very passionate in their beliefs and will try to inspire others to 'sign up' to their beliefs and ideas. These leaders are usually charismatic people who lead by example. They demonstrate good practice to show the team how they should behave.

Advantages of trans-formational leadership

- Team members will look up to these leaders and try to copy them.
- They boost morale among the team members.

Disadvantages of trans-formational leadership

- If the leader's vision and beliefs are wrong, the team may still follow the example they are setting.
- They sometimes fail to consider the detail by looking only at the overall finished picture.

Task-orientated

This is a style of leadership where the task is given the utmost importance. This style of leader will plan the task, put structures in place and make every arrangement necessary to complete the task without giving any thought to the needs and wishes of the team members.

Case Study

Love him or hate him, you have to admire the achievements of Alan Sugar. Born in 1947, his passion and enthusiasm have enabled him to rise above his humble beginnings in London's East End to become one of the UK's most successful businessmen, with an estimated net worth of £800 million.

Always able to detect an opportunity, Sugar started out in business at the age of 12, making ginger beer and selling it to neighbours. At the age of 21, Sugar set up his own company, Amstrad, and what started out as a small enterprise soon became an international consumer electronics, telecommunications and computer group. It now has wholly owned subsidiaries across Europe and a worldwide presence through a network of distributors.

Sugar's experience and expertise are highly valued and he is one of the UK government's team of figureheads travelling around schools and universities encouraging entrepreneurial spirit among young people.

His success is definitely not based on popularity; in fact, Sugar readily describes his personal style as up-front, sometimes belligerent, with high expectations of

Figure 2.2 Sir Alan Sugar

everyone. Viewers of the BBC series *The Apprentice* have witnessed his direct honest style as he ruthlessly exposes the weaknesses of the final 14 (out of 10,000 individuals) fighting for a place at his side.

A strong believer in the power of ownership, Sugar understands the importance of inclusion and good communication. Leading from the front, he expects self-discipline, relentless effort and 'hard graft' from all those on his team. Those who live up to his expectations are rewarded with both his respect and his loyalty.

By Melanie Smith
Source: www.leader-values.com/Content/detail.asp?ContentDetailID=1097
© Melanie Smith at www.leader-values.com

People-orientated

This style of leadership is the opposite of task-orientated leadership. The happiness of the team members is paramount and more importance is placed on the wellbeing of the team than on the completion of the task. Leaders of people-orientated teams will find out the strengths and skills of team members and will then work with these. This ensures that members feel valued and supported, and this style of leadership promotes good teamwork and high team morale.

The role of the team leader in public services

Just as there are many different teams in the public services, there are also many different team leader roles. In the uniformed public services there are teams within teams, and each team has a leader. Each team leader will be part of a team of leaders and they, in turn will also have a team leader.

Position

When referring to the position a person holds, we are referring to the rank, the office or the post held by the leader. The uniformed public services have a very clear rank structure, as shown in Table 2.1.

Table 2.1 The rank structure of the Police Service

	Rank
9	Chief Constable
8	Deputy Chief Constable
7	Assistant Chief Constable
6	Chief Superintendent
5	Superintendent
4	Chief Inspector
3	Inspector
2	Sergeant
1	Police Constable

Figure 2.3 Chief Constable of Police

Commanding Officer

Leaders in the armed forces are usually called Commanding Officers. They may be in charge of a post, base, camp or station and will be responsible for the wellbeing of service personnel, and the control of finances and equipment. Commanding Officers have usually worked their way up through the ranks to attain this position of responsibility.

Case Study

The person in charge of a prison is called the Governor.

A Governor's work may involve supervising security, making inspections, carrying out disciplinary procedures, writing reports and liaising with other professional staff who visit the prison, such as medical staff, probation officers and social workers. Other responsibilities include training, working on admissions and sitting on parole boards.

Responsibilities

The responsibilities of Commanding Officers will vary, depending on the position they hold and the people they command. Responsibilities could include:

- strategic management
- making mission statements
- identifying and setting goals
- maintaining discipline
- monitoring and reviewing performance
- delegating tasks to others.

Coordinate multi-agencies

Multi-agency teams are teams combining members of different services or agencies, which have been set up for a particular purpose, e.g. Crime Reduction Partnerships. The Commanding Officer must be flexible and be able to adapt to the different needs and priorities of the new team that has been created.

Grading Tip!

To achieve the P1 grade you should describe the different styles of leadership, and explain which styles could be used in the public services, giving examples.

To obtain the M1 grade you need to compare the different styles of leadership and explain how they would be used in the public service, giving examples. For example, which leadership style is the most appropriate to be used in the armed forces? Which would be most suitable for a local council organisation? Comparisons should point out the similarities and differences in the styles used, noting any impacts that these styles may have on the roles they perform.

To achieve the D1 grade you should evaluate the different leadership styles that are used in the public services. Give examples of these and explain why different styles may be

needed in different services and different situations. Analyse how effective these different styles are.

2.2 Be able to communicate effectively to brief and debrief teams

P3 M2

Effective communication is essential in all public services, and especially in the uniformed services where lives may be at stake.

Communication

Communication is only effective where information is conveyed, received and understood. It is most important that a leader possesses good verbal (speaking) communication skills in order to brief and debrief teams effectively. However, in addition to good verbal skills, a good leader will demonstrate good non-verbal communication skills (or body language) while speaking to the team. Other communication skills, such as reading, writing and listening, will also be used at various times.

Key terms

Brief – when a senior officer gives information and instructions to team members, usually before some type of operation

Debrief – when a team gathers together after an operation to review and discuss how things went and what lessons have been learned

Activity

How do we communicate? Write down as many ways as you can of how we communicate with each other.

Verbal communication – speaking

When speaking to a group the leader must check that everyone understands the information that is being conveyed. Effective speaking must be:

- clear
- concise
- simple
- prepared.

The content of the information can be affected by the tone, speed and pitch of the speaker's voice. Skilled speakers vary these for emphasis and to avoid monotony. When briefing and debriefing the team, confirmation of the team's understanding should be sought throughout the speech. The group can demonstrate this by using certain body language, such as nodding, or by answering questions from the leader. Appropriate vocabulary should be used.

Listening skills

Communication is a two-way process. In a briefing or debriefing session the team leader must be prepared to listen to comments from the members of the team. A good leader will take note of what the team members are saying and value their contribution.

Non-verbal communication – body language

It is not always what we say that sends out messages, but the way we say it. Our body language can give out strong signals to other people which could mean the total opposite of what we are saying.

Ninety-three per cent of all communication is non-verbal:

- body language (55%)
- tone of voice (38%)
- verbal (7%).

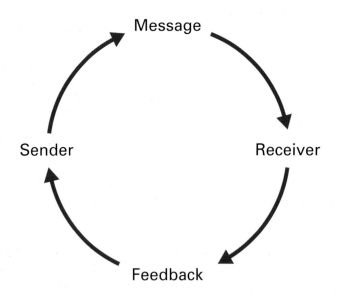

Figure 2.4 Four elements of effective verbal communication

Figure 2.5 Non-verbal communication

People use body language unconsciously to communicate information to another person. It is often our body language that reveals our emotions even if we do not intend this to happen.

Activity

What are the following examples of body language 'saying'?

- **folding or crossing arms across the chest**

- **tilting the head to one side**

- **raising the eyebrows**

- **avoiding eye contact**

- **narrowing the eyes**

- **leaning forward**

- **hunching the shoulders**

Being aware of your own body language and being able to interpret the body language of others can be very useful in the public services. Police officers are skilled in interpreting body language when they interview suspects. Avoiding eye contact, sweating and shaking could all indicate that a person is not telling the truth. Officers need to be aware of their own body language, for example, when trying to calm down a situation where someone is behaving aggressively.

Briefing a team

Team briefings are extremely important as a way of verbally communicating information within the team, so it is vital that the verbal communication is effective. When delivering a team briefing a team leader should ensure that there is open, two-way communication where questions can be asked and answered in a fairly informal way.

The main purposes of a team briefing are:

- to give information to the team
- to motivate the team
- to obtain feedback from the team.

To give a successful briefing a leader will be:

- in control – observing the team and noting the body language
- clear and concise – avoiding the use of unfamiliar jargon or terminology

- brief – only communicating the information required
- positive – will appear confident, which in turn will give the team confidence.

Team briefings can take different forms – there is no set model, but if the format is consistent, team members will know what to expect and will be able to concentrate on the information being shared.

Successful briefings will probably include:

- Ground orientation:
  - the location is described, often involving the use of models
  - often used in the armed forces before deployment.
- Safety points:
  - a comprehensive risk assessment
  - any risk is minimised to decrease likelihood of injury, e.g. wearing safety equipment, etc.
  - risk assessments are regularly reviewed and updated throughout any operation to take account of changing circumstances.
- A summary of the situation – the primary aims of the operation should be established by a concise statement giving the main points of the situation.

One way of remembering the main points of a successful briefing is to use the mnemonic **SMEAC**:

Situation – explanation of why the operation is necessary.
Mission – this is where the operation is explained in brief.
Execution – this is where the details of the operation are explained fully.
Any questions – this is where the personnel can ask questions to clarify any queries.
Check understanding – the senior officer will check that everyone understands the information which has been given.

Roles

The team leader will delegate roles, based on members' strengths and skills wherever

possible. The needs of the team must take priority, however, when this is being considered.

Equipment

Availability of equipment and resources needs to be considered as part of the briefing session when making decisions.

Case Study

There is an explosion and a large fire breaks out at a fireworks factory near the centre of a town. The scene is attended by the Fire Service, police and paramedics. A briefing session is held which is led by the Chief Fire Officer. He has a plan of the building and uses this to direct his team of firefighters. He instructs the police officers to cordon off the site and to block the nearby roads and also to evacuate nearby buildings. He advises the paramedics to remain on standby and to be ready to deal with any civilian or Fire Service casualties. This is all done quickly, calmly and efficiently.

One hour later a further briefing takes place where the situation is reassessed. The fire is spreading, there is a danger of further explosions and the possibility of the roof collapsing. Additional firefighters and appliances are required, and a wider evacuation is necessary.

Eventually the fire is controlled and extinguished. Residents are told they can return to their homes.

1. What might have happened if no briefing had taken place in the above incident?
2. Why would the police and paramedics obey instructions from the Fire Officer in the above incident?

Timings

Briefings often take place in emergency situations which are stressful and dangerous and where every second counts. The situation needs to be assessed, the primary aims need to be established and decisions will need to be made, all extremely quickly.

Debriefing a team

A debriefing meeting will be held after an operation or task has been completed. This is where the operation will be reviewed to find out how the task went, and how everyone performed. Debriefings are used in the uniformed public services, for example, the armed forces use them to allow troops to give feedback after a mission.

Debriefings are an important way of reflecting on the completed task and of learning from this for future personal and professional development. Strengths and weaknesses of the team are clearly identified.

Open communication within the team is a vital part of analysing and evaluating the task. This helps to prepare the team for future operations and to feel more engaged and involved. This can only happen, however, if good feedback is received by the team. Feedback should be given in a constructive and supportive way, as soon as possible after completion of the task.

Grading Tip!

In order to gain P3, you must demonstrate the necessary skills that are needed to brief and debrief teams.

Expanding from P3, to gain M2, you will demonstrate your own communication skills in briefing and debriefing a team. This means you should think about your verbal skills, body language, consider ways to boost team morale and confidence, check the listening and understanding of the team. Evidence for M2 should be witnessed by the assessor or another appropriate observer, and an observation sheet should be completed and signed by the assessor detailing evidence that was presented for this criterion, i.e. how and when effective communication skills were used, and ensuring that the correct procedures have been followed. The briefing and debriefing assessment could be related to the team leading exercise but does not have to be.

2.3 Be able to use appropriate skills and qualities to lead a team

P4 **M3** **D2**

Skills and qualities

'Skills' can be described as abilities that a person can learn and develop. 'Qualities' could be described as part of a person's character. A good leader needs to have certain skills and qualities to be effective. Some of these are listed below.

Qualities

Decisiveness

Many decisions need to be made in the uniformed public services – it is vital that these are made in a calm, professional manner, but as speedily as possible.

A good leader needs to be proactive in making effective decisions before problems develop. In any emergency, decisions need to be made as quickly as possible. This requires leaders to be decisive and able to make clear, firm and valid decisions.

Integrity

A good leader should receive respect from the team, and displaying integrity is one way of commanding this respect. The team needs to know that it can trust its leader to act in an honest, honourable and ethical manner.

Courage

A good team leader may earn the respect of the team by demonstrating bravery and courage in difficult situations. The team will often look to the leader to set a brave example when asked to take part in difficult or dangerous operations

Accountability

All leaders are accountable for their own actions and for the actions of others who are under their leadership. This means that when things go wrong a team leader is ultimately responsible and must take full responsibility for any failings by the team. If things go well, however, a good leader should give credit and praise to the team.

Trust

A good leader must have the trust and respect of the team and must, in return, trust and respect them – it must be a two-way process. This can be achieved by valuing each other's opinions, being open and honest with each other, and being loyal to each other. A good leader should support the team and a good team should support the team leader – everyone involved should know that they can rely on each other.

Adaptability/flexibility

Good team leaders should be able to adjust thier plans when new information is received.

This is particularly important in the uniformed public services where conditions and priorities can change with very little warning.

Skills

Time management

Good time management is a necessary skill for successful public service team members and leaders. This means managing time effectively, and prioritising the most important tasks and the order in which they should be done. Every second counts when the emergency services respond to an alarm call, and their training prepares them to act in the most effective way in the shortest possible time when called upon.

Activity

Make a list of things you could do to improve your time management.

Motivation

A good team leader will realise that motivation and good team morale are closely related. It is important that good performance by the team is recognised and acknowledged by a team leader as this can contribute to raising the morale of the team. This, in turn, will motivate the team to perform well in future. Team members will be motivated if they are allocated roles according to their personality and strengths. One demotivated team member can affect the performance of the whole team.

Delegation

A good leader knows when to delegate to others. This does not mean handing over authority and accountability, but it does give others empowerment and ownership. This works well when leaders look at the strengths and skills of the team members and allocate tasks accordingly. If team members do not feel they are being trusted to carry some responsibility, they can start to feel devalued and under-utilised. This can affect the morale of the whole team.

Planning

The planning process for any task or operation is a very important stage. The following steps should be taken when any planning is done:

- Step 1 – identify the primary aim – this is the main aim of the task.
- Step 2 – consider factors. These are the things that will affect the way a task is carried out.
- Step 3 – consider available resources. These are the people, equipment, materials and time that need to be considered.
- Step 4 – consider team member skills and abilities. What are the strengths and skills of team members?
- Step 5 – select a course of action. The team considers and decides which way to go about completing the task.

The plan can then be implemented. Implementing a plan means putting it into action.

Personal organisation

Leaders need to have good personal organisation skills. They are often responsible for organising the circulation of information, ensuring adequate equipment and resources, and scheduling activities. Leaders of uniformed public services teams, especially, need to be able to organise and coordinate many different operations quickly and effectively.

Leading a team

The following stages would be required to lead a team activity effectively.

- *Carry out briefing* – check understanding of overall aim (see section 2.2 on effective team briefings).

Case Study

Army Royal Engineers and local Territorial Army members were involved in building a footbridge over the River Derwent in Workington, Cumbria, after floodwaters destroyed the existing bridge. The bridge had connected the two sides of the town, which were then completely cut off from each other. Two hundred soldiers were involved in the building of the new bridge, which only took one week to complete. This was a very good example of teamwork where teams who had never previously met worked together to build the bridge in a very short space of time.

1. When planning the above operation what factors would have been considered in Step 1 and Step 2?
2. Looking at Step 4, which teamwork skills would have been required in the above operation?

- *Allocate individual roles* – team leaders should, where possible, allocate roles according to the strengths of team members.
- *Implement plan* – the planned operation should now be carried out.
- *Ongoing quality control* – the team leader should play an ongoing role in the work being carried out, giving encouragement and praise as required. When things are not going well the team leader should be on hand to provide help and guidance.
- *Safety* – the safety of the team members must be a priority for any leader – risk assessments to identify potential hazards should always be carried out when planning to lead an activity.

- *Evaluating performance* – the leader should confirm to the team when the aim of the task has been achieved. A debriefing should then take place, once the team has had time to rest and to reflect on its performance. All those involved should then review and evaluate the team's performance, feeding back any comments. Members should reflect on their own performance and make recommendations for future tasks. Although there may be aspects of the team performance that could be improved upon in future, the leader should ensure some positive feedback is given and state which goals were achieved.

Grading Tip!

To achieve the M3 and D2 grade you will be expected to lead a team activity and then to evaluate your own abilities to do this effectively.

By taking the role of team leader, you should demonstrate your skills and qualities in leading a team in the practical implementation of a plan. You should demonstrate that you are leading the team to a specific plan to meet a specified aim. You should lead a team of no less than five people, ensuring that they are correctly briefed and debriefed to meet criterion P4. An example of a practical task could be the planning and execution of a long expedition (e.g. Duke of Edinburgh's Award), or planning a charity fundraising event.

To achieve M3, you must show a higher level of skill than that

at P4, i.e. that of effective command and control techniques when leading the team. You should be able to lead the team to implement a plan, showing a level of critical and creative thinking as a team leader.

Evidence for D2 will be based on your ability to self-reflect and evaluate your effectiveness in providing team leadership. This should be based on your performance in leading a team to implement a plan. You should make realistic and achievable recommendations for your future development and improvement in providing team leadership and supervision.

2.4 Be able to participate in teamwork activities within the public services

P5 P6 M4 D3

Types of teams within the public services

One definition of a team is 'a group of people working together for a common purpose'. The public services, both uniformed and non-uniformed, is made up of many different teams. Some teams can be very small, consisting of three or four people; other teams may contain hundreds of people, as in the case of a regiment, for example. The size of the task will determine the size of the team required. Small teams may be part of large teams, and team leaders may themselves be members of a team of team leaders. Examples of different types of teams are shown in Table 2.2.

Table 2.2 Types of teams

Formal teams	<ul><li>A formal team is a team that is clearly structured and closely monitored to ensure that goals are achieved.</li><li>Formal teams may be set up by senior management to look at a particular issue.</li><li>An example of this would be where a multi-agency team is created under a government initiative to reduce crime in a particular area.</li></ul>
Informal teams	<ul><li>The opposite of formal teams. There are few rules, no uniform, and minimum discipline and structure. This can allow for innovation and new practices.</li><li>A voluntary group which is set up to help deprived families would be an example of this.</li></ul>
Temporary project/task teams	<ul><li>These teams may be set up at short notice, for example, after the 2005 London bombings.</li><li>These are often multi-agency teams, which means team members have to work with others who they would not normally work with. This can cause some strain among members.</li><li>Teams can then be disbanded when a project is completed.</li></ul>
Permanent groupings	<ul><li>The uniformed public services consists of many permanent teams. Team members will work alongside one another every day; they will form a bond and can become very close, almost like family.</li><li>This is particularly true of the armed forces. Many forces regiments are very traditional and have deeply rooted practices which they are reluctant to change.</li></ul>

Figure 2.6 Fire Service watch

Public service teams come in all shapes and sizes. Their formation will depend on:

- the type of organisation
- position within the organisation
- number of people in the organisation
- the role in the organisation.

Activity

List some of the types of teams that exist in the public services.

Some of the different teams found within the public services are described below. These will vary greatly in size and composition, and the meaning differ from one service to another.

- Divisions – some public services have 'divisions'. The British Army has five divisions, which are the largest units within the Army. Each division has lots of other teams within it. The Fire and Rescue Service is also divided into divisions.
- Departments – many public services organisations comprise different departments. For example, a local council may have an Education Department, Social Services Department, Parks and Leisure Department, Highways Department, Planning Department and others. A Police Constabulary will have departmental teams such as CID (Criminal Investigation Department), Traffic Department, Forensic Department.
- Sections – a section can be a small part of any department or organisation. The work of the section is usually specialised. For example, a Finance Section would handle the financial aspects of an organisation.
- Geographical teams – these types of teams work in particular areas or regions. Many services such as the Police and Fire and Rescue Services cover a geographical area, which could be a city or a county.
- Multi-disciplinary teams – these are teams that comprise people with different specialisms which may be required for a particular operation or project.
- Regiments and brigades – an army regiment is a very large type of team comprising around 650 soldiers. Regiments are usually steeped in history and tradition and members have a very strong sense of pride. The 22nd (Cheshire) Regiment, the Staffordshire Regiment and the Worcestershire and Sherwood Foresters were very old regiments that were combined as the Mercian Regiment as a result of army funding cuts. There was a lot of sadness about this among everyone connected with the old regiments.
- A brigade is a large group consisting of several regiments and around 5,000 soldiers.
- Forces – the police used to use this name, but now prefer the word 'service'. The term is sometimes still used in military situations.
- Multi-agency teams –these are teams consisting of several different agencies working to a common purpose. Crime Reduction Partnerships are one example of this.
- Specialist teams – these are teams of experts dealing in a specific area of work, e.g. a forensic team.
- Search and rescue teams – these can be volunteer teams, such as Mountain Rescue, or could be part of a Royal Navy team.
- Project teams – these types of teams are set up for a specific operation or purpose and may then be disbanded when this is completed.

There are other teams which are specific to the uniformed public services. For example:

- The Fire Service has 'watches' named by colours, e.g. Blue Watch, White Watch, Green Watch etc.
- The Police Service uses teams, which are known as squads, for some operations, e.g. Drugs Squad. Other teams that operate together are known as 'shifts'.
- The navy uses the term 'crew' for different teams.

Benefits of teams

It is widely accepted that teamwork brings several benefits to an organisation – in fact, it could be argued that an organisation consisting of more than one person would fail to function as an organisation without teamwork. There are obvious examples of when several pairs of hands will be more effective than one pair, e.g. when members of the Army Logistics Corps build bridges or erect accommodation buildings, but even in less manual situations the use of teamwork can lead to increased productivity when different skills and talents can be utilised.

Contribution to organisational productivity and effectiveness

All organisations, whether public or private, need to be productive and effective, and give value for money. Good teamwork can help organisations to achieve their aims and objectives effectively and efficiently.

Reduction of alienation

Most humans are fairly social beings and we like to 'feel we belong' and be part of a group. This is the reason why many of us join social clubs, sports clubs, churches and other interest groups. Many people see going to work as a way of interacting socially, in addition to being a financial benefit. People who work together sharing tasks and common goals also share a bond with each other and often form friendships that continue outside of their working life. This is particularly true of many of the uniformed services, such as the armed forces, the police and the Fire Service.

Fostering innovation

Innovation is a way of finding new solutions for new or old problems. The use of teamwork can assist this process as team members can pool and share their ideas and 'bounce' them off each other.

Sharing expertise

The sharing of skills, abilities and specialist knowledge is one of the great benefits of being part of an effective team. When all team members are allowed to contribute equally, not only will the team goals be achieved more easily, but members will feel valued and the morale of the team will improve.

Implementing change

All organisations need to change in today's ever-changing society. This is even more true of public service organisations which are subject to changes in governments, changes of policies, and social and global demands. Teams can be instrumental in bringing about necessary changes in an organisation – team leaders should be positive when communicating any proposed changes, to help team members to embrace the changes in an enthusiastic manner.

Grading Tip!

P5 asks you to identify the types of teams within a named public service, using examples from different team activities. You can look at functions that naturally lend themselves to team activity.

Identification and development of talent

A good team leader will identify the individual talents of team members and will take steps to ensure that these talents are developed further. This could mean arranging for members to undergo further training. Individual team members will gain fulfilment and job satisfaction from this, and the team will also benefit from the improved skills and talents within the team.

Meredith Belbin, a British expert on management and team roles, showed how the diverse talents and abilities of a team can greatly add to the effectiveness of the team. He identified nine different types of team members – this theory is covered in more detail in section 2.5 of this chapter.

Types of teamwork activities

Teamwork activities are tasks or exercises where people work together for a common purpose. These activities can be divided into *task-centred* activities, *team-centred* activities and *paper-based* activities.

- Task-centred activities focus on a particular task or operation and team members will look at the most effective way of completing this.
- Team-centred activities are aimed at team-building – forming a bond between members.
- Paper-based activities are used for a number of reasons when planning exercises or events. Activities can be broken down and divided up, with each group looking at a different aspect, such as cost and logistics. Disaster scenarios can also be used on paper for training purposes.
- **Military/emergency** (or tabletop) exercises are scenario-based, simulation exercises which are often used by the uniformed public services for training and planning purposes.

Grading Tip!

For P6, you need to take part in five team activities. This will be based on the learning acquired from learning outcome 4 and show that you can work within a team using appropriate communication and personal organisational skills, with tutor support.

To obtain P4 you should look at your own performance in the team activities. How do you rate yourself? Could you have performed better?

D3 requires you to evaluate the performance of the other team members in the activities undertaken. Relate their performance to theory, where possible.

2.5 Understand team development

P7 M5

Team members

Teams can consist of members with different skills, qualities and personalities. Not all members will be leaders, but they will have a specific role within the team which is just as important. Dr Meredith Belbin carried out extensive research into team roles. He identified nine team roles and concluded that these roles should be fulfilled in order for a team to be effective:

1. Plant – a creative individual who generates new ideas and innovative solutions to problems.
2. Resource investigator – usually very enthusiastic at the start of the project and are excellent networkers. They will use their contacts and other external resources to obtain their ideas, but may lose enthusiasm towards the end of the project.
3. Co-ordinator – the co-ordinator often becomes the chairperson of a team.

They are usually confident, mature individuals who will clarify decisions, identify the skills and talents in others, and delegate tasks accordingly.

4. Shaper – committed to achieving the aims of the team, they will motivate others to do the same. Shapers will argue and disagree with others in order to achieve the aims, and can be sensitive to the needs of other team members.

5. Monitor evaluator – usually fairly logical and detached individuals who can make unbiased decisions. They act slowly and analytically and usually arrive at the right decision, but they are not usually very good at motivating others.

6. Teamworker – a good listener and diplomat, helping other team members understand one another without becoming confrontational. Because of an unwillingness to take sides, a teamworker may not be able to take decisive action when it is needed.

7. Implementer – takes the ideas and suggestions of others and puts them into action. They are efficient and self-disciplined, and will always meet deadlines. They are very loyal to the team and may take on the tasks that no one else wants. However, they may be seen as being inflexible since they may have difficulty deviating from their own well thought-out plans.

8. Completer/finisher – this team member is a perfectionist who will want everything to be 'right'. They set themselves and the team very high standards and may be reluctant to delegate work to others as they fear it will not be done as well as they could do it themselves.

9. Specialist – brings a high level of knowledge, concentration, ability and skill in their particular field to the team,

but tends to be uninterested in anything other than this. They enjoy imparting their superior knowledge to others.

A simpler way of identifying roles within a team has been proposed by Peter Honey, with the five team roles as described below:

1. The leader – ensures that the team has clear objectives and makes sure that everyone is involved and committed.

2. The challenger – questions the team's effectiveness and pushes for improvement and achievement.

3. The doer – carries out practical tasks and will urge the team to get the job done.

4. The thinker – produces well thought-out ideas and analyses and improves ideas from others.

5. The supporter – maintains team harmony and prevents conflict.

Team building

A successful organisation will recognise the value of training and developing its staff, and promoting team building.

Recruitment

When organisations recruit new staff who are going to be part of an existing team, they have to consider how the new person will fit in. This can be difficult because until the new person is recruited there is no way of knowing if they will fit in with the rest of the team. A new member can be recruited from inside the organisation or by advertising externally, but any candidate would need to be carefully assessed as to their skills, qualities and personality. This could mean that the person they recruit may not necessarily be the person with the most qualifications, but they could be the person thought most likely to complement and fit in with other team members. Public service organisations, particularly the uniformed services, have very thorough recruitment processes which can last several months, to ensure that they recruit the right person.

Induction

This is the process which new staff will go through to help them to settle into their new role. They will be introduced to the people they will be working alongside and they should also be provided with any information they will need to help them to carry out their job. Organisational policies and procedures will be explained to them at this stage. The induction process may be fairly informal in some organisations, but public service organisations tend to have a lengthy training or probationary period.

Training/coaching

Most public service jobs will require a period of training – in certain jobs, such as firefighting, the training is ongoing for the duration of a person's employment. New legislation, new equipment and changes in procedures mean that refresher training is needed on a regular basis.

Mentoring

New members of staff are often allocated a 'mentor'. This will be someone who is experienced in the job role who will help the new member to 'settle in' to their role by offering advice and assistance.

Motivation

Motivation is what helps a person to strive to do a job to the best of their ability. There are two kinds of motivation: intrinsic and extrinsic. Intrinsic motivation is a personal desire to perform well, which will lead to job satisfaction. Extrinsic motivation comes from external factors, such as salary and promotion. If a team is not motivated, it will not perform at its best.

Team knowledge

It is important that the leader of a team knows the strengths and weaknesses of the team, and uses this knowledge when allocating tasks. Similarly, team members should share their skills to help others who may have different strengths.

Table 2.3 Tuckman's theory of how teams develop

Stage	Behaviour
1. Forming	This is the stage where the team first get together. At this stage they may not know what their roles and responsibilities within the team are. They will be dependent on the leader to give them instructions.
2. Storming	This is the stage where team members start to get to know each other and friendships may be formed. There may also be conflict as individuals may be fighting for position and power, and the leader's authority may be questioned or challenged. The team needs to be focused on the task and not become distracted by these issues.
3. Norming	Team members are feeling more secure in their roles at this stage. The rules of the team are formed and there is a strong commitment to the team.
4. Performing	The team is working well by this stage. Team members are task-focused, they communicate well and share knowledge and resources with one another.

Team development

Bruce Tuckman, an American management expert, developed a theory of how teams develop, as shown in Table 2.3.

Weaknesses

If a team member is under-performing, this can affect the success of the team task. This needs to be addressed using one of the following options:

- Ignore the weakness and hope that things will improve.
- Change the role of the weaker member.
- Retrain and help the weaker member to improve.
- Dismiss the weaker member.

Sensitivities

When a team is working effectively, members will be very dedicated and emotionally involved, and will take a real pride in their work. If members feel under-valued or neglected, they will be emotionally affected and feel 'hurt'.

Supporting team members

All team members must be treated fairly and equally by the leader and by each other. Public services team members regularly support one another, e.g. army soldiers on the front line and firefighters or police when dealing with emergencies.

Team building is an integral part of the uniformed public services. During the training period, recruits will learn about team building theory and will put this into practice throughout their career.

Team performance

There are several different ways of measuring the performance of the team, including monitoring, self-evaluation, appraisal, target setting and performance indicators. Performance indicators for the public services are usually set by the government to measure things such as crime statistics, emergency response times, customer or public satisfaction.

Team cohesion

The word 'cohesion' means 'sticking together'. When a team is operating under difficult circumstances, e.g. soldiers in Afghanistan, team members pull together. A lack of cohesion would lead to poor performance by the team. Team goals should be clearly defined when new members join the team.

Group conflict

Conflict can occur in any team, and finding ways to resolve the conflict can lead to a stronger team. If there are tensions and strains in the team, it is usually better to bring these out into the open. If conflict is not resolved this could lead to team members leaving and, if there is a high turnover of staff, this can unsettle the rest of the team. Too much change in the team could lead to a lack of experienced members. On the other hand, if members stay in the team for too long they could become 'stagnant', reluctant to change or implement new ideas, and resentful of any new members. Ideally, teamwork should give people the opportunity to gain new skills and enable them to move on and progress in their careers.

Recognition of contributions

Most people respond positively to praise or recognition of their work. Good team leaders should not forget to give credit where it is due and also to pass on the thanks of other people, e.g. other teams or members of the public.

Grading Tip!

For P7 you should look at the key stages in the development of an effective, cohesive team. You should refer to how team building and performance are conducted in the public services and explain how teams are developed, relating this to the relevant theories.

For M5, you will need to analyse the importance of team cohesion in effective team performance with reference to relevant theorists. You should provide examples to support your analysis from at least two named uniformed public services. This is an extension of P3 and P4. You should therefore include details of how personal organisation and communication skills can contribute to developing a cohesive team.

End-of-unit knowledge check

1. What is a team?
2. List three benefits of using teams in the uniformed public services.
3. What are the main purposes of a team briefing?
4. Give a brief summary of Belbin's team roles.
5. List the four stages of Tuckman's theory.

Grading criteria

In order to pass this unit, the evidence that you present for assessment needs to demonstrate that you can meet all the learning outcomes for the unit. The criteria for a pass grade describe the level of achievement required to pass this unit.

To achieve a pass grade the evidence must show that you are able to:	To achieve a merit grade the evidence must show that, in addition to the pass criteria, you are able to:	To achieve a distinction grade the evidence must show that, in addition to the pass and merit criteria, you are able to:
P1 Describe the different leadership styles used in the public services	**M1** Compare the different leadership styles used in the public services	**D1** Evaluate the effectiveness of different leadership styles used in the public services
P2 Identify the role of the team leader in the public services [IE3]		
P3 Brief and debrief a team for a given task	**M2** Brief and debrief for a given task using effective communication	**D2** Evaluate your own ability to lead a team effectively
P4 Carry out a team task using the appropriate skills and qualities [TW5]	**M3** Effectively lead a team task using the appropriate skills and qualities	
P5 Describe the different types of teams that operate within a selected public service	**M4** Appraise your own performance in team activities	**D3** Evaluate team members' performance in team activities
P6 Participate in team activities [TW1]		
P7 Explain how team building leads to team cohesion in the public services, with reference to relevant theorists	**M5** Analyse the impact of good and poor team cohesion on a public service, with reference to relevant theorists	

Unit 3
Citizenship, diversity and the public services

Introduction

The concepts of **citizenship** and diversity are central to modern society. Understanding their importance is fundamental for employees within the public services. This chapter will guide you towards an understanding of the meaning behind these concepts. You will also investigate the benefits to public services of good **citizens** as employees and members of society. You will have the opportunity to explore the legal rights and humanitarian rights that citizens are afforded.

A large part of this unit is concerned with diversity and equal opportunities. You will examine the various laws that exist in relation to discrimination, and consider ways in which unlawful discrimination might be contested. You will explore case studies that have been reported in the media, and consider the impact of media reporting on citizenship and diversity. You will also review the work of statutory public services and voluntary groups in relation to these issues, and judge the effectiveness of the support they provide to citizens.

Learning outcomes:

By the end of this unit, you should:

1. Understand the meaning and benefits of citizenship and diversity.

2. Know the legal and humanitarian rights that protect citizens and promote diversity.

3. Understand the role of public services in enforcing diversity and providing equality of service.

4. Be able to investigate current affairs, media and support.

3.1 Understand the meanings and benefits of citizenship and diversity

Key terms

Citizen – a person who lives in, has loyalty to and contributes to a community

Citizenship – the state of being a citizen of a particular social, political or national community

Citizenship

There are many different ways of describing citizenship, depending on who is providing that meaning. Here we will consider some of the most widely accepted understandings of the term, and the ways in which citizenship might be achieved. Citizenship is a status that is awarded to citizens; 'citizens' is the collective term for members of a specific community.

British citizenship can be gained legally either by birth or naturalisation. Anyone who was born in the UK before 1983 was automatically considered to be a British citizen; this rule also applied to children whose parents carried out a diplomatic role in the UK. After 1983, a person could become a British citizen by birth only if they had a parent who was a British citizen, or if one of the parents was allowed to stay in the UK permanently. If neither of these criteria is met, application can be made for British citizenship by means of naturalisation, which involves a set of regulations.

Six steps to naturalisation

To be granted British citizenship by naturalisation, the applicant must:

- have lived in the UK for at least five years
- be at least 18 years of age
- not be of unsound mind
- be of good character
- know sufficient English, Welsh or Scottish Gaelic
- stay closely connected with the UK.

Activity

Consider the criteria for naturalisation listed above. What reasons can you provide to explain them? Record your responses in a table similar to the one below. The first one has been started for you.

Table 3.1 Criteria for naturalisation

Criterion	Reason
Five years in UK	Understanding of how to behave appropriately. Life experience of how the UK operates, e.g. work, taxes, benefits.
At least 18 years old	
Not of unsound mind	
Be of good character	
Knowledge of language	
Keep close connections	

Each public service has its own view on citizenship, and imposes restrictions on who may join the service. In general, all public services reflect the views of the government on citizenship. This is not surprising, as the public services represent the government in society. When an application to join a UK public service is made, the employers must ensure that the applicant has a right to live and work in the UK.

The police service will consider applications from an individual who is a British citizen, a citizen of the European Union or other states in the European Economic Area, a Commonwealth citizen or a foreign national with indefinite leave to remain in the UK.

Think about it!

Did you know that, 'Contrary to popular belief, you don't have to be British to join the Met. In fact, you can be of any nationality to apply, as long as you have the legal right to remain indefinitely and without restriction in the UK.'

Source: www.met.police.uk/careers © Crown copyright material is reproduced with the permission of the Controller of HMSO and the Queen's Printer for Scotland

Eligibility requirements for the British Army are very similar to those of the police; potential recruits might include those who have British overseas territories citizenship and are a 'British protected person'. Additionally, regardless of nationality, *officers* in the British Army must have resided in the UK for at least five years immediately prior to entering officer training. The maritime and coastguard agency invites applications from any nationality; all applicants must, however, satisfy Home Office conditions of entry permit and visa conditions.

Diversity

Diversity is a term used to describe the differences between individuals and groups of people in society. Areas that are included in this description include gender, age, race, ethnic origin, ability and religion.

Every ten years a census is carried out in the United Kingdom which is designed to provide an accurate picture of the population. On a selected date every household is required to provide information of who is at the property. At the most recent census, in 2001, the total population of the UK was 58,789,194; this is the third highest in the European Union.

Activity

It was estimated that by mid-2008 the UK population had grown to over 61 million. Can you estimate what this figure will be when the next census is carried out, in 2011?

There are many reasons for the rise in the UK population, one of which is immigration, when people decide to move to the UK from another country. Citizens of the European Union (EU) have the right to live and work in any member state. In recent years, one in every six immigrants to the UK was from Eastern European countries that joined the EU in 2004.

When individuals settle in the UK they bring with them a wealth of skills, cultures, language and traditions. People are often identified by *ethnicity*, that is, their shared origins and traditions. This might include religion, language, the way they dress and the food they eat.

For the first time, the 2001 census included questions about the ethnic origin of the UK population. The results showed that there were

4.6 million people from a variety of non-white backgrounds; furthermore, the information gathered demonstrated that they are not distributed evenly across the UK. In Leicester, 37.4% of the population was non-white, with a slightly lower proportion (30.4%) in London. By contrast, less than 5% of the population of Wales, North East and South West England were from ethnic minorities.

Table 3.2 Ethnic groups in 2001

White (mainly of British descent)	92.1%
South Asian	4.0%
Black	2.0%
Mixed	1.2%
Chinese	0.4%
Other	0.3%

Source: www.statistics.gov.uk © Crown copyright material is reproduced with the permission of the Controller of HMSO and the Queen's Printer for Scotland

It is essential that members of all public services understand the composition of their community, so that they are able to provide the best service for everyone, according to their particular needs.

The figures in Table 3.2 include 1,575 over 90 years of age, and nearly 2,000 whom were away from their usual home.

Since the middle of the 20th century there has been a steady increase in the numbers of people settling in the UK. This has led to reactions from the **indigenous population** that range from anger and hostility to unconditional approval. As the UK became recognised as a multi-cultural society these responses continued to be mixed; generally business people welcomed the arrival of young and well-skilled people, while others felt there were already too many people living in the UK, and that there would not be enough jobs for everyone.

Table 3.3 Population characteristics of Swansea (2001 census)

Total population	223,301	Ages	
Males	108,075	Under 10	25,185
Females	115,226	10–19	29,060
		20–29	28,128
		30–59	88,481
		Over 60	52,547

Marital status (16 years and over)		Knowledge of Welsh	
Single	53,741	Speaks Welsh	2.47%
Married	78,690	Understands spoken Welsh	5.99%
Divorced	15,872	Speaks and reads Welsh	1.37%
Widowed	17,285	No knowledge of Welsh	77.53%

© Crown copyright material is reproduced with the permission of the Controller of HMSO and the Queen's Printer for Scotland

Activity

Nearly 25% of the population of Swansea was under 20 years of age. Which other group was closest to this?

Why do you think so many people were away from their usual home on the date of the census? (clue – Higher Education)

Other available data tell us that four out of every five people in these figures were born in Wales. Can you think of any reason why more than ¾ said they have no knowledge of the Welsh language?

The major problems associated with disapproval of newcomers to the UK have involved **racism** – this is the hostility demonstrated towards people of other races. Prejudices (pre-judging someone, because of a certain trait) are often held by people as a result of their upbringing or previous experiences. **Prejudice** and bias are rooted within each one of us; from the moment we are born we learn about ourselves, our environment and the world. Families, teachers and friends influence what we perceive as right and wrong. These early experiences shape our views and how we respond to new things. In the same way we make judgements on things we do not understand. Often these prejudices are irrational and get in the way of making sound judgement, based on facts. This can be described as *labelling*. It can also involve not recognising that within any social group there are many people who have different attitudes, behaviours and skills.

The most common forms of prejudice relate to:

- race
- colour
- nationality
- religion
- gender
- sexual orientation
- age
- disability.

In the next section of this chapter we will consider ways in which these prejudices can manifest themselves, and the problems that occur when people are discriminated against. You will also have the opportunity to carry out research into the many laws that exist in the UK to protect people from this form of unjustified treatment.

Key terms

Indigenous population – people originating from the country they live in

Prejudice – an attitude (usually negative) about a group of people

Racism – the theory that one group of people (one race) is superior to another

Good citizens

Good citizens include those who are involved in activities that assist others, and could include working within or alongside one of the public services. These roles might be evident, for example a Special Constable or member of the Territorial Army. Other examples could be working on a project to improve the environment, or assisting in a charity shop.

Activity

How many public services can you identify that offer an opportunity for 'good citizens' to be involved? Complete a table like the one opposite.

Table 3.4

Public service	Role
Police	Special Constable; Cadet
Army	Reserve Officer; Cadet

The National Health Service (NHS) has introduced a term 'Good Corporate Citizenship' to describe how NHS organisations can reduce the negative impact of its activities on the environment. It is also committed to taking an active role in maintaining improvements in health and equalities for all, by utilising its resources in ways that benefit the social, economic and environmental situation. With almost 300 hospitals, mental health and ambulance trusts, and 152 Primary Care Trusts (PCTs) in England alone, there is opportunity for this approach to result in a wide range of benefits for many citizens.

In 2009 the budget for the NHS was almost £100 billion. The NHS has identified good corporate citizenship as a priority for all its establishments – by adopting these principles it is hoped that the service will become more efficient and any financial savings can be re-invested in local services.

Sometimes citizens are identified by the group to which they belong, for example, a youth club, political party, religious or pressure group. There are many ways in which citizens can contribute to making society better; these might include helping others, gaining knowledge or protecting the environment. By promoting fairness and challenging injustice, good citizens can make a positive difference to society.

Table 3.5 Elements of NHS plans for Good Corporate Citizenship

Area identified	Ways to improve
Transport	Use environmentally friendly vehicles; walk, cycle, use public transport to get to work
Purchasing	Reduce packaging and waste; ethical trading; healthy food choices; supporting local suppliers
Facilities	Examine use of chemicals; manage water and energy use more efficiently
Employment	Recruitment; training; childcare facilities

Grading Tip!

To achieve P1 you will need to explain the meanings of citizenship, diversity and the terms associated with them. You will also need to link these concepts to the work of public service organisations.

For P2 you will consider the key issues associated with citizenship and diversity, and demonstrate the ways in which public services can benefit from 'good citizenship'.

Evidence for P3 will need you to include an assessment of the extent to which these elements benefit the public services, and society.

To achieve M1 you are required to *analyse* the importance to public services of good citizens, and respecting equality and diversity.

For D1 you will *evaluate* the role of good citizens in dealing with issues of equality and diversity.

Remember, it is your views that count; it does not matter if your analysis and evaluation provide different responses from those of your classmates.

3.2 Know the legal and humanitarian rights that protect citizens and promote diversity

P4 **M2**

All citizens are protected by legislation (laws). However, these laws are also balanced by certain responsibilities that every citizen has. This section provides an introduction to this important issue.

Human rights

In 1948 the first piece of present-day legislation, the United Nations Universal Declaration of Human Rights (UDHR), was introduced. This document was developed soon after, and directly from the experiences of the end of the Second World War. The Declaration set out for the first time the rights to which all human beings are entitled. Within the UDHR there are 30 articles, each dealing with a separate area of the ways in which *all* citizens should expect to be treated.

Key term

Human rights – rights set out under the United Nations Declaration of Human Rights 1948

Activity

Working in small groups research the UDHR. Following discussion in class, produce a poster that sets out the main points of the Declaration. Display the poster in your classroom.

Fifty years after the introduction of the UDHR a piece of legislation was introduced in the United Kingdom that further enhanced the fundamental rights set out in the Declaration. Whereas the UDHR focused in many parts on the issues of life and death, the Human Rights Act (1998) also affects the rights you have in your everyday life, including what you can say and do, how you express your beliefs and your right to a fair trial.

If any of these rights or freedoms are violated, you have a right to an effective resolution in law. This applies even if the person who breached your rights was someone in authority, for example, a police officer or a senior person in your public service.

Other rights, such as the right not to be discriminated against, are given not because someone is a citizen, but because it is accepted that all people should be treated fairly, according to their needs. As more people relocate between different countries, national legislation has needed to be more flexible, to allow for social integration.

While the Human Rights Act affords many rights to every citizen, one of the most basic responsibilities is that you have to respect other people's rights (even if you do not agree with their view).

Equal opportunities and diversity

There is much confusion within society about the meaning of *equal opportunities*. Many people will say it is about treating everyone the same; in fact, the real meaning is that everyone is treated fairly *according to their needs*. This means making allowances, for example, for those who speak a language different from the majority of the population, those who need assistance with walking or those who belong to a particular religious group and need to pray at certain times.

The issues of equal opportunities and diversity are important to individual citizens, society and the public services which serve that society. It is necessary for every member of the public services to treat everyone (whether they are a British citizen or not) fairly, and to not be prejudiced towards them as a result of their sex, race, disability or any other aspect of that person. This is equally important when dealing with members of society as it is when dealing with colleagues.

Within organisations that embrace the true meaning of diversity, people will feel empowered and the organisation will perform effectively because it capitalises on all the strengths of every employee.

Discrimination

This involves putting into action the prejudices we hold; it could affect people we work with or members of the public. There are two types of discrimination – direct and indirect.

Direct discrimination occurs when one person is treated less favourably than another, purely on the grounds of sex, race or gender reassignment, disability or age – and it is illegal. Examples of this might include not offering a person a job because she is a woman, or deliberately harassing a person because of their nationality. It does not matter if the person carrying out this act was having a 'bit of fun', or if the person affected had not previously complained about the behaviour. Under legislation, an employer discriminates against a disabled person if they treat the person less favourably because of their disability and the less favourable treatment cannot be justified.

Indirect discrimination means putting in place a requirement or condition that is applied to everyone, but results in a disadvantage to a particular group in society. For example, there might be a rule which stipulates that applicants for a job must be a minimum height (as was the case in the Police Service). If this rule was still in force today it would indirectly discriminate against those men and women who had not met the height requirement imposed.

Legal rights

The government has introduced legislation that seeks to outlaw discrimination in the workplace and in public life. The main Acts that have been passed are outlined below.

Examples of equal opportunities legislation

Equal Pay Act 1970
Race Relations Act 1992
Disability Discrimination Act 1996
Sex Discrimination Act 1997
Human Rights Act 1998
Employment (Age) Regulations 2006

Examples of reasonable adjustment might include relocating an employee with limited mobility to the ground floor, especially if no lift is available; another example could be buying a specially adapted keyboard for someone with arthritis in their hands. If an employer fails to make such adjustments, without reasonable cause, it is unlawful discrimination.

Activity

Carry out research into the following aspects of equal opportunities. For each area, provide a summary of the purpose of the related Act, and describe *at least two* of the duties of an employer:

- **Sex**
- **Race**
- **Age**
- **Pay.**

Many companies fail to comply with equal opportunities requirements; in most cases this is because they do not fully understand exactly what is involved.

A variety of laws exist to provide equal rights to males and females in the UK. The Sex Discrimination Act protects individuals from being discriminated against in employment and education. The Equal Pay Act should ensure that males and females are paid the same *for comparable work*.

Age discrimination is relatively new; the Act that protects people on these grounds became law very recently. The Equality (Age) Regulations 2006 protect people aged 50 and over from being discriminated against in the workplace. Employment equality for younger workers is dealt with in other legislation.

Unfair treatment of people with disabilities is also illegal in the UK. The Disability Discrimination Act 1996 forbids discrimination on the grounds of disability in employment, services and education. This Act also requires public bodies to promote equal opportunities for every individual regardless of ability, and sets minimum standards for all users of public transport. Employers must also make *reasonable adjustments* for people with disabilities to help overcome the practical effects of their disability.

Grading Tip!

To achieve P4 you will need to describe key legislation that has been implemented to protect the rights of citizens within society. This should focus on the range of legal and humanitarian rights that are currently available and should also deal with different areas, and include race, age, culture and gender.

For M2 you will also consider how well these measures work to protect rights of citizens, and provide reasons for your answer. This will involve research before you begin your assessment, and explaining the legislation in your own words.

3.3 Understand the role of public services in enforcing diversity and providing equality of service

The public services in the UK have a duty to ensure that they provide a service to all sections of the community that is free from bias and discrimination, and provides equal access to all of their services. Examples of these services include education and training, employment, housing and also the right to be protected from crime. You will learn more about the initiatives that are provided in this respect in Unit 12, Crime and its effects on society.

In addition to satisfying the needs of the community, the public services are required to take care of their own organisations, and the personnel within them. This includes demonstrating that they are equal opportunities employers.

As we have already discovered, the Metropolitan Police invites applications from a wide range of citizens. All public services need to ensure that their recruitment policies do not discriminate against any section of society, and that all applications are dealt with fairly; this fairness must also form the basis of the careers that public service personnel achieve.

The UK public services employ a wide range of methods to ensure that their policies and procedures offer employees and others the best opportunity of receiving equality in the services they provide.

Activity

Investigate the recruitment processes of public services. Your class could split into groups and each group be responsible for one service. Remember to include statutory and non-statutory services in your research. Within your research, consider how under-represented groups within society might be encouraged to apply to that service.

Collate your results so that you are able to provide results that cover all groups and many public services.

Tip: this information will be extremely useful in providing evidence for P5.

Key term

Harassment – unwanted behaviour or attention that causes harm or distress to the victim

The British Army considers that promoting equality and diversity will improve its operational effectiveness, believing it balances the rights of the individual with the needs of the entire team.

Many of the public services in the UK accommodate bodies that represent minority groups within the service; one of these is the National Black Police Association (NBPA). The objective of the NBPA is to

Think about it!

Did you know that, 'The British Army is an equal opportunities employer committed to ensuring a working environment free from **harassment**, intimidation and unlawful discrimination, in which each individual is respected and encouraged to realise their full potential.'

Source: www.army.mod.uk © Crown copyright material is reproduced with the permission of the Controller of HMSO and the Queen's Printer for Scotland

Figure 3.1

promote good relations and equality of opportunity within the police services of the UK, and between the police and wider community. The NBPA meets regularly with the Home Office and strategic committees in government, and seeks to promote schemes that will benefit staff and officers from minority groups within the service. The performance of the NBPA is monitored and documented, so that there is transparency and accountability in its work.

On occasions organisations have been criticised for the culture that exists within their ranks. Such a condemnation was voiced against a UK public service in 1999, by Sir William Macpherson. In his report into the investigation of the murder of black teenager Stephen Lawrence in London in April 1993, MacPherson stated that the Met was '**institutionally racist**'.

Key term

Institutionally racist – when there is a 'collective failure of an organisation to provide an appropriate and professional service to people because of their colour, culture of ethnic origin'

There will be occasions when a public service is the subject of a complaint. Consider the response when, in March 2009, a memory stick that contained information relating to police investigations had 'gone missing' in Edinburgh. Further information revealed that the data had not been encrypted – and it became unaccounted for inside the police headquarters!

A short time before this, a disk that held the personal information of about 2,000 British Council staff had also gone missing. The information included names, National Insurance details, salaries and bank account numbers of the employees. On this occasion the disk had been encrypted. Further cases reported in the media reveal that the theft of information stored in electronic format is not unusual, with theft of laptops from cars being one of the main methods by which this information can get into potentially dangerous hands.

Within public services there are policies that set out ways in which employees may seek redress (a remedy or compensation) if they feel that they have not been treated properly. If their complaint is not dealt with satisfactorily, they may invoke (use) what are known as grievance procedures. The reasons why employees invoke grievance process are varied, and might typically include the belief that they are not being paid an appropriate salary for the job they perform; that they have been passed over for promotion; that they have been the subject of bullying or harassment, or have been discriminated against. Once a formal complaint has been made, there are rules laid down in law that have to be followed. Often these cases are resolved internally, but on other occasions they result in a case being heard in a tribunal, before a judge.

Public services are required to monitor the success of their recruitment policies, in respect of numbers within their workforce who belong to different groups within society. As the public services recruit from the whole community, it should realistically follow that their workforce reflects that community.

As discussed at the beginning of this chapter, the number of people entering the UK has risen dramatically over many years. The vast majority of these entrants are allowed to be here, however, some people enter the UK illegally. Some of these will have travelled into the UK undercover, while others will have entered openly, and their status has not been detected.

Activity

Obtain application forms for as many UK public services as you can – remember to include statutory and non-statutory services, not just the main ones you might be interested in. Develop a database that includes all the information requested from potential employees or volunteers. Do all organisations ask for the same information? Why do you think this information is needed? Do you believe any of the information is not needed?

Discuss your results with others in your class. What are the outcomes of this research?

Grading Tip!

To achieve P5 you will need to examine the recruitment policies that are used within public services and comment on how they combat under-representation of specific groups in those services. You should also consider how equality and diversity are promoted within the services in order to help retain recruits from diverse backgrounds.

P6 requires an investigation of the methods used by public services to ensure that all members of society can access their services, as well as receive protection from discrimination within society.

To achieve M3 you will need to *analyse* how well the methods chosen by public services to promote equality and diversity work, both in society and within the services.

An *evaluation* of why these methods work well (or not) will provide some of the evidence for D2; you will also consider the advantages and disadvantages of the methods, and make recommendations for change that you consider necessary.

Many allegations have been concentrated on the UK Border Agency, the government department responsible for investigating the suitability of entrants to remain in the UK. Recent headlines include revelations that illegal immigrants have been employed at government offices and that, in 2009, the Attorney General (Baroness Scotland) was found guilty of employing an illegal immigrant as a housekeeper. Figures released under the Freedom of Information Act show that this situation is repeated in more than 30 local authorities and NHS Trusts across the UK.

3.4 Be able to investigate current affairs, media and support

In the final section of this unit you will explore in greater depth the ways in which the media inform the public of incidents involving many of the public services. Media is the term used to describe the many ways in which news is brought to the attention of the public; this includes methods such as newspapers, magazines, television, radio and the internet.

National issues and media representations of uniformed public services

All these forms of media provide information relating to the UK public services in their reporting of current affairs. The extent to which the media represents the public services changes over time, depending on the event or situation that is being covered.

Another factor that might help to explain why the same story is represented in different ways by diverse publications is that each of the television channels, newspapers, magazines and other media have allegiances similar to political preferences. Examples of these is provided Table 3.6.

Some of the more reputable media provide diverse opinions within the same issue or programme. In this way readers and viewers can decide for themselves which version they wish to accept.

In January 2010, the following headline appeared in the *Daily Telegraph*: 'Illegal immigrants employed at UK Border Agency'. At first sight this would appear to many to be impossible; after all,

Table 3.6 Examples of political allegiances in the media

	Newspaper	Television	Internet	Magazine
Left wing	Guardian			New Internationalist
Central	Independent Observer Daily Mirror	Newsnight BBC News 24	Yahoo! news	Economist New Statesman
Right wing	Times Sun Telegraph Mail			Spectator

the Border Agency is the government department responsible for ensuring that any immigrants who stay in the UK are eligible to live and work here.

Research identified that no fewer than ten illegal workers were employed at the headquarters of the Agency, while a further two illegal immigrants (one of whom was employed as a security guard) secured positions at the headquarters of the Home Office. Eight of the 12 have since been deported, three were detained pending appeals and one was later granted leave to remain in the country.

When these figures were released, the *Mail on Sunday* quoted the shadow Home Secretary (Chris Grayling) as saying: 'This is an absolute scandal. The government has taken tough action against private companies … it is clear the public sector has taken on bogus workers and escaped any form of censure.'

The number of workers from other countries who had secured employment in the UK unlawfully since 2006 was 349. This included six secondary school teachers and ten who were employed within the social care sector. A further four qualified as doctors and 13 were employed as nursing staff in NHS hospitals.

The true number of people in the UK who have entered illegally is not known (after all, they would prefer to remain undetected). It is widely believed to be in excess of 500,000.

Support provided to citizens by statutory and non-statutory public services

Many public services, both statutory and non-statutory, work to support those individuals who belong to minority groups within society. The case study on page 58 is an example of how Victim Support in Wales has formed an association with another charity to highlight the plight of victims who have been targeted because of their sexuality, and have become victims of hate crime.

Key terms

Transphobic – hostile actions towards transsexual or transgendered people

Homophobic – having an irrational hatred, intolerance and fear of lesbian, gay and bisexual people

Sometimes the media report incidents in such a way that people believe the individual within the report has already been found guilty of whatever the subject of the story is. For example, some people believe that young criminals, whatever their age, do not deserve privacy and that if they have done wrong their identity should be revealed. Others are concerned about the effect that naming individuals could have on their future life. The media's motivation for wishing to reveal such details has been called into question – some would say the public have a right to know, while others suggest it is merely to boost the readership.

Two young boys (not yet in their teens) who killed a toddler in Liverpool spent a total of just eight years in custody. Upon release they were provided with new identities and began a life apparently like any other young men in the UK. In March 2010 headlines in newspapers, on television and radio announced that one of these men had been 'recalled to custody' because he had broken the terms of his licence.

The Children's Rights Alliance for England (CRAE) has set up the campaign group Report Right, which calls for an end to

Case Study

At the beginning of 2010, Victim Support Cymru entered into a partnership with another charity, Stonewall Cymru, to provide a service in Wales to help and support victims and witnesses of **homophobic** and **transphobic** crime. Staff at Victim Support have undergone specialist training for this work. The support offered is adapted to meet individual needs and could include advice on personal safety, along with ensuring the victims are supported in court if

Figure 3.2 It's no joke leaflet

necessary. This service is funded by the Equality and Human Rights Commission. Gaynor McKeown (Victim Support Regional Manager for Wales) said: 'With more staff and volunteers we will now be able to give a more robust service to victims and witnesses of homophobic and transphobic crime. It's essential that all victims have someone they can turn to for support, someone who will understand the issues and challenges they may face.'

Jenny Porter (Community Liaison Officer, Stonewall Cymru) appealed to victims of homophobic crime to take advantage of this service, adding that receiving support and information at an early stage can have a positive effect on coping with the experience.

Source: www.stonewallcymru.org.uk

Activity

Hold a discussion within your class about whether anyone has the right to anonymity when they have committed a crime. You should be very careful to record all relevant points, so that at the end of the discussion you are able to provide evidence of occasions when you believe this is justified and when the wishes of individuals might be overshadowed by the needs of society as a whole to have access to the facts.

the naming of young criminals and greater protection of young people's privacy.

CRAE head of policy Sam Dimmock says the campaign group, which is led by young people, is looking to stage a discussion between members of the media and young people about privacy versus freedom of speech.

Grading criteria

In order to pass this unit, the evidence that you present for assessment needs to demonstrate that you can meet all the learning outcomes for the unit. The criteria for a pass grade describe the level of achievement required to pass this unit.

To achieve a pass grade the evidence must show that you are able to:	To achieve a merit grade the evidence must show that, in addition to the pass criteria you are able to:	To achieve a distinction grade the evidence must show that, in addition to the pass and merit criteria, you are able to:
P1 Explain the range of meanings attached to citizenship, diversity and the associated terminology [IE]		
P2 Discuss the key concepts associated with diversity [CT]	**M1** Analyse the importance to public services of good citizens respecting equality and supporting them by respecting the key concepts associated with diversity	**D1** Evaluate the role of good citizens in supporting the public services in dealing with issues of equality and diversity
P3 Assess the benefits of good citizens to public services and society in respecting equality [RL]		
P4 Describe the legal and humanitarian rights that protect citizens in the UK [EP]	**M2** Analyse the effectiveness of legal and humanitarian measures to protect citizens in the UK	
P5 Review the methods used by public services to ensure they have a diverse workforce [IE]	**M3** Analyse the effectiveness of the methods used by public services to promote equality and diversity in society and within the service	**D2** Evaluate the effectiveness of the methods used by public services to promote equality and diversity in society and within the service
P6 Explain the duty of public services to provide equality of service to all citizens [CT]		

To achieve a pass grade the evidence must show that you are able to:	To achieve a merit grade the evidence must show that, in addition to the pass criteria you are able to:	To achieve a distinction grade the evidence must show that, in addition to the pass and merit criteria, you are able to:
P7 Report on three examples of current affairs that affect public services and citizens [RL]	**M4** Analyse the effects on citizens and public services of the way that three current affairs examples have been reported by the media	**D3** Evaluate the impact that media reporting has on citizens and on the level of support from public services in relation to examples of current affairs
P8 Present information on how the media reports current affairs involving public services [TW]		
P9 Demonstrate how support is provided to citizens by statutory and non-statutory public services [EP]	**M5** Justify the involvement of statutory and non-statutory public services in providing support to citizens	

Unit 4
Understanding discipline in the uniformed public services

Introduction

All the uniformed public services – that is the emergency services, the armed services and other services such as the prison service – place great emphasis on discipline, to ensure that each service operates efficiently. Orders and instructions must be obeyed immediately and carried out to the letter – lives could be lost otherwise. This unit will explore what discipline is, why discipline is so important in the uniformed services, and how conformity and obedience play a part. The unit also examines **self-discipline** and why this is necessary for members of the uniformed public services.

The unit will provide you with the opportunity to demonstrate skills, such as self-discipline and acceptance of authority through practical activities, and increase self-awareness of these skills, which are vitally important in the context of the public services

Figure 4.1 An Army regiment marching on parade

Learning outcomes:

By the end of this unit, you should:

1. Understand the need for discipline in the uniformed public services.

2. Be able to demonstrate self-discipline as required in the uniformed public services.

3. Know what conformity and obedience mean, highlighting their place in the uniformed public services.

4. Know the complex nature of authority in the uniformed public services.

4.1 Understand the need for discipline in the uniformed public services

P1 **M1** **D1**

Key terms

Discipline – (noun) calm, controlled behaviour; order and control; training to ensure proper behaviour
– (verb) to punish somebody, to teach somebody obedience
Self-discipline – the ability to do what is necessary or sensible without needing to be urged by somebody else

Discipline is vital for the uniformed public services to operate effectively. All the services are organised in a similar way, with a clear rank structure and clearly defined roles and responsibilities, which rely on discipline to work effectively. Each rank brings with it the respect of all the ranks below it. People of higher ranks can give orders, commands or instructions to people of lower ranks. Providing that the orders are reasonable, lower ranks are expected to carry these out promptly and professionally, without question. Discipline does not just apply to the lower ranks, however – all ranks and personnel are subject to the same disciplinary code.

Key term

Hierarchy – an organisation or group whose members are arranged in ranks, e.g. in ranks of power and seniority

The hierarchical command and rank structure of each service

A **hierarchy** (or rank structure) within an organisation is a chain of command with the 'bosses' usually shown at the top. Every uniformed service has its own rank structure, but these are all different, even if some of the rank names are the same.

Table 4.1 Rank structures in the armed services

Army	Royal Air Force	Royal Navy
Field Marshall	Air Force Marshal	Admiral
General	Air Chief Marshal	Vice-Admiral
Lieutenant-General	Air Marshal	Rear Admiral
Major-General	Air Vice-Marshal	Commodore
Brigadier	Air Commodore	Captain
Colonel	Group Captain	Commander
Lieutenant-Colonel	Wing Commander	Lieutenant Commander
Major	Squadron Leader	Lieutenant
Captain	Flight Lieutenant	Sub Lieutenant
Lieutenant	Flying Officer	
Second Lieutenant	Pilot Officer	Midshipman
Warrant Officer Class 1	Warrant Officer Master Aircrew	Warrant Officer
Warrant Officer Class 2	Flight Sergeant Chief Technician	Charge Chief Petty Officer
Staff Sergeant		Chief Petty Officer
Sergeant	Sergeant	Leading Rate
Corporal	Corporal	
Lance Corporal		Able Rate
Private	Junior Technician	Rating

Table 4.2 Rank structures in the emergency services

Police	Fire and Rescue Service	Ambulance Service
Chief Constable	Brigade Manager	Director of Operations
Deputy Chief Constable	Area Manager	Assistant Director of Operations
Assistant Chief Constable	Group Manager	
Chief Superintendent	Station Manager	Duty Station Officer
Superintendent		
Chief Inspector	Watch Manager	Team Leader
Inspector		Emergency Care Practitioner
Sergeant	Crew Manager	Paramedic
		Emergency Medical Technician
		Emergency Medical Dispatcher
Police Constable	Firefighter	Ambulance technician

Ask Yourself!

Can you think of other organisations or groups, including family groups, where there is a 'hierarchy'.

The armed forces

All the UK armed forces, which include the British Army, the Royal Air Force, Royal Navy (including the Royal Marines) share the same purpose – to protect the interests of the UK over land, sea and air, as well as carrying out peacekeeping duties overseas. The culture and ethos of the armed forces are extremely disciplined. You can see the rank structure of the different services in Table 4.1.

The police

The main aims of the police are to protect life and property, to keep the Queen's peace, to prevent and detect crime and to bring offenders to justice. Table 4.2 shows the rank structure of the police. A police constable is responsible for carrying out the duties assigned to him or her as a police constable, such as routine patrols, investigating crime, attending road traffic incidents etc. A police sergeant is responsible for the welfare and development of all police constables under his or her command and needs to maintain discipline and ensure that they carry out their duties. A police inspector is responsible for ensuring that the sergeants under his or her command are carrying out their duties effectively, and is also ultimately responsible for ensuring that the police constables are working effectively. Similarly, the Chief Inspector and Superintendent are responsible for all the officers below their ranks. The Chief Superintendent is the head of the Division, so his or her chain of command goes from the top to the bottom.

The ranks above Chief Superintendent are usually based at Divisional Headquarters and are non-operational. This means that they are not involved in everyday police work, but are responsible for strategic planning, implementing government policies and achieving the targets set by central government.

The Fire and Rescue Service

All fire service personnel, regardless of rank, have a duty to protect life and property from fire and other hazards. Other duties include carrying out risk assessments, enforcing fire legislation and educating the community.

The firefighter's duties include attending emergency incidents, dealing with fires, flooding, chemical spillages, terrorist incidents and checking water hydrants.

In addition to the above duties, a crew manager will be responsible for supervising the crew. A watch manager has responsibility for several crews, known as a 'watch'. The station manager manages all the watches and crews at a particular station.

The Ambulance Service

This service is part of the National Health Service and provides a response to emergency calls. It also provides transport for patients to and from hospital.

The need for discipline

Great emphasis is placed on discipline by all the national public services. This is because if orders and instructions are not obeyed immediately, lives could be lost. The uniformed services are, by nature, very structured, orderly and controlled, and this is mainly due to the enforcement of discipline. The major way in which discipline is instilled into public service employees is via effective training.

The necessity for rules and regulations

It would be difficult to enforce discipline without **rules** and **regulations**. The making

Key terms

Regulation – an official rule, law, or order stating what may or may not be done or how something must be done

Rule – a principle which has been made to guide behaviour or action

of rules creates boundaries for people to live and abide by. Most people prefer to have some rules to live by to ensure some order, and discipline, in their lives. Rules can be written or unwritten.

Why orders need to be followed

In the uniformed services the consequences of someone not following orders could be very serious, even life-endangering. It is essential, therefore, that strict discipline and the obedience of order should underpin everything. Orders, so long as they are reasonable, must be obeyed unquestioningly. In a conflict situation an army officer may have to give an order which might place soldiers in a potentially dangerous situation. They are trained to obey that order, aware that the officer will have assessed the risk from a position of knowledge.

Maintenance of order

The UK uniformed services have a reputation for high standards of organisation and order. This would not be the case without high levels of discipline. The rank structures in the services promote discipline. People of higher ranks have the 'power' or authority to command people of lower ranks, and the lower ranks are expected to have respect for the higher ranks, and to acknowledge that rank, even if they do not know the person who carries the rank. People of lower ranks will salute the wearer of a badge of higher rank – this is one way in which discipline is instilled in new recruits to the armed services.

Rewards and punishments

Rewards and punishments can be used to instil discipline. In the armed services medals are given to personnel who carry out their service in accordance with the rules, as well as for people who carry out actions which are over and above the call of duty. This way of giving rewards can be seen as a positive reinforcer, a way of motivating members of the uniformed public services to behave in the correct manner.

Punishment can be seen as the negative reinforcement for breaking the rules. Acts of indiscipline can be punished by a reprimand, by the cancellation of leave, confinement to quarters, reduction in pay or rank, or a dishonourable discharge.

Consequences of a lack of discipline in the public services

If discipline was lacking in the uniformed services this would soon lead to a lack of control and order. The effectiveness of the services relies on members abiding by the rules and regulations. Without discipline, as a means of ensuring that this happens, the whole structure would be undermined. This would then affect the effectiveness of the service, the morale of the members of the services and would also have a detrimental effect on the way public services are viewed by members of the public.

Effect on social order

Our uniformed services help to keep social order in the UK by enforcing the laws of the land. If this breaks down in any society people start to take the law into their own hands. **Anarchy** (a total lack of control) would be the result.

Key term

Anarchy – 'a situation in which there is a total lack of organisation or control'

Figure 4.2 Lack of discipline in the uniformed services could lead to anarchy

The role of discipline

Team spirit

Members of the uniformed public services will experience a sense of belonging and camaraderie with other colleagues. This is known as *esprit de corps* or team spirit. Team spirit carries the responsibility not to discredit the service or bring the reputation of the service into disrepute.

Sense of duty and honour

As a member of a uniformed public service you will come into contact with many people in the course of your duties. Whatever your role, you will have a duty to your colleagues, the public and the service.

The British armed services have an excellent reputation and are well respected throughout the world for their strength and fairness. The UK emergency services are also admired and respected by others. Members of the services have real pride and a sense of honour and duty in their particular service.

Serving the public

All the uniformed public services exist to serve the public. When you join a public service you undertake to serve the public in a fair, efficient manner and to ensure that everyone is treated equally, without prejudice or reward. Discipline plays a part in ensuring that all public service employees carry out their duties in a fair and courteous manner.

There are rules, procedures, policies and legislation governing the uniformed public services to ensure that all members carry out their duty in a professional manner.

The code of Professional Standards for Police officers, drawn up in 2006 by a working party of the Police Advisory Board, sets out ten principles which govern the professional conduct of serving police officers, as shown in the box below.

Principle 1 – Responsibility and Accountability

Police officers are personally responsible and accountable for their actions or omissions.

Principle 2 – Honesty and Integrity

Police officers are honest, act with integrity and do not compromise or abuse their position.

Principle 3 – Lawful Orders

Police officers obey lawful orders and refrain from carrying out any orders they know, or ought to know, are unlawful.
Police officers abide by the law.

Principle 4 – Use of Force

When police officers use force it is only to the extent that is necessary and reasonable to obtain a legitimate objective.

Principle 5 – Authority, Respect and Courtesy

Police officers do not abuse their powers or authority and respect the rights of all individuals.
Police officers act with self-control and tolerance, treating members of the public and colleagues with respect and courtesy.

Principle 6 – Equality

Police officers act with fairness and impartiality. They do not discriminate unlawfully on the grounds of sex, race, colour, language, religion or belief, political or other opinion, national or social origin, association with a national minority, disability, age, sexual orientation, property, birth or other status.

Principle 7 – Confidentiality

Police officers treat information with respect and access or disclose it only for a legitimate police purpose.

Principle 8 – Fitness for Duty

Police officers when on duty or presenting themselves for duty are fit to carry out their responsibilities.

Principle 9 – General Conduct

Police officers, on duty, act in a professional way.
Police officers do not behave in a manner which brings, or is likely to bring, discredit on the police service or that undermines or is likely to undermine public confidence in the police, whether on or off duty.
Police officers report any action taken against them for a criminal offence, conditions imposed by a court or the receipt of any penalty notice.

Principle 10 – Challenging and Reporting Improper Conduct

Police officers challenge and when appropriate take action or report breaches of this code and the improper conduct of colleagues.

Activity

Refer to the Code above and answer the following questions:

1. If a police officer arrives at work suffering from a hangover from the night before, which principle would this breach?

2. If a police officer sees a colleague breaking a law and does not report it, which principle is breached?

The Armed Forces Act 2006 underpins service discipline across all three services so that all personnel are subject to the same system wherever in the world they are serving. The Act aims to increase fairness and efficiency, particularly in joint units, and thus support operational effectiveness. The key principles of this Act are as follows:

- Be fair and be seen to be fair.
- Be conducive to the expeditious application of justice.
- Be efficient and simple to use – it should not overburden commanding officers.
- Reinforce the link between command and discipline.
- Be 'transportable' anywhere in the world.
- Be compliant with the European Convention on Human Rights (ECHR).
- Provide for consistency in treatment within single and joint Service environments.

Grading Tip!

For P1, you should explain the need for and role of discipline within the uniformed public services.

M1 requires you to investigate the need for discipline and explain why it is that discipline plays an important role in the various public services. You will be expected to give reasons, or support the need for and the importance of discipline, using case studies.

For the D1 grade you should expand on the M1 grade by adding some evaluation, weighing up the positive and negative aspects of discipline, comparing and contrasting different case studies.

4.2 Be able to demonstrate self-discipline as required in the uniformed services

P2   M2   D2

If a person has **self-discipline** it means that they have the ability to control their own behaviour without help from anyone else. It is something which everyone can learn and develop if they really want to. It is a quality which the uniformed public services place great importance on.

Personal grooming and presentation

All the uniformed services insist that their members are well groomed and of smart appearance. This is particularly relevant in the armed services. New recruits are trained to take a pride in their appearance, to have good hygiene habits and to take care of their own uniform and kit. Uniform and kit inspections are carried out regularly. There are good reasons for doing this, as it promotes:

- good health and hygiene
- morale and *esprit de corps*
- disciplined habits
- the public image of the service.

Ask Yourself!

Do you take care of your own clothes/ uniform for college? Why do you think personal presentation is important in the uniformed services?

Punctuality

Great emphasis is placed on punctuality in all the uniformed services for the following reasons:

- It demonstrates respect.
- It helps you to organise your time.
- It prevents other people's time being wasted.

Organisations need to keep to tight deadlines to be able to run efficiently and effectively, and this is difficult to do if people do not arrive at the time they are supposed to. If a member of a team is constantly late this affects the performance of the whole team.

Time management

Good time management skills are very useful skills to have. Someone who manages their time well can be far more productive than someone who may appear to be very busy, but who is, in fact, not being very productive at all. Often, there is not enough time to do all the work that needs to be done. This means that an employee will need to be able to prioritise work, and this is part of good time management. To prioritise means to sort out which tasks are the most urgent and which need to be completed first. It is often very easy to be distracted and to lose concentration when completing a task, and it requires a high level of self-discipline to keep on track.

Reliability

In the uniformed services reliability is an essential quality to possess. Being reliable means doing what you have agreed to do, and not letting others down. This is particularly important in the public services, where good teamwork is essential and team members need to be able to rely on each other.

Attendance

All employers, both in the public services and also in the private sector, expect their employees to attend work regularly. Poor attenders can expect to be disciplined or even dismissed. This is because work rotas are planned around the number of people who will be available, and this cannot work if people do not turn up. No team or organisation can operate effectively in this way.

Composure

If a person is described as being composed, it means that they remain calm, even in stressful situations or times of crisis. This can be extremely important for members of the uniformed public services who need to think quickly and clearly at such times.

Attitude

Having the right attitude can be very important when you attend a job interview. Uniformed public service employers will be looking for someone who shows that they are enthusiastic without being overbearing, confident without being cocky and who are polite and courteous, not aggressive or 'stroppy'. Having a good attitude can be equally important when you are employed as a member of the uniformed services. You will need to be able to listen to members of the public and to empathise with them without letting your own feelings or attitudes show.

Performance

Conscientious employees will carry out their job to the best of their ability. Public service workers will always be expected to provide a first-class service and to give the public good value for money. If you are self-disciplined you will do this without someone watching over you to do it. Most public services, however, will have performance targets set for them which they will be expected to meet. These targets are set either by national government or by the authority or body which governs the service. If these targets are realistic and achievable (see SMART targets in the glossary), they will be challenging, but motivating. However, if targets are too challenging and impossible to achieve, employees will become demotivated and there is a real danger that performance may be geared purely towards meeting targets.

Case Study

Police officers are being forced to make 'ludicrous' arrests in an attempt to hit Home Office targets, it has been claimed.

Ridiculous examples include the case of a Cheshire man who was cautioned for being 'found in possession of an egg with intent to throw'.

In Kent, a child was arrested for throwing a slice of cucumber from a tuna sandwich at another youngster, while a boy was arrested for throwing a cream bun on a school bus.

Now the Police Federation, which represents rank-and-file officers, has called on the Government to reverse the target-chasing culture.

Source: www.dailymail.co.uk/news/article-454889/Nicked-throwing-cream-bun-police-dossier-dubious-offences.html#ixzz0lBVLSP6z

Personality

A person's 'personality' is what makes them unique. No two people are the same. A group of uniformed service workers may look similar in their uniform and they may have had exactly the same training, be working to exactly the same rules and regulations, and be carrying out the same duties, but it is the way in which they carry out these duties which makes some people more popular than others. Some people are naturally 'warmer' and more approachable than others, and some will empathise with the public more than others. Some will wish to lead, others are happy to follow. That does not mean that everyone needs to be similar. The best teams contain a mix of people with different personalities.

The effects of self-discipline and the consequences on the individual and organisation of a lack or total absence of self-discipline

The UK uniformed public service workers have a reputation for being self-disciplined and are respected throughout the world.

Our services have often been called upon to train uniformed services overseas. It is therefore very important that everyone maintains a high standard of self-discipline. When all members of a team are self-disciplined this is good for the individual, for the team and for the organisation – and members of the public can benefit also.

A high level of self-discipline will result in improved performance and productivity, and also raised morale within an organisation. Individuals will know that they can depend on one another to do their fair share of the work to a good standard.

If one individual is lacking in self-discipline the effects can be great, both on other individuals and on the organisation. Increased stress, frustration, lowering of morale and poor performance are only some of the effects that a lack of self-discipline in one person will have on other individuals.

Effects on the organisation overall could include low levels of efficiency and productivity, poor attendance, poor health and safety and missed performance targets. This then has an effect on the members of the public, who will lose confidence in the service, and can result in a high level of complaints directed at the organisation.

Activities requiring self-discipline

The uniformed public services are seen as disciplined organisations. Certain characteristics of the uniformed services will enforce this.

Drill

Drill is an activity which is used by most uniformed public services as a method of promoting and improving self-discipline. It is used more in the military services as a form of training used in marching manoeuvres and weapons handling, which involves the constant repetition of a set pattern of movements or tasks.

Uniform maintenance

It is an expectation of all uniformed service workers that they will look smart and take a pride in their appearance at all times. This is emphasised particularly in the armed services. New recruits will be shown how to wear and care for their uniform. New Royal Marines recruits will spend much of the first week of their training ironing and folding their kit, polishing their boots and even being shown how to shower themselves properly. Maintaining a smart appearance is an aspect of self-discipline.

Figure 4.3 Uniforms are worn with pride

Adhering to a team code

Most formal teams will have a team code which can be written or unwritten. The code will set out negotiated rules for team members to adhere to, such as:

- open communication
- share issues with one another
- respect for one another
- honesty
- integrity.

> **ⓖ Grading Tip!**
>
> For P2 you should participate in relevant activities such as drill manoeuvres, uniform maintenance and checks, presentation of self, and simple aspects such as punctuality and attendance. These could be tracked through a personal record as well as clear registers and witness statements from tutors, peers and public service personnel.
>
> For M2 you should demonstrate relevant tasks (as agreed with your tutor) with a high standard of self-discipline.
>
> D2 expands on M2, requiring you to increase your self-awareness of your own levels of self-discipline and consider the areas for development if you are to be successful in entering the public services

4.3 Know what conformity and obedience mean, highlighting their place in the uniformed public services

P3   **M3**   **P4**

> **Key terms**
>
> **Conformity** – behaviour or thought that is socially acceptable or expected
> **Obedience** – the act or practice of following instructions, complying with rules or regulations, or submitting to somebody's authority

Conformity

Conformity means behaving as others around you are behaving without being told to do so. We often conform and adopt the behaviour of our peers as a way of being accepted.

Compliance with common practices

Compliance is a kind of conforming which is linked to 'social control'. It can mean doing what other people in the same social group as yourself do, in the way of speaking, dressing, eating etc. Family, peers, education, religion, employment and the law all encourage conformity.

> **Key term**
>
> **Norms** – standard patterns of behaviour that are considered normal in a society

Social norms

Social **norms** are the behavioural expectations within a society or group. They could be defined as 'the rules that a group uses for appropriate and inappropriate values, beliefs, attitudes and behaviours'. Failure to follow the rules can result in exclusion from the group.

Social norms indicate the established and approved ways of doing things, such as norms of dress, of speech and of appearance. These vary from one age group to another and between social classes and social groups. What is acceptable dress, speech or behaviour in one social group may not be accepted in another.

Not sticking to the social norms risks one becoming unacceptable, unpopular or even an outcast from a group.

The role of self-esteem

Self-esteem could be defined as the opinion we have of ourselves. If you have high self-esteem you consider yourself to have self-respect and a sense of worth. Low self-esteem is linked to feeling insecure, and also to a person's background and upbringing.

The purpose of uniforms

Some public service employees wear a uniform which makes them instantly recognisable to the public, e.g. police. Some uniforms offer protection to the wearer, e.g. the special protective outfits worn by firefighters and the combat gear worn by soldiers. Uniforms also serve another purpose – they are symbols of unity and authority. A uniform can also be a source of pride to the wearer, e.g. the green beret which is presented to a Royal Marine on completion of his training is a much coveted possession.

The relevance of conformity in the public services

People who join the uniformed public services do so knowing that they are going to be part of a team. Teamwork and camaraderie are very important in any public service. All members want to be accepted into the team, and in order to be so they must conform to the norms of the team. If one team member does not conform, not only does that member risk not being accepted, but there is a danger that this will upset the dynamics and the performance of the rest of the team.

Obedience

Members of the uniformed public services are expected to obey orders and commands from those in authority. If you do not obey a command from a high authority, then you are likely to face disciplinary proceedings. **Obedience** is the act of obeying orders given by someone of a higher rank and is an essential practice in the uniformed services. Every uniformed service has a hierarchical rank structure which relies on discipline and obedience for its effectiveness. Without the practice of obedience, the uniformed public services could not operate.

In the uniformed services orders are given for a reason. Some orders can be linked to life and death situations. If an order is given by someone in authority, it is not acceptable for anyone to question that order and decide whether or not to obey it. Orders must be obeyed, without question. These orders can be verbal or written.

Obedience can be conscious or unconscious. New recruits in the uniformed services may find obeying orders a little strange at first and really have to think hard about what they are doing. After a while, however, obeying orders will become second nature. This then becomes unconscious obedience. This form of obedience is necessary in emergency situations when an instant response is needed.

Status is a factor in obedience. As we have discussed, most of the uniformed services have a clear hierarchical rank structure. Each rank carries a certain status and authority which means that lower ranks must obey orders from higher ranks. This is an accepted norm in the uniformed services. An exception to this would be in the case of a road traffic accident where the police would normally assume overall charge and would give orders and directions to other emergency services at the scene. However, if there was a fire or chemical spillage then the Fire and Rescue Services would take control and give the orders, as they are the experts in such situations.

Influences

Certain influences can change the manner in which orders are obeyed.

Reward

Members of the uniformed public services do not receive 'bonuses' or other material incentives for obeying orders and carrying out their duties. They can receive medals for certain conducts and behaviours, but self-fulfilment and personal job satisfaction can be the normal 'rewards' received.

Fear

Fear of punishment, loss of rank, pay or privileges, or fear of being ridiculed by others can lead to some service members obeying orders which they would not otherwise do. A certain element of fear is sometimes necessary to ensure discipline in the public services.

Love

'Love' may not be a term which is used by members of the uniformed services to describe their feelings for their colleagues and for the service itself. However, camaraderie, mutual trust, respect, admiration and a deep affection for other team members can all help to ensure obedience.

Respect

There is a saying that respect has to be earned. This can be very true on a personal level. In the uniformed services, however, there is another form of respect – that which comes with rank. Members of lower ranks are expected to show respect to those of higher ranks and there does not need to be a personal respect. This respect for rank is demonstrated by a system of salutes.

The relevance of obedience in the uniformed public services

Obedience is very relevant in the uniformed services. The whole structure of rank and discipline relies totally on absolute obedience by the members. Also, any disobedience by a team member could be completely demoralising. In life-threatening situations everyone needs to have total trust in one another, and to know that orders which have been given by those in authority will be obeyed immediately and unquestioningly.

Research studies

Many research studies have been carried out into conformity and obedience. These include the following:

- Asch – in 1951 Asch carried out an experiment to find out if people's behaviour was a response to group pressure, either real or imagined.
- Milgram – in 1974 Milgram carried out an experiment to see how far people would obey reasonable and inhumane commands.
- Zimbardo – psychologist Zimbardo carried out an experiment in 1971 to investigate the human response to being held captive.
- Hofling – in 1966 Hofling conducted an experiment to see if nurses would obey orders from a doctor, even when they knew that by doing so, harm would be caused to a patient.

Activity

1. In groups of four, each carry out research into one of the four experiments above.

2. Produce a summary of each experiment to say what was studied and what the results were, then feed back to the rest of your group.

Grading Tip!

For P3, you should outline the meaning of conformity and obedience and how they are represented in the public services. Your work should make reference to the influences affecting conformity and obedience, fear, reward.

For P4, you are required to participate in conformity simulations such as moral dilemmas or ethical questions.

M3 requires you to analyse why conformity and obedience are important to the public services, considering the consequences of not conforming and obeying orders with reference to research studies.

4.4 Know the complex nature of authority in the uniformed public services

Authority

What exactly does the word 'authority' mean? Authority can be defined as 'the right or power to enforce rules or give orders'. The uniformed public services need to have the legal right or power to enforce their rules and orders, so there are laws (legislation) in place to provide this.

Legislation

Police and Criminal Evidence Act 1984

This Act, known as the PACE Act, governs the powers and behaviour of the police when stopping, searching, arresting and detaining suspects of crime. The Act was formed to ensure that police evidence would be properly obtained for court and that suspects are treated fairly.

Police Act 1997

This Act set up the National Criminal Intelligence Service and led to the formation of the Serious Organised Crime and Police Act 2005 and the Serious Organised Crime Agency.

Activity

Carry out research to find out what the Serious Organised Crime and Police Act 2005 actually says.

Armed Forces Discipline Act 2000

This was the first of several Acts which were formed to merge the discipline framework of all three armed forces

Fire and Rescue Services Act 2004

This Act set up new fire and rescue authorities to create a more modern Fire and Rescue Service. The term 'Fire Brigade' was replaced by the term 'Fire and Rescue Service' to reflect the provision of a community service structured on the roles of individuals rather than a rank structure.

Conduct of services

No public service is above the law and there are organisations which oversee the conduct of the services, as follows.

The Independent Police Complaints Commission (IPCC)

The IPCC is an independent body which investigates any complaints made against the police, or any issues such as where a member of the public has died as a result of police action, e.g. while in custody or in a police car chase.

Activity

Go to www.ipcc.gov.uk and look at some of the cases which the IPCC has investigated.

HM Chief Inspector of Prisons

The Ministry of Justice funds independent teams of inspectors who can carry out inspections into prisons to check the conditions and to regulate the way in which they are managed.

See www.hmprisonservice.gov.uk.

Chief Fire and Rescue Adviser's Unit

The Chief Fire and Rescue Adviser's Unit was established in 2007 to provide independent, professional advice on fire and rescue issues to ministers and civil servants. The unit, established by Communities and Local Government, will have a key role in further developing the improving fire and rescue service to meet the challenges of today's world.

See www.communities.gov.uk/news/corporate/newadvisoryunit

The nature of authority

Power

Power does not mean the same as authority. Someone who exerts power over someone else may not have the authority to do so, e.g. a bank robber holding a gun may have power to control the bank staff, but they do not have the authority to do so. To be in a position of authority you should have power and morality on your side.

Position can be linked to power – in the uniformed services a person of higher rank has authority over a lower-ranking person, and also has morality on their side.

Status and position mean almost the same thing. However, neither status nor position are transferable from one service to another, meaning that there is no authority over lower ranks in other services. The exception to this would be an operation involving multi-agencies where authority has been agreed.

Influence

Some people can exert influence over others for a variety of reasons. Some people can be a good influence, a 'role model', while others can be a bad influence.

Corruption

Corruption can occur when people in authority abuse their authority and are tempted to make money dishonestly. When corruption occurs at the highest level it can have a detrimental effect on members of the public who see no reason why they should play by the rules if the public servants do not. This has been highlighted recently by a scandal over Members of Parliament who have been claiming expenses which they were apparently not entitled to.

Disobedience

Disobedience means refusing to obey an order. It is seen as a serious offence in the uniformed public services and can result in loss of rank, privileges and/or salary.

Blind obedience

This means obeying an order without question, however unreasonable or bad the order may be. This is different from the kind of unconscious obedience which occurs in an emergency. There are both positive and negative aspects to this.

Ask Yourself!

Can you think of any examples of when atrocities have been carried out by people who said 'they were just following orders'?

Moral dilemmas

A moral dilemma is a problem to which there does not appear to be a clear solution. It may be a case of weighing up which action would be the better one to take in the circumstances – this could be the lesser of two evils. Take a look at the following case study, which illustrates this.

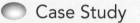

Case Study

Ambulance workers face 'moral dilemma'

Figure 4.4 Paramedics are at risk of attack when attending emergencies

UNISON is calling for a review of ambulance service blacklists which warn staff about addresses where they may be at risk of attack.

Ambulance services across the UK hold records of more than 8,500 homes deemed dangerous, where there is a history of violence against paramedics.

Staff responding to emergency calls at these addresses are advised to wait until a police escort can accompany them inside.

UNISON says assaults on health workers are unacceptable. However, the union is concerned about the way the blacklist system works.

Head of Unison Health Karen Jennings said paramedics were faced with a moral dilemma, forced to choose between their own safety and that of their patients.

'I think there are serious questions to ask about whether ambulance crews should sit outside if somebody inside is having a heart attack,' she said.

'Having said that, if that household has a history of attacking people when they go in, then it doesn't do anybody any good if they were just to rush in and put themselves at risk.'

Source: With kind permission from UNISON www.unison.org.uk/news/news_view.asp?did=4957

The responsibility for making decisions such as this lies with the senior officer or team leader, and a good leader would accept responsibility for such decisions. These decisions may involve considering the ethics involved. Ethics are to do with what is right and wrong.

Types of authority

(Similar to leadership styles, see Unit 2 for more information.)

Authoritarian

Authoritarian discipline is based on a strict hierarchy where orders are given and must be obeyed unquestioningly without any discussion. This style of authority is used in most uniformed services, particularly at the initial training stage, to ensure the high standard of discipline that is required, but this may be relaxed slightly when training is complete. Although things have changed, this style is still found in the armed services.

Dictatorial

This type of authority is used by commanders who want absolute power. It can lead to low morale and, in the armed services, can lead to bullying and human rights abuses.

Consultative

This is a democratic style of authority where leaders consult and seek the opinions of others before making decisions. It is mainly used in the emergency services and non-uniformed services.

Participative

This style of authority endeavours to include everyone in decision-making, which may be difficult when quick decisions have to be made.

Grading Tip!

To achieve the P5 you should describe authority in the public services. This should include the structure of authority, the nature, different types of authority and the legislation which is in place to support decisions made by those in positions of authority.

End-of-unit knowledge check

1. Explain five reasons for wearing a uniform.
2. Name three research experiments into obedience.
3. What is meant by blind obedience?
4. What is a moral dilemma?
5. Explain the difference between a rule and a regulation.

Grading criteria

In order to pass this unit, the evidence that you present for assessment needs to demonstrate that you can meet all the learning outcomes for the unit. The criteria for a pass grade describe the level of achievement required to pass this unit.

To achieve a pass grade the evidence must show that you are able to:	To achieve a merit grade the evidence must show that, in addition to the pass criteria, you are able to:	To achieve a distinction grade the evidence must show that, in addition to the pass and merit criteria, you are able to:
P1 Explain the need for and role of discipline in the uniformed public services	**M1** Justify the need for and the role of discipline in the uniformed public services	**D1** Evaluate the impact of discipline on the uniformed public services
P2 Demonstrate self-discipline through relevant activities	**M2** Perform relevant activities with a high standard of self-discipline	**D2** Evaluate personal levels of self-discipline for entry to the uniformed public services
P3 Outline what is meant by the terms 'conformity' and 'obedience' with reference to the public services	**M3** Explain why conformity and obedience are important in the public services, with reference to research studies	
P4 Participate in conformity simulations		
P5 Describe 'authority' as it relates to the uniformed public services		

Unit 5
Physical preparation, health and lifestyle for the public services

Introduction

Being physically fit is a major requirement for anyone wishing to join the uniformed public services. You do not need to be super fit or extremely strong, but you do have to be in fairly good condition to carry out the regular active and physically demanding roles. Therefore you will need to know your current fitness levels and how they measure up to the requirements of the public services and, possibly, how you can improve your fitness levels.

You will start the unit by examining three of the major human body systems and extend this into the effects of exercise on these body systems, giving you the knowledge to understand how the body works when taking part in physical activity. From there you will study the effects of different **lifestyle factors** on your health and fitness and why participating in exercise is only one way of controlling your physique.

You will be required to research the advice given by the professionals on lifestyle improvement strategies and the guidelines and recommendations for leading a healthy lifestyle. From all the information gathered you are asked to plan a personal health-related physical activity programme.

Learning outcomes:

By the end of this unit, you should:

1. Know the fitness requirements for entry into the public services.

2. Know the major human body systems.

3. Know the importance of lifestyle factors in the maintenance of health and wellbeing.

4. Be able to provide advice on lifestyle improvement.

5. Be able to plan a health-related physical activity programme in preparation for the public services.

5.1 Know the fitness requirements for entry into the public services

P1 M1 D1

Fitness assessments for each component of fitness

There are 11 components of fitness. These are broken down into health-related and skill-related components:

- Five **health-related components of fitness**: aerobic endurance, muscular endurance, strength, flexibility and body composition. These relate to those which make up our health status.

- Six **skill-related components of fitness**: speed, power, agility, balance, reaction time and coordination. These relate to those skills used in sporting performance.

All the fitness components are tested in one way or another before joining the uniformed public services, but only some of them have specific tests that can be assessed against national results.

- Aerobic endurance – otherwise known as stamina. This is tested in a number of ways, the most common of these being the multi-stage fitness test (the bleep test or beep test). Another method is the Chester step test.

- Muscular endurance – this is required when muscles make a number of continuous movements. Again there are a number of different tests that are used, mainly for muscles of the upper body. Press-ups and pull-ups are the tests most often used by the public services.

- Strength – known as muscular strength, this is the ability to exert a specific muscle or muscle group in a single maximal contraction against resistance. Pull-ups or using a barbell to push the maximum lift can be used to test this, as can a grip strength dynamometer to test forearm strength.

- Flexibility – also known as suppleness, this is the ability of a joint to move through a full range of movement. The sit-and-reach test is a popular public service test for flexibility.

- Body composition – this is the amount of body fat in an individual. Skin-fold callipers are used to measure this but can be unreliable, so more sophisticated methods are now used.

- Speed – this is not really tested for entrance to the uniformed public services, but a 30 m or 40 m distance can be useful to time and compare runs.

- Power – again, this is not usually tested but can be assessed using the horizontal or vertical jump.

- Agility – this is the ability to change direction quickly and accurately. It is tested by some police forces as part of a scenario or using the Illinois agility run.

- Balance (being able to maintain stability), reaction time (reacting to a stimulus) and coordination are not usually formally tested by the uniformed public services.

Key terms

Health-related components of fitness – aerobic endurance, muscular endurance, strength, flexibility and body composition

Skill-related components of fitness – speed, power, agility, balance, reaction time and coordination

Figure 5.1 Aerobic endurance, muscular endurance, speed and balance are among the fitness components tested in one way or another before joining the uniformed public services

Measure results against a public service test

You must take part in all, or some, of the fitness assessments for each of the major components of fitness mentioned above so that you can explain the results you have achieved. Once you have done this you must research the entrance fitness requirements for your chosen public service and measure your results against those required.

British Army entrance fitness requirements

1.5 mile run completed at a time set by the particular Regiment or Corps you wish to join:

- Infantry – 12 minutes 45 seconds or less

- Royal Armoured Corps, Royal Artillery, Royal Engineers and Royal Logistic Corps – 13 minutes 15 seconds or less

Think about it!

You have to be fit to join the uniformed public services and each service has its own entrance fitness test but they all differ in one way or another. For the Armed Forces the entrance fitness tests are relatively simple, as you are only usually tested on your aerobic endurance to see if you have the stamina required and a basic fitness level to begin training. However, once you join there is a Basic Training Fitness Programme for each of the specific services, which will test more of your all-round fitness. However, in the 'Blue light' (emergency) services the fitness tests are more specific to the job role.

How fit are you? How much effort are you prepared to put into getting fitter? Which service do you want to join?

- Parachute Regiment – two time targets (1.5 mile run between 9 minutes and 18 seconds, and 9 minutes and 40 seconds), followed by a static weight lift of 116 kg or more.

Royal Navy entrance fitness requirements

1.5 mile run on a treadmill with times dependent upon your age and gender:

- male – between 12 minutes 20 seconds and 13 minutes 49 seconds
- female – between 14 minutes 35 seconds and 16 minutes 40 seconds.

Royal Air Force pre-joining fitness test

1.5 mile run on a treadmill:

- male – 12 minutes 12 seconds
- female – 14 minutes 35 seconds.

For all the Armed Forces above you may also be asked to complete a multi-stage fitness test (beep test) and do as many sit-ups and press-ups as you can in a minute. You can find out more by going to the website www.hmforces.co.uk.

Police Service entrance fitness test

You need to be physically able to carry out your duties, which includes being able to run for a reasonable distance and constrain a person. Therefore there is a thorough test of two key fitness requirements:

- aerobic endurance – run to and fro along a 15 m track in time to a series of bleeps
- dynamic strength – perform five seated chest-pushes and five seated back-pulls on a dyno machine.

You can find out more by going to the website www.policecouldyou.co.uk.

Prison Service job-related fitness test

- Grip strength test – squeezing a dynamometer to measure the strength of your forearm.
- Dynamic strength test – using a dyno machine to measure the strength of your upper body and arm muscles.
- Endurance fitness – reaching 5.4 on the multi-stage fitness test.
- Speed–agility run – running around cones and changing direction in a slalom fashion to a set time.
- Shield test – hold up a 6 kg shield in front of the body for a minute.

You can find out more by going to the website www.hmprisonservice.gov.uk.

Once you have the results of the fitness assessments, you need to measure them against the relevant public service entrance test, some of which are shown above, others of which you will need to search for on the internet. You must explain why you did well on some of the tests and not so well on others (most people struggle with the upper body tests), or how you completed them all extremely well, and what you are going to do next.

Evaluate your results and analyse the strengths and recommend improvements

If you have achieved, or even surpassed, the required scores for your public service entrance fitness requirements then you need to maintain these levels and consider them to be your strengths. For those assessments where you did not reach the necessary results you must set yourself some targets to achieve and practise regularly, ready for the next opportunity you have to re-take the entrance test.

This could mean setting up a physical activity programme with specific exercises to practise in order to attain the necessary results to pass the relevant public service entrance fitness test.

Grading Tip!

First you need the results of all the fitness assessments you have taken part in and the entrance fitness requirements from your chosen public service.

For the Merit grade you need to look at your results and see how they measure up against those required.

For the Distinction grade you must break down each of the results and show which ones you are good at, which ones you need to improve on and how you are going to do this.

5.2 Know the major human body systems

P2 P3 M2

Structure and function of the major human body systems

The skeletal system – the bones

- **Structure** – the adult skeleton is made up of 206 bones. There are four different types of bone: long, short, flat and irregular.

  Many of the bones meet at joints to help us move. There are three different types of joint: immovable, slightly movable and freely movable. The five types of movable joints are: ball and socket, hinge, pivot, gliding and condyloid.

- **Function** – the skeletal system has five main functions: it gives us our body shape, supports the body, protects the vital organs, allows movement and makes new blood cells.

Key terms

Function – the natural action of something; the specific role of each structure

Structure – the way in which something is constructed; the framework around which things are added

---

The muscular system – the muscles

- *Structure* – there are three different types of muscle: cardiac, involuntary and voluntary. Muscles are made up of many fibres. We all have the same number of fibres, but a different number of voluntary muscle fibres called fast twitch and slow twitch.

- *Function* – the muscles pull on the bones of the skeletal system to provide movement. Muscles work in pairs that pull in opposite directions. There are two types of muscle contraction: isometric and isotonic.

The respiratory system – breathing

- *Structure* – the respiratory system is made up of six components: mouth and nose cavity, trachea, bronchi, bronchioles, alveoli and lungs.

- *Function* – to breathe in oxygen from the air, taking it into our lungs where it exchanges with carbon dioxide, which we then breathe out.

The cardiovascular system – blood and circulation

- *Structure* – the cardiovascular system has three main functions: to transport blood around the body; to keep your body temperature under control; and to protect you against disease by platelets forming blood clots when a blood vessel is damaged. There are three types of blood vessel: arteries, veins and capillaries. Plasma carries platelets, red and white blood cells in the blood stream.

- *Function* – double circulation: the heart pumps oxygenated blood around the body in arteries and returns deoxygenated blood back to the heart through veins. The deoxygenated blood flows from the heart to the lungs to be oxygenated and then returns to the heart to begin the process again. Capillaries carry food and oxygen to the tissues of the body and take waste away from them.

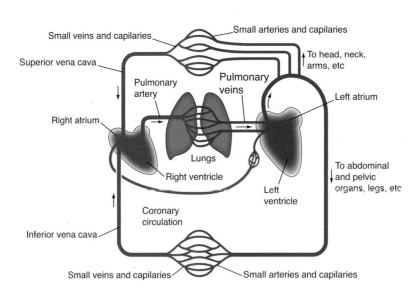

Figure 5.2 The cardiovascular system

Record results from a fitness activity and identify the short-term effects of exercise on the major human body systems

Activity

Take part in any fitness activity, for instance a circuit training session, which lasts for a minimum of 20 minutes, and record the results. Also note the short-term effects of the activity on your heart rate and your breathing.

The short-term effects of exercise on the muscular-skeletal system

There are no real short-term effects of exercise on the skeletal system, but there are a few long-term benefits such as your joints remaining flexible through regular use, and the strengthening of cartilage, ligaments and tendons that join the muscles to the bones – as long as you do not over stretch them! The bones are strengthened and it can improve your posture. There is also a continuous formation of white blood cells from bone marrow. These help to fight disease by destroying bacteria. There is a slight improvement in muscle tone and strength each time you exercise, but you must be sure not to overuse the muscles in one go or they can tear.

The short-term effects of exercise on the respiratory system

Immediately you start to exercise your respiratory system begins to start working harder. You start to breathe more deeply and much faster, therefore taking in more oxygen and breathing out more carbon dioxide. As your oxygen intake increases it makes the muscles work harder.

The short-term effects of exercise on the cardiovascular system

Similar to the respiratory system, the circulation of blood around the body starts to increase immediately you start to exercise. Your heart starts to beat faster to circulate more blood, and this is diverted from the minor organs of the body to the muscles so that they can work harder. As you begin to get warmer, the blood moves closer to the skin and you begin to sweat.

Over a period of time exercise will increase the number of red blood cells, your arteries grow bigger and your heart increases in size so that it beats more slowly. Your heart rate will also return to normal much more quickly after exercise.

The short- and long-term effects of regular exercise on the major human body systems

When you exercise you make your body work harder than normal and put a greater stress on it. This in turn makes your major body systems respond and you will see and feel immediate changes to your breathing and heart rate. These are the short-term effects, or benefits, to your body. If you exercise on a regular basis you will notice some longer-term effects on your body and the major body systems.

Short-term effects

As you start to exercise you start to breathe faster and more deeply. This means that your lungs and respiratory system are working harder to draw oxygen from the air and remove the carbon dioxide from your lungs. The oxygen goes to the muscles and muscular system so that they keep working by producing movement.

Your heart beats faster to circulate the oxygen in the blood (oxygenated blood which is bright red) around the circulatory system. Blood that normally goes to some of your internal organs is diverted to the muscles to keep them moving.

The blood vessels will widen to cope with the extra blood supply and keep your blood pressure at the correct level. This means the blood gets hotter and moves closer to the surface of the skin so that heat can escape. Your skin starts to turn red as you start to sweat; this helps you to keep cool and prevents you from overheating.

The circulatory and respiratory systems work together (the cardiovascular system) to provide oxygen for the muscular system to continue working until you begin to rest.

Long-term effects

Your body systems will adapt and even change permanently as you participate in exercise, fitness or physical activities. You will become stronger, faster or more flexible, depending upon the types of work you choose to make your body do.

Cardiovascular system

The heart becomes larger and stronger as the walls get thicker and more blood is pumped per beat. Your resting heart rate falls as each heartbeat pumps more blood. Blood vessels increase in size and number and your body produces more red blood cells to transport oxygen more efficiently. Your heart beats more slowly but pumps the same amount of blood so your blood pressure falls.

Respiratory system

The lungs get bigger and so increase their capacity to let in more oxygen. The rate of carbon dioxide being exhaled increases and the muscles used for breathing, including the diaphragm, make your chest cavity larger.

The increase in efficiency of the cardio-vascular and respiratory systems makes the exchange of gasses much quicker and therefore you can exercise for longer and at a higher tempo.

Muscular-skeletal system

Muscle tone is increased and body fat is reduced. The muscles adapt to use more energy and work more efficiently and for longer. A larger network of blood vessels is developed to feed more oxygen and energy to the muscles.

Grading Tip!

For the Pass grade in this outcome you have to describe the four main body systems and identify the short-term effects of exercise on the systems once you have participated in an activity.

For the Merit grade you will need to research the long-term effects of exercise on those four systems. It could take years before you notice any difference in the long-term effects, especially on the internal organs, but you should be able to see a difference in your muscle tone and weight, or feel your breathing and heart rate being more efficient i.e. slower.

5.3 Know the importance of lifestyle factors in the maintenance of health and wellbeing

Lifestyle factors that have an effect on health

Lifestyle is everything that you do in life, your hobbies, work, study, relaxation and physical exercise. A healthy lifestyle will enable you to perform to your potential. The main healthy lifestyle factor is what you put into your body, so you need to avoid all that which is not good for your body and replace it with that which is good. A few simple lifestyle changes can keep your heart healthy by reducing the risk of heart disease, heart attack and strokes. The body was made to be physically active – the heart needs to pump fast once in a while to keep its muscle tone and your lungs need regular exercise to function properly.

> ### Key term
>
> **Lifestyle factors** – these include stress, smoking, alcohol, family history, sleep and rest, physical exercise, drugs, diet, personal hygiene, environment

The way you live will influence your chance of developing allergies, especially what you eat and being aware of your personal hygiene. There are other factors which all have a part to play in your style of living, so let's have a look at them in more detail and then find some strategies to try and improve your lifestyle.

Stress

Most people experience stress at some time in their lives and it is a normal part of work. However, if the stress level gets too high it has a negative effect on health. Feeling good is important, so try to avoid too much emotional stress and worry.

Smoking

Most people recognise that smoking cigarettes can damage your health. It is the single greatest cause of preventable illness and premature death in the United Kingdom. Smoking is also known to affect people in some of the following ways:

- It is the prime cause of cancer and heart disease.
- It lowers resistance to illness.
- It raises blood pressure.
- It lowers life expectancy.
- It reduces your sense of taste and smell.
- It reduces lung efficiency.
- It lowers fitness levels.
- It reduces your appetite.
- It makes your breath and clothes smell.
- Passive smoking (breathing other people's cigarette smoke) also leads to poor health.

Is there anything good to be gained from smoking? It would seem not.

Alcohol

Alcohol is part of the normal diet of many people, as an alcoholic drink at the end of the day may help to make people relax. However, excess alcohol is harmful to health and can lead to very serious internal problems and, for some people, death. Drinking too much alcohol leads to dehydration and will affect your performance in activities, and in the outdoors could lead to hypothermia. From a physical exercise perspective, drinking alcohol will:

- reduce your coordination
- slow down your reaction times
- affect your movement in performing skills and techniques
- lead to poor balance.

Figure 5.3 A maximum of 2 units of alcohol per day is recommended (this equates to one pint of beer or two small glasses of wine)

Alcohol is a drug which is best taken in moderation during the evening and never before, during or after physical exercise.

Family history

Some people suffer illness because of a family predisposition, for example, heart disease. You need to ask about your parents' and grandparents' health and consider whether they have lived to a good age.

Sleep and rest

It is important to get between seven and nine hours of sleep each night. If your pattern of sleep is disrupted by drinking alcohol or caffeine, smoking or eating a high-protein meal before sleeping, your performance will be affected. If you are tired from a lack of sleep or rest, you do not reach your full potential and fatigue will set in, so you slow down and your ability to perform skills and techniques is affected. Rest is essential to recover physically and mentally, as is your need to eat carbohydrates to replace your energy supplies and improve your motivation.

Figure 5.4 Rest and relaxation are very important after physical activity

Physical exercise

Exercise is associated with keeping healthier for longer – it reduces coronary heart disease, strokes, diabetes, colon cancer and hypertension. You should aim to do 30 minutes of physical exercise at least four times a week if possible, leaving a rest day in between sessions.

Drugs

The misuse of substances can lead to poor health. This includes the use of performance-enhancing drugs which are used to gain an extra advantage but are in fact illegal and harmful.

Diet

A good diet is essential to overall good health, so it is imperative that you know which foods to include in your meals and which ones are best avoided. A balanced diet is one of the best routes to healthy living, and though it may not be possible to balance your food correctly at every meal, it may be possible to get it right over a whole day or week. Choose options that are lower in fat, saturated fat, salt and sugars and drink approximately 1.2 litres (6–8 glasses) of fluid a day to replace that lost through waste products, sweating and evaporation through breathing – the warmer it gets the more you lose.

Obesity is accompanied by serious conditions such as non-insulin dependent diabetes, cardiovascular diseases and other complications. It is difficult and expensive to treat and reduces your life expectancy by eight to ten years. Sensible eating and the right balance of nutrients are essential to remaining at your healthy weight.

Figure 5.5 Ensure you eat plenty of fresh fruit and vegetables

Personal hygiene

Cleanliness is one defence against disease, and the body builds up internal defences against specific bacteria and viruses. Personal hygiene is about keeping yourself clean by regularly washing your hair, cutting your nails, cleaning your skin and brushing your teeth. Wear correctly fitting footwear and wash and dry your feet carefully to avoid athlete's foot and verrucas. Change and wash clothes daily and change clothes immediately after exercise.

Environment

Pollution can cause respiratory problems and noise can cause stress and affect your much-needed sleep.

Activity

Log onto www.food.gov.uk and find out about the 'eatwell plate', which shows the types and proportions of foods we need to have a healthy and well-balanced diet. Describe the 'plate' and match its contents against what you eat every day, including snacks. Can you honestly say you eat well?

Grading Tip!

To gain the Merit grade for this outcome you have to explain in detail the effects of the lifestyle factors on health and fitness that you described for the Pass grade, giving reasons why they are so important.

For the Distinction grade it is necessary to evaluate the factors, giving the strengths and weaknesses of each one and a conclusion to justify your comments.

Fruit and vegetables should make up one-third of your diet, as should starchy foods such as bread, potatoes, rice and pasta. The rest will include dairy products, meat, fish, eggs, beans and non-dairy sources of protein, as well as some fibre, both soluble and insoluble, which comes from plants.

5.4 Be able to provide advice on lifestyle improvement

Lifestyle improvement strategies that have a positive effect on health

Stress

You must ensure a good balance between work and leisure, making sure you get enough sleep – it is recommended we have eight hours per night to rest the body and the mind – and not to take drugs or medicine to help you sleep, relax or to affect your mood. If you have severe personal or emotional problems you must seek help from professionals. There are some stress management techniques such as goal setting, time management and physical exercise which can be used to reduce stress when it begins to build.

Smoking

It is not easy to stop smoking as it is habit forming and nicotine is addictive, but it will bring health benefits if you start to cut down the number of cigarettes you smoke and eventually stop. Again, there are professionals who can help, and the NHS has a free 'Quit smoking' campaign and can offer help in the form of patches, fake cigarettes and other methods designed to stop you smoking, as well as a 'smoking helpline'.

Physical exercise

Physical health is when your body is functioning as it was designed to function, and being active is important in keeping your body healthy. Walk or cycle, don't drive; use stairs instead of the lift; go out for long walks; join a gym or a jogging club. Start off at an easy level if you have not done much exercise before and always consult your GP if you are aware of any medical history which may prevent you from starting strenuous activities.

Diet

Eat three good meals a day. Breakfast is your most important meal and should be eaten as soon as you rise each morning, to refuel after the many hours without food while you slept. Try to eat as balanced a diet as possible. Lunch should be the second biggest meal of the day and contain energy foods in order for you to train and keep your mind sharp, while your evening meal really should be eaten before 7 p.m. to allow your digestive system to get to work before you go to bed.

Figure 5.6 A healthy salad – part of a balanced diet

If you must snack between meals, try to have fruit or juice and other healthy snacks. Eat foods rich in iron to help the blood flow around your body, and keep well hydrated, especially before, during and after exercise.

Other factors

● Environment – the body requires a stable environment away from pollution and toxins to sustain your health.

Eight tips for eating well

1. Base your meals on starchy foods.
2. Eat lots of fruit and vegetables.
3. Eat more fish.
4. Cut down on saturated fat and sugar.
5. Try to eat less salt – no more than 6 g per day.
6. Get active and try to be a healthy weight.
7. Drink plenty of water.
8. Don't skip breakfast.

Source: www.eatwell.gov.uk © Crown copyright material is reproduced with the permission of the Controller of HMSO and the Queen's Printer for Scotland

- Personal hygiene – regular dental checks, eating fresh fruit, being in sunlight and avoiding sugary drinks will help to improve your personal hygiene. Our clean lifestyles and reduced exposure to infectious diseases mean that our immune systems are more likely to react to otherwise harmless allergens.

5.5 Be able to plan a health-related physical activity programme in preparation for the public services

A personal health-related physical activity programme

Using all the information collected previously in this unit, you need to set out a health-related physical activity programme. First set yourself a main aim and then some objectives for how you are going to achieve this. Check out your present lifestyle and make any necessary changes – think about your present physical activity schedule (if

> ### Key terms
>
> **FITT** – an acronym for four of the principles of training: frequency, intensity, time and type
> **SPORT** – an acronym for five of the principles of training: specificity, progression, overload, reversibility and tedium

you have one) and set some SMART targets (specific, measurable, achievable, realistic and time constrained – these are explained in more detail in unit 6). For a physical activity programme of appropriate activities, you need to think about the nine principles of training. You can remember these by using the two acronyms explained below.

FITT

- Frequency – how often you need to exercise each week. You should train at least three times a week for a minimum of 30 minutes and spread the sessions out so you allow yourself some rest days.
- Intensity – how hard you need to work. You will only get fitter if you make your body systems work hard enough for them to adapt, but you must know your

- limits, such as the training threshold of 80%.
- Time – the amount of time you intend to spend in each session. Training sessions should gradually last longer to make the body systems work harder
- Type – which type of activities you will include to keep it fun and interesting. For instance, try cross-training, swimming or cycling.

SPORT

- Specificity – each person will need a different training programme because everyone is different and does different things. Therefore the programme is specific to you and only includes the specific exercises and activities that you will be participating in. The programme should be set at the correct level for you, and designed so that it conditions your body to develop the correct type of fitness.
- Progression – you need to ensure that you slowly and gradually increase the amount of training, exercise and activities that you carry out in order that your body adapts to the changes. Your fitness levels usually increase quite quickly at the beginning of the programme but then slow down as

you get a routine going, eventually, sometimes, staying at the same level for a while.

- Overload – the idea of setting up a programme is to make your body work harder, so you must do one of three things: increase the number of times you participate, increase the intensity (how hard you make your body work) or increase the amount of time you spend on the activity. If you do not overload the programme, you will see very little improvement, but be careful not to overload it too much or you will cause an injury.
- Reversibility – your fitness levels can drop again very quickly, so it is important not to stop training and competing. Once your fitness levels have gone down it will be much harder to get back to where you were originally. However, if you are injured or ill you must stop immediately and return to the start of the programme once you are fully fit.
- Tedium – if the activities and the exercises are boring you will not want to take part. Try to use a variety of methods and exercises to keep the programme exciting and ensure that you will continue to participate and improve.

Table 5.1 A typical health-related physical activity programme

Week 1 Date	Aim	Objectives	Targets	
	Activity	Meals	Change to lifestyle	Comments
Monday				
Tuesday				
Wednesday				
Thursday				
Friday				
Weekend				

End-of-unit knowledge check

1. List three health-related and three skill-related components of fitness.
2. What is the average time for males and females to run 1.5 miles in the Armed Forces?
3. Why does your heart beat go faster when you exercise?
4. Which is the best type of training to join the public services, bodybuilding or cardiovascular training?
5. List six lifestyle factors.

Grading criteria

In order to pass this unit, the evidence that you present for assessment needs to demonstrate that you can meet all the learning outcomes for the unit. The criteria for a pass grade describe the level of achievement required to pass this unit.

To achieve a pass grade the evidence must show that you are able to:	To achieve a merit grade the evidence must show that, in addition to the pass criteria, you are able to:	To achieve a distinction grade the evidence must show that, in addition to the pass and merit criteria, you are able to:
P1 Describe a fitness assessment for each of the major components of fitness [EP, IE]	**M1** Explain the results of the fitness assessment and measure against the relevant public service entrance test	**D1** Evaluate results of the fitness assessment, analyse strengths and recommend improvements
P2 Describe the structure and function of the muscular-skeletal, cardiovascular and respiratory systems [SM]		
P3 Undertake a fitness activity, record and identify the short-term effects of exercise on the major human body systems [CT, EP, IE, RL]	**M2** Explain the short- and long-term effects of exercise on the major human body systems	

To achieve a pass grade the evidence must show that you are able to:	To achieve a merit grade the evidence must show that, in addition to the pass criteria, you are able to:	To achieve a distinction grade the evidence must show that, in addition to the pass and merit criteria, you are able to:
P4 Describe the lifestyle factors that can affect health [CT, IE, TW]	**M3** Explain the effects of identified lifestyle factors on health and fitness, when applying for public service and long-term employment	**D2** Evaluate the effects of identified lifestyle factors on health and fitness, when applying for public service and long-term employment
P5 Provide lifestyle improvement strategies that can have a positive effect on health [CT, EP, IE]	**M4** Explain lifestyle improvement strategies to justify their positive effect on health	
P6 Plan a six-week health-related physical activity programme based on personal results [CT, EP, IE, RL]		

Unit 6
Fitness testing and training for the uniformed public services

Introduction

Fitness is a fundamental entry requirement for the uniformed public services and for the continued physical development of staff. A key component of preparing yourself physically is to understand how to plan, undertake and review a personal fitness training programme to ensure you are capable of performing the complex and difficult tasks that service life will demand.

This unit looks at the fitness requirements and physical fitness tests of the different uniformed public services, as well as the methods of fitness training and components of fitness. From this knowledge you are required to plan your own fitness training programme using the principles of training, monitoring your progress and evaluating the results. This will require using a training diary and receiving feedback to set new targets and goals in preparation for your fitness test with the service of your choice.

Learning outcomes:

By the end of this unit, you should:

1. Know the fitness requirements for entry into the uniformed public services.

2. Know different methods of fitness training.

3. Be able to plan a fitness training programme.

4. Be able to monitor and review a fitness training programme.

6.1 Know the fitness requirements for entry into the uniformed public services

Entrance fitness requirements and tests for three different public services

The entrance fitness requirements and tests for the three Armed Forces are reasonably easy to achieve, much more so than some of the emergency services (also known as 'Blue light' services), because once you have joined the British Army, Royal Air Force or the Royal Navy, you will be asked to complete a rigorous and specific basic training course to prepare you for action in each of those services. The training for specialist roles within the Armed Forces, such as the Royal Marines, is even more demanding once you have passed the entrance tests.

Activity

Why do the uniformed public services have entrance fitness tests? In a small group, discuss the reasons why you think each of the public services have their own entrance requirements and different tests.

Fire Service

Many people have no idea that fire fighting is only part of what the Fire Service does. Just as important is the work on preventing fires and accidents from happening in the first place, and of course the unpredictable environmental factors such as floods and storms, oil spills, terrorism threats and transport accidents. So the Fire Service recruits people with special skills and abilities, especially that of being able to work with the public, as they visit schools, colleges, businesses and the community as a whole. You will be given the right training and development once you have been recruited.

Key term

Aerobic fitness – this refers to endurance, or the ability to sustain work for prolonged periods

The physical and job-related fitness tests are just a small part of the entry requirements, but they will determine whether you have the required levels of **aerobic fitness** and strength to carry out the role of a firefighter. You will need to be fit as you will need to use ladders, hoses and other equipment, but it is not just a case of sheer strength; you can achieve many things by employing the right technique.

Figure 6.1 Fitness test for the Fire Service

The tests include:

- The ladder climb – tests your confidence and ability to follow instructions.
- Casualty evacuation and ladder lift – tests your upper and lower body strength and coordination.

- Being placed in an enclosed space – tests your confidence and agility while identifying any claustrophobic tendencies.
- The equipment assembly – looks at your manual dexterity.
- The equipment carry – tests your aerobic fitness, upper and lower body strength and your coordination.

Royal Air Force

Everyone who joins the RAF must have a basic level of fitness, so you are requested to take part in a pre-joining fitness test. The test is a 1.5-mile run on a treadmill to be completed in an allocated time, plus a specified number of press-ups and sit-ups, all of which will depend upon your age and gender. For someone just leaving school, the maximum time for the run is 12 minutes 11 seconds for a male and 14 minutes 26 seconds for a female.

Men will have to complete four press-ups and seven sit-ups while women will need to complete two press-ups and six sit-ups.

Once you have achieved these results you are invited to a Potential Recruit Training Course where you will undergo further fitness assessments, which include the multi-stage fitness test and a series of press-ups and sit-ups.

To join the RAF Regiment Gunners, however, you will need to attend a Potential Gunners Selection Course where you are expected to pass a number of fitness tests. These include a 3-mile run to be completed in less than 24 minutes, a multi-stage fitness test, 10 press-ups, 25 sit-ups and a 50-m swim. There is also a 'skirmish exercise', which will test your endurance as you simulate casualty evacuation, tactical movement and transporting equipment as a team.

Royal Marines Commando

Once you have been considered for the Royal Marines you will have to attend the Potential Royal Marines Course (PRMC) at the Commando Training Centre at Lympstone, Devon for three days. In two of those days you will be expected to participate in four sessions of physical training which will include a 3-mile run in 22.5 minutes (1.5 miles as a group then run back in your own time) and a body weight circuit of press-ups, squats, pull-ups, box jumps, triceps dips and lunges, among other things.

You should be able to cope with running 4–6 miles at a 7 minute per mile pace, three times a week, completing 60 press-ups in 2 minutes, 80 sit-ups in 2 minutes, 6 pull-ups and a minimum of level 11 on the multi-stage fitness test. In addition you may have further physical activity sessions to build up your cardiovascular fitness. For example: a 35-minute run followed by three sets of 3 pull-ups; a 45-minute bike ride and three sets of 3 pull-ups; 35-minute swim followed by three sets of 3 pull-ups.

If you are unsuccessful first time around you may be offered another chance at the PRMC a few months later, but if you have shown the required potential to undergo 30 weeks of rigorous training, then you will be invited to join and try to attain the famous 'Green Beret'.

A fitness test for the main components of fitness and comparison of results

Each of the main components of fitness has a number of physical tests you can perform in order to measure your results against those required by each of the public services as an entry requirement.

Multi-stage fitness test

This test, sometimes referred to as the 'bleep' or 'beep' test, is used to test your aerobic endurance. It is a maximal test used by nearly all the public services as it easy to use, gives instant results and can be done by a number of people at one time. It involves a progressive run of 15–20 metres between two markers or cones in time with a series of bleeps from a tape/CD player, which gets progressively faster. You have to keep in time with the bleeps and record your score once you fail three times to reach the end in time or are too tired to carry on. The test measures your VO2 maximum score, which will give an indication of your aerobic or cardiovascular endurance. (VO2 max is maximum cardiovascular fitness or aerobic capacity.)

Figure 6.2 One of the fitness training methods used by the public services

Grip dynamometer test

For this strength test you are required to squeeze a handgrip dynamometer in order to measure the force of your forearm grip. Hold the dynamometer in your dominant hand, set the dial to zero or switch on, and squeeze tightly while lowering your arm from 45 degrees to rest at your side. Record your result, re-calibrate the dynamometer and take a reading from your non-dominant hand using the same technique. This will measure your isometric strength in kilograms.

Sit-and-reach test

This is a simple check on the flexibility of your hamstrings and lower back. Using a specific 'sit and reach box', or a bench and a yardstick, you sit with your feet flat against the box and, keeping your knees straight, reach slowly forward, keeping your hands parallel, and hold at the furthest point. Your result will be recorded for three successive attempts and the mean (average) score calculated

Sit-ups, pull-ups or press-ups

These tests vary in length of time and will measure your muscular endurance. Using the correct techniques, perform each of the tests for a specific time or until you cannot go any further. Some public services require you to continue for one minute or two minutes, while the Royal Marines prefer you to participate for as long as you are physically able and record your score.

Vertical or horizontal jump tests

Either of these activities can be undertaken to test the anaerobic power in your legs, and a measurement recorded from your starting position to the one you reach. For the vertical jump you mark the wall by reaching as high as you can then leap upwards to make a mark at the top of the jump. The difference between the two marks is known as the jump distance. The horizontal jump is similar, but a mark drawn at your toes is measured to a mark at your heels once you have leapt forward with both feet together, and the difference between the two is calculated. Three attempts at each are recommended to get a mean score.

Sprint tests

A variety of distances can be used to test your speed, depending upon the requirements for your public service entrance test. On response to a whistle you should sprint as fast as possible over the distance, which is timed in hundredths of seconds, and record the result. Perform the test three times using a stop watch or electronic timing gates.

These are just a few of the simple tests you can undertake to gain some baseline measurements of your fitness. They must be performed at regular intervals to show your improvements, but remember, you are testing against yourself and not someone else, so do not compare your results with another person. Once you have undertaken the relative fitness tests for each of the main components of fitness, you will need to compare them with those required on public service entrance tests.

Figure 6.3 Training to pass a public service entrance test

Activity

Research the entrance fitness test requirements for the public service of your choice and compare them with another service, preferably of a different type, such as a blue light service and one of the Armed Forces. See which ones are near to your own results.

Strengths and areas for improvement

In order to confirm your strengths and areas for improvement you must have the results from your baseline measurements and any subsequent testing. Compare the results for each of the tests and note which ones have shown an improvement, which have remained constant and any that show a decrease. Explain the reasons for each of the test results and the differences that have occurred, and state how you can make improvements to all of them, even those considered to be strengths. You may decide to carry out further regular testing or participate in specific training.

6.2 Know different methods of fitness training

P3   M2   D1

Methods of fitness training for the main components of physical fitness

Key terms

Anaerobic system – this is the body system that is used to increase non-endurance fitness, such as strength, speed and power
Components of fitness – aerobic endurance, strength, flexibility, muscular endurance, power, speed

There are six main **components of fitness**.

- *Aerobic endurance or cardiovascular endurance* – this is the ability to exercise at a steady pace over a relatively long period of time without becoming tired. Otherwise known as 'stamina', it involves the heart and lung systems coping with activity of the whole body, such as running, swimming, skiing, rowing or cycling.

- *Strength* – this is the ability of your muscles to apply a maximum force on an immovable object in a single contraction. It requires training with weights or resistance machines for a number of sets and repetitions.
- *Flexibility* – this is the ability to move your joints through a full range of movement. You need to be flexible in order to perform the required movements, prevent injuries and develop more strength and power.
- *Muscular endurance* – this is the ability to make your muscles work hard over a period of time. The muscles should produce repeated contractions at a low intensity, and training is performed by a number of repetitions.

- *Power* – this is the ability to produce strength at speed or to move a heavy load. Muscular power comes from the **anaerobic system**.
- *Speed* – this is the ability to move the body or individual limbs quickly. You supply energy to the muscles rapidly and they have to contract in the shortest possible time.

Methods of fitness training
Continuous and Fartlek training

Continuous training is also referred to as 'steady state' training as it is long, slow distance training. It is of moderate intensity and uses the principle of overload so that you can train for a considerable period of time and either increase the duration or distance of the training. It is ideal for beginners to exercise and when recovering from injury.

Fartlek is a different method used to improve your aerobic fitness. The intensity

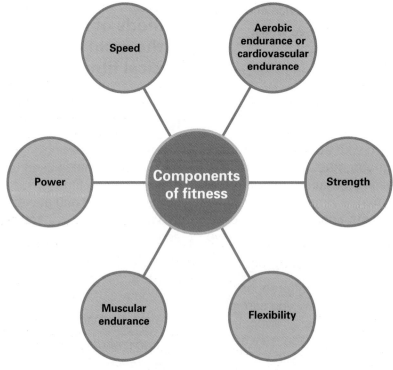

Figure 6.4 The six components of fitness

of the work is varied to suit individuals and is carried out over different terrains such as grass, hard paths, uphill, wooded areas and can include sprints interspersed with jogging.

Weight and resistance training

Weight training allows you to have a constant resistance during a dynamic action, which will increase your strength and help you to specialise in certain movements or muscle groups. Using barbells and dumbbells you can alter the type of training by using higher weights for fewer repetitions or lower weights for more sets of repetitions, depending upon your requirements.

Fixed resistance machines are much more popular now as the number of gyms increases. They provide much more safety than free weights yet still allow you to change your load base in order to overload or progress to suit your training programme.

Stretching

There are a number of different methods of stretching to improve the amount of movement possible around a joint or a number of joints. You need to overload the specific muscle group by stretching the muscles beyond what they normally do. Static stretches, either passive or active, are controlled and slow. Once you have stretched the muscle, you hold the position for ten seconds while slowly overloading it beyond its normal range. Passive stretching requires someone else to apply an external force to stretch the muscle.

Ballistic stretching involves fast, jerking movements by bobbing and bouncing through a full range of movement. This method is specific to certain activities and must be performed carefully to avoid injury. Proprioceptive neuromuscular facilitation (PNF) stretching also requires two people but is much more controlled. You hold a stretch in position while your partner gently forces the muscle further and you force them back to produce overload in opposition.

Circuit and core stability training

In a circuit training session a number of exercise stations are arranged where you undertake a particular activity. Either a time limit or number of repetitions for each station is used, depending on the type of fitness you are improving, e.g. aerobic fitness, muscular endurance, strength or a combination of these. The circuit should be designed to exercise different muscle groups and a rest should be allowed between exercises. You can easily overload or progress the exercises by changing the time limits or repetitions and even increasing the number of stations.

Core stability training strengthens the muscles of the abdominal area and allows you to generate more force and power through your arms and legs. The Swiss ball is being used increasingly to perform exercises to load the core muscles, though you can still use the old favourites such as press-ups and sit-ups.

Plyometrics

Previously known as jump training, plyometrics is used to improve explosive leg power and is increasingly used with the speed, agility and quickness (SAQ) method of training. You are required to jump, hop or bound from benches or over hurdles to stretch and contract the muscles of the legs.

Interval training and pyramid training

The concept of interval training is that you participate in an exercise at a very high threshold for a short period of time, followed by a rest period then a further exercise and rest. This is undertaken a number of times and allows for progression and overload by increasing the length of training and rest periods.

Evaluating the methods of fitness training for the components of fitness

For each of the methods of fitness training you are required to evaluate the effect on the main components of physical fitness. You can either assess the different training methods first and then match against each of the components of fitness or, if you wish, explain each of the components of fitness first and match them to the range of fitness training methods available. In either case you need to ensure full coverage of all the elements with an analysis and conclusion.

 Grading Tip!

To achieve the Merit grade for this outcome you have to explain in detail a method of fitness training for each of the components of fitness that you described for the Pass criteria. For a Distinction grade it is necessary for you to evaluate those training methods giving the strengths and weaknesses for each one and a conclusion as to which ones are the most effective for you.

6.3 Be able to plan a fitness training programme

Collecting information and other considerations

There is information to be collected and certain considerations to be taken into account before you can start to plan your own fitness training programme. The first thing to decide is what goals you are going to set yourself. You will need short-term goals of a few weeks, some medium-term goals to achieve in months, and a long-term goal overall, perhaps in a year or more.

Ask Yourself!

What kind of goals do you need to set yourself? Are they particular fitness targets such as 'get fitter', or are there specific components of fitness that you need to improve? For example, do you need to improve your cardiovascular endurance or your upper body strength? Is your flexibility as good as it should be? Do you need to improve your Body Mass Index (BMI)?

Look at the entry requirements and fitness tests that you will be required to complete in order to join the public service of your choice and build your goals around the results needed.

You must ensure that you do not start vigorous physical activity or training immediately, especially if you have never done any before or if it is a while since you did so. You must look at your present lifestyle and see if there are any changes that need to be made first, and then consider what you can put into your fitness training programme.

Lifestyle includes your diet and nutritional intake. To train correctly it is important to have a balanced diet and consume plenty of liquids. A balanced diet contains plenty of fruit and vegetables as well as starchy,

Table 6.1 A balanced diet

Types of food		Examples
50–65% of carbohydrates for energy production	1. Simple – sugars which provide quick energy	Fruit, sport drinks, jam, sweets, milk, honey, sugar
	2. Complex – starches with a slow release of energy	Bread, potatoes, rice, pasta, cereals, vegetables, crackers
25–30% of fats for energy and insulation	1. Saturated – full fat	Dairy products – cream, cheese, milk, butter; plus – meat, pies, cake, biscuits and chocolate
	2. Unsaturated – mono and poly	Oils, peanuts, low-fat spread, oily fish, nuts
10–15% of protein for growth and repair of cells		Red meat, eggs, poultry, fish, nuts

energy-giving foods such as pasta, rice potatoes and wholegrain bread, with very little fat, salt and sugar. Another food type to consider is fibre, which aids the digestive system and can help prevent/treat certain diseases.

Other lifestyle factors include the consumption of alcohol and illegal drugs, smoking, stress and your family or medical history.

Alcohol is a legal drug that may be consumed by people aged 18 or over. There is plenty of information available regarding the recommended daily intake of units of alcohol (though these may gradually be changed to millilitres) and the diseases associated with drinking too much. Illegal drugs should not be taken by anyone at any time.

Stress is something which we all suffer from some time or another; in fact, a small amount of stress is good for you. The secret is not to have too much stress at any one time.

The targets you set yourself to attain your goals must be SMART:

Specific – to focus attention
Measurable – to be able to assess progress
Achievable – to be able to reach them
Realistic – to be challenging
Time bound – to be set within a time limit for completion.

Or even SMARTER! The above, plus:

Exciting – to be fun and enjoyable
Recorded – to evaluate progress, provide feedback and set new targets.

Principles of training

There are several principles of training that should be followed, as listed below.

- *Overload* – you can overload the fitness on your body systems by working them harder than normal so that the body will adapt and become fitter. This can be done by training more often, spending more time on each element of fitness or just working harder.
- *Progression* – as the overload adapts to the extra stress, you gradually or progressively increase the exercises, but not too quickly or you will risk injury or it will become too difficult to reach

your targets. The fitter you become the harder it is to progress.

- *Reversibility* – you cannot store fitness, so if you stop due to injury or you lessen the overload and progression, it does not take long to get out of condition and lose the fitness you have worked hard to gain.
- *Tedium* – vary the fitness training programme to avoid boredom. Make changes where necessary to keep the exercises and training enjoyable and interesting. You could change the venue or type of training.
- *Specific* – it has to be the right type of training to achieve your targets and goals. Each method of exercise will affect different components and you must overload and progress slowly to see the difference. Do not over train by doing too much as it can have negative effects; ensure you get plenty of rest and enough sleep between training sessions.
- *Type* – this is referring to the kind of training you participate in and the types of activity that will develop your fitness.
- *Time* – this is how long you train for. Each session needs to be a minimum of 30 minutes in order to raise your heart rate and for you to feel any benefit.
- *Frequency* – you need to train at least four times a week to improve your fitness, with a rest day in between each session in order for your body to recover.
- *Intensity* – depending upon your present fitness you need to start at the right level and work your body systems gradually to make them adapt.
- *Periodisation* – this is a progressive change in the type of training to gain the maximum fitness benefits. A micro-cycle represents each individual training session, a meso-cycle would cover the six-week training programme, while a

macro-cycle is the culmination of all the targets that you set at the beginning and your ultimate goal.

Now you can begin to put together your six-week fitness training programme.

Activity

Design your six-week training programme using all the information you have gathered. Draw up a table for seven days – remembering to rest every other day as recommended – with exercises for morning, afternoon or evening, depending upon other considerations such as work, study, sport and leisure. Use a variety of training methods and exercises throughout your programme and try to use all components of fitness for overall improvement.

Undertaking your fitness training programme using a training diary

Now it is time to put your fitness training programme into practice. You need to keep a diary of all the physical activities you take part in: date, day, time, warm up, activity, venue, how long you participated for, cool down and some immediate self-evaluation – how you felt afterwards and what you could possibly do next time. If you begin to feel tired or are finding it to be too much at any time, review the programme immediately and make some changes in order for you to continue the training programme.

If you are injured at any time – stop! There is no point continuing a fitness training programme if you are unfit to do it. The vital thing is to rest and recuperate. Analyse how you were injured. If it is linked to your training schedule, you will need to make changes. However, if the injury has no relation to the programme then you must terminate the training immediately and go back to week one once you are fit enough to start the programme again.

Any information relating to your fitness – your feelings, your mood, any injuries or changes – must be recorded in your training diary on a regular basis as this will enable you to review and evaluate the programme accurately once the six weeks of training have been completed.

Think about it!

What headings will you require in your training diary? Will it need to cover every day of the week? How will you link it to the training programme?

6.4 Be able to monitor and review a fitness training programme

Report and explanation of the six-week training programme

With your six-week fitness training programme completed, you can use your fitness training diary entries to review, evaluate and analyse all the results. You can establish whether you have achieved your goals, identify the strengths of the programme and decide upon areas of improvement for your next six-week fitness training programme. You could also have feedback from someone who

has been observing you while taking part in the programme to help in future modifications and improvements to the new programme.

You should be able to learn something new about your fitness after every session. This will supply you with information on the strengths and weaknesses against which the improvements can be assessed. You should develop your own self-assessment techniques, paying particular attention to what needs to be improved and in what order.

Key terms

Extrinsic factors – factors which are not directly related to you personally, e.g. training indoors or outdoors, time of training, weather, footwear, clothes

Intrinsic factors – factors which are directly related to you personally, e.g. age, diet, health, motivation, self-confidence, level of ability and previous training

The effectiveness of your fitness performance comes down to a range of factors, some of which will be **intrinsic factors** (which come from within yourself) and others of which will be **extrinsic factors** (which come from elsewhere).

It is very difficult to improve or change unless you receive feedback. There are several ways of getting feedback:

● It can be done immediately or be delayed until later.
● It could be your own knowledge of your performances and the results.
● It can come from you and anyone else who has witnessed your training.
● It can be carried out at the end of each training session and at the termination of the programme.

Once all the feedback has been gathered you need to decide how to use the information. The first step is to set yourself short-, medium- and long-term goals, then set some new SMART targets (as you did when setting up the original fitness training programme) to enable you to set up a new programme with the strengths and improvements included.

Evaluation of strengths and areas for improvement with recommendations for future activities

So what were your strengths in each of the particular activities? Strength is not about being strong but refers to knowledge or understanding, a skill or technique that you feel confident and competent in carrying out on a regular basis, and maybe one that you could teach to others. It may be that you are fully aware of the safety or environmental factors that have to be considered before and during the activity, which is a strength; or one of your strengths may be completing a risk assessment correctly. Strengths do not exclusively relate to the physical and mental factors of carrying out a particular activity.

Areas for improvement are those skills and techniques in which you do not feel so confident. It is understandable that you cannot be excellent at everything – we are all learning all the time, so improvements can always be made to some areas of our knowledge or physical prowess. Is there any particular area of knowledge or understanding that you need to research before trying out an activity again?

Activity

Make a list of all the strengths that you presume to have and another list of all the areas for improvement. Discuss the list with a leader from the activities, your peers and any other observer of the activities to confirm or change any of them. Then you can evaluate the list and recommend changes for the next time you take part in any of the activities.

Grading Tip!

In order to move up to a Distinction grade for this outcome you may need to complete a performance profile to analyse your physiological fitness. Draw up a table and list all the components of fitness that you covered in your fitness programme. Include ten columns numbered 1–10. Give yourself a mark out of 10 on each of the components, with 1 being the lowest. This will give you a profile of your current level of fitness and will identify your strengths and weaknesses.

End-of-unit knowledge check

1. List the six main components of fitness.
2. Describe three methods of fitness training.
3. Why is a balanced diet important during fitness training?
4. List six of the principles of fitness.
5. Who can provide you with feedback on your training programme and diary?

Grading criteria

In order to pass this unit, the evidence that you present for assessment needs to demonstrate that you can meet all the learning outcomes for the unit. The criteria for a pass grade describe the level of achievement required to pass this unit.

To achieve a pass grade the evidence must show that you are able to:	To achieve a merit grade the evidence must show that, in addition to the pass criteria, you are able to:	To achieve a distinction grade the evidence must show that, in addition to the pass and merit criteria, you are able to:
P1 Describe the entrance fitness requirements and tests of three different public services [IE]		
P2 Outline a fitness test for the main components of fitness and compare results based on a public service entrance test [EP, RL]	**M1** Explain the strengths and areas for improvement of the fitness test	
P3 Undertake a fitness activity, record and identify the short-term effects of exercise on the major human body systems [CT, EP, IE, RL]	**M2** Explain one method of fitness training for six different components of physical fitness	**D1** Evaluate for the different components of physical fitness
P4 Plan a six-week personal fitness training programme to incorporate the principles of training [CT, RL]	**M3** Explain in detail strengths and areas for improvement following completion of the training programme	**D2** Evaluate strengths and areas for improvement following completion of the training programme, providing recommendations for future activities

Unit 9
Outdoor and adventurous expeditions

Introduction

To understand the need for **expeditions** and their role in outdoor adventure you need to be familiar with their history, their aims and their successes and the way that they demonstrate teamwork, endeavour, humanity, leadership and tenacity. To undertake an expedition you need the appropriate practical knowledge and **skills**, and in this unit you will have the opportunity to demonstrate your competence and proficiency in a wide range of practical expedition skills as well as leadership and teamwork skills.

You will undertake at least two expeditions, which will complement and build on any other outdoor and adventurous expeditions that you have participated in, either in a similar programme of study or in a wider context of expeditions such as that through the Duke of Edinburgh's Award, the Armed Forces cadets or local Scout and Guide association.

Throughout this chapter you will find ways to develop your self-confidence and self-esteem and improve your inter-personal skills in a safe learning environment. These skills and qualities will be developed through the practical participation in planning, carrying out and evaluating day and overnight expeditions, which will enhance your physical, social, spiritual, emotional and intellectual development.

Key terms

Expedition – an organised journey or voyage; for exploration; for scientific or military purpose

Skills – practical ability; a craft requiring skill

9.1 Know the types of expedition

Through the ages expeditions have taken place for many different reasons. You may have heard of Christopher Columbus, Hannibal, Ernest Shackleton, Marco Polo or Ellen MacArthur, all of whom led expeditions of a very different kind at different times in our history. Not that you will be going to quite such lengths in this unit! Researching expeditions from the past will give you an excellent insight into some of the challenges you may face when carrying out your own expedition.

Different expeditions from the past

Expeditions come in a variety of guises, be they via land, sea or air. They are undertaken by individuals, teams and armies. They may be for conquest, trade, exploration, scientific or even for corporate reasons. They can be organised as part of education, to help disaffected youth, run by various clubs or as a form of training. Whatever their reason and whoever is taking part, expeditions are exciting, interesting, hard work and very intriguing. In all expeditions you are part of a team – you will grow in confidence, your skill set will improve, your appreciation for the environment will increase and you will test yourself against nature. And it is these factors that have made people go out and try to do something that has either never been done before or to do it better, faster or against the odds.

Dame Ellen MacArthur

Ellen became an overnight star when she returned from a solo circumnavigation of the globe in record time, claiming a world record. She was born in Derbyshire, which has no coast, but became a sailor and bought her first boat when she was at school. In 1995, when she was 17, Ellen sailed single handed around Great Britain – she circumnavigated it.

Ellen started her attempt of the solo world record on 28 November 2004, sailing over the equator, around the Cape of Good Hope and back around Cape Horn to the finishing line in France on 7 February 2005, beating the previous record by over a day. This expedition was a culmination of previous round the world voyages, both single handed and with a crew, over the previous two years.

Sir Ernest Shackleton

Shackleton was a crew member on Scott's famous *Discovery* expedition to the Antarctic in 1901, but had to be sent back due to illness. In 1908 he returned to Antarctica as head of his own expedition to reach the South Pole and the South Magnetic Pole, aboard the ship *Nimrod*, for which he received a knighthood. Six years later Shackleton announced his new venture, the 'Imperial Trans-Antarctic Expedition', which was to cross the continent on foot, a journey of 1,800 miles. It was to be one of the most famous expeditions of all time.

The ship *Endurance* set sail for Antarctica in December 1914, but a month later and only one day from land, the ship became trapped in sea ice which would not melt until September, in the Antarctic spring. However, the pressure on the hull from the ice it was trapped in was so great that it started to break up, and they had to abandon ship, getting all the equipment onto the ice before it sank. They camped on the floating ice for two months, then got into lifeboats to sail to solid ground. From there Shackleton made two open boat journeys with four of his men, one to a whaling station to organise a rescue party for the rest of the crew, the other an 800-mile ocean crossing to South Georgia Island.

Figure 9.1 Shackleton's expedition ship *Endurance*

Activity

Research four other famous expeditions from the past to get an idea of what people will do to test their resolve, put their leadership skills to the test and try to beat others in achieving a dream. Your expedition may not be so famous, but it could be the start of something much bigger than you anticipated before you started this qualification.

Compare and contrast different expeditions

Once you have carried out your research into at least four different expeditions, it is necessary to compare and contrast them and show the differences between each of them. Try to use expeditions that are very different from each other, for example, across lands, on the sea, up mountains, and even use one you may have taken part in yourself, so that you can really show the differences in the planning, preparation, participation and review with plenty of detail.

Start with the aims of each expedition:
- Why did they take place at that particular time?
- What was the reason for such a venture?
- Was it to break a record, to beat someone else, for monetary reasons, to achieve an award?
- Was it educational, commercial, military or exploratory?

Then look at the planning of the expedition:
- How much time was spent on planning?
- How much did it cost to organise and participate in?
- Did everyone have the right clothing and equipment?

- Did everything run according to the timeline given?

On the execution of the expedition:
- Did everyone return safely?
- Did everyone carry out their roles and responsibilities?
- Where was the base camp set up?
- Was there enough food and water?

9.2 Be able to plan expeditions

Planning a one-day expedition without support

Expeditions involve joint planning and preparation by all members of the group and should have a clearly defined purpose. The first task is to have an initial briefing to decide on the type and length of expedition. This will help the participants to consider the options available and clarify the commitment required by all members of the group. The purpose, aims and objectives of the expedition should relate to the interests and abilities of those taking part and not just to fulfil the requirements of the unit or the qualification. You may wish to test yourself on a physically demanding journey, or see the countryside environment close up; you may need to find a way of bonding your group (so they work better as a team), or just to learn more about your course outside the normal environment of your centre.

If you are travelling on foot, the routes you take should make as little use of roads as possible and avoid villages. Cycling expeditions should involve minor roads, lanes, tracks, bridleways and disused railway tracks. Cycling on footpaths is illegal unless there are marked cycle ways. Expeditions involving water should use safe waterways such as inland waters, lochs, estuaries or sheltered coastal waters.

First decide where the expedition will take place and find the map that relates to the area. All route finding should be based on the 'Explorer' 1:25000 scale maps as they have precise details of footpaths, tracks, lanes and field boundaries, making instruction and learning easier. A compass should then be studied to take precise bearings for the route card.

Figure 9.2 Equipment needed for an expedition: map, compass and route card

Ask Yourself!

What is a route card?

For those learners who have never undertaken an expedition previously it is useful to understand what a route card is and why it is so useful when out in the countryside.

A route card gives all the important information of your expedition on one sheet of paper or card – names of the people taking part, dates, location, details of the journey, approximate times, emergency routes, features of the expedition etc.

A copy is left wherever you start your journey and one at your centre, so that if you do not arrive at your destination by the given time, someone will be alerted. There are usually two or three route cards among the walking group so that you can keep a check on where you are and where you are going.

Identify and avoid any hazards, while taking environmental issues into account such as not trespassing on private land. The route card can now be completed.

Key term

Techniques – methods of achieving a purpose; the manner of execution

Map reading **techniques** are largely used when you are off the beaten track in mountainous or difficult terrain, where excellent navigation skills are essential. These techniques can be used effectively once you have learnt to interpret the features of a map. Some methods will rely on your eyesight while others use a compass. Pinpointing your location is a useful technique to make sure you are travelling in the right direction, or can help you to relocate if you are lost.

Think about it!

Pinpointing your location

1. Transit lines – when you know two or more features on a map will line up with one another along your journey you can form a transit line. As you walk along a track on the map, there will only be a single point where two features are in a direct line with each other.
2. Back bearings – using a compass you can take a bearing from a feature on the landscape to locate your position.
3. Resection – used when you are in the middle of the countryside by taking the bearings of three features in sight and located on your map – one to your right, one to the left and one in front of you.
4. Aspect of slope – when lost you can use slopes of the land to find your location. Find the km square on your map, face down the slope and use your compass to take a reading of the direction the hill is sloping.

You need to take into account your destination, how you will get there and the costs involved. Ensure that everyone is available for the day(s) planned for the expedition and that they all have the necessary equipment prior to leaving. Participants under the age of

18 will be required to have their parents sign a consent form agreeing to the expedition.

A risk assessment of the route should be completed well before the intended trip by someone in authority who will be travelling with you. A long-range weather forecast of the area should be checked a week before setting out. This should be up-dated the day before leaving and if there are any doubts regarding the conditions, the trip should be cancelled.

Planning an overnight expedition without support

The more thought and care you put into your planning the more likely you are to enjoy a successful experience. Once you have consulted with everyone in the group as to the possible location of your overnight stay, you should assess thoroughly the potential of the area and identify specific objectives, features, places of interest, summits to climb etc. It is advantageous if someone – possibly the leader – has some familiarity with the area for your first overnight expedition. You should obtain plenty of information about the area from various sources, especially a good map – Ordnance Survey Explorer 1:25000 being one of the best.

Preparation

While all the planning is going on for your second expedition, you need to ensure that your fitness is good enough to take the extra stress that will be placed on your body compared with the previous one-day expedition. You do not want to let your team down by being at the back all the time, unable to keep up with the pace of the leaders.

There are obviously more things to take into consideration for an overnight expedition than there were for your previous one-day trip. There will be travel arrangements to make, with the extra baggage that will

Activity

During the planning stage of your expeditions you will have to consider the personal clothing and equipment you may need to take with you. Remember, you have to carry everything that you pack, so do not take too much – you are not packing to go on holiday! Lay out all the clothing that you will need on the bed and then halve it. You will really only need to change your underwear, unless your outer clothing is too wet to wear again. Practise packing your backpack and then do it at night without the light on, as this is how it can be on some early mornings.

g Grading Tip!

It is quite easy to gain a Merit grade for this outcome as all you need to do is avoid support. That is, you should not ask for help from the leader or organiser of the expeditions. The emphasis is on teamwork and for you to all work together to plan, organise and undertake the two expeditions. However, you could always ask an expert for 'advice or guidance' on a particular query, and phrase your question in a way that the answer will not be seen as supportive! Ask before you pose the question if it will be considered as support. Remember, everyone has to contribute to the planning, otherwise you could say that they were being supported.

inevitably come with the increased amount of clothing and equipment that will be required – tents, sleeping bags, camping mats, stoves, food, fuel, spare clothing etc.

9.3 Be able to undertake expeditions

Taking part in the expeditions, demonstrating skills and techniques

After all the planning, debating, researching and training it is time to get out and participate in your expeditions, both the one-day venture and the overnight stay. You now have the chance to show what skills and techniques you have learnt and which ones you need to improve on. Don't be the one to constantly drag behind the rest of the group, or moan about everything to do with the expedition; rather, be the one who volunteers to take the lead, or helps to pitch other people's tents. Show your willingness to be a team worker, even a leader – enjoy the experience.

Navigation is the art of moving from one *known* place to another. When you don't know where you are, you are lost. If you intend to go out of sight of a road or feature you must know how to navigate back again. Mists descend rapidly and restrict visibility, and even a slight accident may delay you until after nightfall. If you ignore common-sense precautions, the hills have some stern lessons.

You will have already demonstrated various navigational skills while planning the two expeditions, including:

- orientation of a map
- plotting a route onto a route card
- using a compass to take bearings
- learning grid references

- interpreting scale and distance
- identifying map symbols
- obtaining a weather forecast.

You will now use some of these skills while in the great outdoors. Always know where you are on the map. Keep checking your precise location and moving the map to the direction of your travel. Double-check with your compass bearings, work out your pace and check with the timings that you are on course to complete the section as predicted, or make the necessary adjustments. Look at the features of the landscape and match them with the symbols on the map. Keep an eye on the weather and any recent changes in temperature, wind strength or direction, cloud formations and darkness.

If you are unfortunate and find that you are lost, there are a number of ways to summon help. You can use your emergency whistle, start a small fire, use a mirror to reflect the sun, flash your torch light, send two people ahead to find help, use your mobile phone or find the nearest water supply and follow it downhill.

On the overnight expedition you will be able to put the following camp craft skills and techniques into action:

- choosing the correct location for your tent – on a slight slope, door away from the wind, near shelter etc.
- erecting the tent
- setting up your sleeping arrangements
- unpacking your backpack
- setting up a stove and cooking food
- waste disposal
- washing up after eating
- keeping the site tidy
- relaxing and sleeping early to conserve energy
- cooking breakfast and clearing up
- packing away tents and backpacks
- leaving the site as you found it.

Also, please think about personal hygiene. You will be sharing with others in close proximity, even cramped conditions, and the last thing you want is to be reminded about your odour!

If you have decided to use different accommodation, such as a lodge, youth hostel or camping barn, you will not have so many tasks to complete, but you will still be required to help others to settle into an unfamiliar environment.

The outdoor environment puts a strain on the human body, so some of the skills you should learn are basic first aid treatments such as what to do for a sprain, blister, cut, shock and even exposure. All expeditions must have a first aid kit – in date and checked before leaving. Know how to raise the alarm if you get lost, where to wait for help and how to fetch help – these are all key to survival in the great outdoors.

Taking part in the expeditions showing advanced expedition skills

'I marvel at what has been achieved in giving so much pleasure and satisfaction to so many young people within reasonable parameters of safety. Reasonable, for safety in mountains is, and should be, a relative term. If you seek to eliminate it altogether, you remove the magnet of adventure, in which an element of risk is an essential ingredient; risk is the honey pot which lures us to the mountains. Most of the satisfaction in every "risk" sport lies, not in courting hazards unprepared, but in matching danger with your skills, and in extending your experience in order to step up the degree of risk which you seek.'

John Hunt, *Mountaincraft and Leadership* ISBN 0-903908-75-1

When venturing out on an expedition, the two basic principles are survival and safety, and as the passage above mentions, sometimes you have to weigh up one against the other and use your advanced expedition skills to make a decision between the two. Experience cannot be taught; you have to grab it and learn from it, and then remember what you have learnt.

Navigation is really observation, and it is a skill that everyone in the group must master. It takes you to a world of adventure and discovery and, on a nice sunny day, finding your route using a map and compass is a pleasant pastime, so everyone should be encouraged to navigate and to keep in touch with the group. However, when the weather or darkness is against you then it requires the skills of an experienced explorer to use the sun, moon and stars for navigation. If you find you are lost, it is important to have someone with you who can take the lead and find the way back 'on route'.

Measuring the time you take to travel a certain distance is fine if you are on firm, level terrain – we walk at around 4 km per hour or 1.5 minutes for 100 metres in these circumstances. However, this is rarely the case, so you need use an effective formula developed by a Scottish climber called Naismith, who took into account the changes in height while calculating speed over the ground. This is: 5 km per hour plus 30 minutes for every 300 metres of ascent (height climbed).

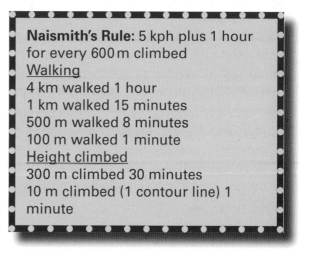

Naismith's Rule: 5 kph plus 1 hour for every 600 m climbed
Walking
4 km walked 1 hour
1 km walked 15 minutes
500 m walked 8 minutes
100 m walked 1 minute
Height climbed
300 m climbed 30 minutes
10 m climbed (1 contour line) 1 minute

Ask Yourself!

Using a map and compass to find direction is another skill that you can all practise in a warm, dry room. Understanding the map symbols, measuring distance, working out the relief and contours and setting the map to ground are techniques to learn before venturing into the unknown environment. You also need to learn, prior to the expedition, how to use a compass, how to work out the 'three' North bearings (true, grid and magnetic), and how to set the map and take compass bearings from the map.

However, once out in the open:

- **Can you estimate how far you have travelled and how far to go?**
- **Do you know the distance travelled by timing?**
- **How much height have you gained or lost?**
- **Can you navigate at night or in bad weather?**
- **Will you be able to keep group discipline?**

- Always play safe. Do not take any risks, do not guess. Double check all the time.
- Have continual reference to a map.
- Use the natural and manmade features to full advantage.
- Ensure your load is not too heavy. When you get tired you begin to lose concentration.
- Be aware of whiteout conditions, which make it impossible to judge scale, distance and steepness of slopes. Snow is a particular problem to be aware of.
- Know the weather forecast predictions.
- Use Naismith's rule.

Grading Tip!

You can upgrade from a Merit to a Distinction in various ways. When out on the expedition, offer to take the lead when no one else will volunteer. Keep talking to all the group members, show your skills in navigation by referring to the map and route card regularly, propose when to stop for a break and when to start off before you get too cold. Let the group know how far they have travelled and how much further there is to go, and help others to set up cooking stoves and tents when they are struggling. Do not moan and groan or show off in front of the group or the leader, and don't try to pretend that you know everything about expeditions, because we all have something to learn. If you can use your experience to help others and lighten the load by using your skills and techniques then you should achieve the top grade.

There are a number of techniques to use that will help you to keep you on the right track:

- Have the map oriented at all times (hold the map in the direction you are travelling).
- Keep the compass legs short. Each section of the journey should not go on for too long.

Figure 9.3 An expedition in the great outdoors

9.4 Be able to review the planning and undertaking of expeditions

P5   P6   M5   D2

The planning and undertaking of the expeditions

The review of the planning and undertaking of the expeditions can take a number of forms. You could have an individual evaluation with the leader of the expedition, or carry out your own self-evaluation as well as taking part in a group review.

A review, or evaluation, is an effective way of gathering information and can be used to set boundaries, it will help to devise improvement strategies and identify individual development issues. Evaluation helps the team to remember the aims initially set and to determine whether they have been achieved. Team members can also praise each other and celebrate success, as well as identifying any problems or weaknesses that can be rectified in a future task.

Individual review

- Acknowledge the benefits of teamwork.
- Reflect on your own performance.
- Plan for future developments.
- Make adjustments to how you work and who with.
- Recall how you interacted and worked within the group situation.

Group review

This is an important part of team development. When a task is going ahead, everyone will make observations about what is going well and how things may be better, but, sometimes, they will not reflect after the event and discuss the issues as a team. So it is imperative to use evidence from the expedition to refresh their memories and, for some group members, let them write down their thoughts anonymously if they are worried about feeding back to the group.

- Question the effectiveness of the planning.
- See what can be learnt from the experience for next time.
- Get responses from every individual.
- Collect the evidence and identify the development needs.

Ask a series of questions to encourage discussion, reflection and improvement:

- How much time was spent on planning, and completing?
- What changes did you make during the planning and participating?
- What elements of the plan were effective or ineffective?
- What additional support did you require and from whom?
- What were the main objectives?
- Did everyone contribute to planning and completing the task?
- Was there good, open communication between the group members?
- Were all team members clear about the primary aim?
- What aspects did not go according to plan and how were they rectified?
- What were the team's strengths and weaknesses?
- What are the areas for improvement?
- How could it be performed better next time?
- Was everyone clear about their individual role within the expedition?
- How did you go about making decisions on how to complete the task?
- Were you successful in completing the task?
- What qualities and skills did you bring to the group?
- What was your best contribution?
- What did the team do well and why?
- What have you learnt and when will you use it again?

Personal development plan

It is not easy to reflect on your own performance unless you have done really well and feel good about what you have done. If some things did not go so well, it is harder to think about what you can do to improve. This, however, is the best way to learn. If you are honest with yourself then you are the best person to put things right – you are

Figure 9.4 The Armed Forces carry out many expeditions as a part of training.

your best critic. It is important to be honest when you reflect on your own performance during the planning, preparation and undertaking of the expedition, otherwise you will not learn from the experience.

You could use Gibb's Reflective Cycle to review your contribution to the whole process, and then set up your own personal development plan.

Gibbs' Reflective Cycle

Description – what, when, where, why and how did it happen? Who was there? What did you do? What did others do?

Feelings – what were you thinking and feeling? How did you feel?

Evaluation – what was good about the expedition? What was not so good?

Analysis – what sense can you make out of the situation? Break it down into smaller parts – which parts went well and which parts did not go so well?

Conclusion – what else could you have done in the same situation?

Action plan – if it happened again, what would you do differently?

A personal development plan will focus on the activity being undertaken and how you performed, and will include actions and targets for you to achieve next time. Here is a typical start to a plan, but you could devise your own to suit what you hope to achieve.

Table 9.1 Personal development plan

The day expedition	What did not go well? (areas for improvement)	Why did it not go well?	How can it be improved? (action plan)	Date to be completed	Comments
Planning					
Clothing					
Equipment					

Strengths and areas for improvement

What you consider to be the strengths of your participation in both the one-day and overnight expeditions may not be mentioned in your development plan. This does not mean that you can forget about them – constantly monitor the areas that you think you are good at and show some improvement over time. Consider what level you achieved in the skills and techniques used; what knowledge and skills you gained and what improvements could be made. Were your fitness levels sufficient for you to keep up with the group? How often do you think you will be able to practise the skills and techniques you need to improve or maintain?

Your strengths and areas for improvement could also be in relation to your lifestyle and not just to the expeditions. Is your diet the correct one for energy-sapping physical exercise? Do you show enough commitment to training and effort? Can you improve your fitness test results, and do you have access to equipment and facilities to practise? Use a SWOT analysis to assess yourself and others. The strengths and weaknesses are intrinsic things (things that you can change), while the threats and opportunities are extrinsic things (things that are out of your control and come from external sources).

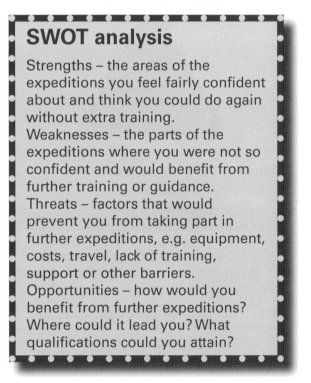

SWOT analysis

Strengths – the areas of the expeditions you feel fairly confident about and think you could do again without extra training.
Weaknesses – the parts of the expeditions where you were not so confident and would benefit from further training or guidance.
Threats – factors that would prevent you from taking part in further expeditions, e.g. equipment, costs, travel, lack of training, support or other barriers.
Opportunities – how would you benefit from further expeditions? Where could it lead you? What qualifications could you attain?

Justification of the suggestions made in the plan

For the top grade in this outcome you must state the reasons why you chose the particular areas for improvement in the development plan. The improvements will require targets for you to accomplish in order to show that you have improved, and dates set to give you the motivation and drive to complete them.

A development plan is based on performance, and performance is judged on three main areas, as shown in Figure 9.5.

Review your current performance and previous experience to see what level you feel you have achieved, what skills you have learnt or even mastered. Note any barriers that could affect your performance, and research any training or competitions that you could be involved in that could help you to improve.

Ask Yourself!

Consider the three points of performance and note in which points you were strong and which ones need more practice and development.

⑨ Grading Tip!

To achieve a higher grade for this outcome it is necessary for you to look at the strengths and areas for improvement that you chose for your personal development plan and give more detail as to why you selected those particular factors, how you are going to maintain or improve them for the next expedition and give a conclusion

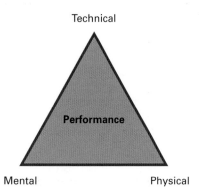

Figure 9.5 The three factors for a performance triangle

End-of-unit knowledge check

1. List ten points to consider when planning a one-day expedition.
2. What extra personal clothing and equipment will you need for an overnight venture, compared with a one-day expedition?
3. What is the average speed of walking when out on an expedition, with a full backpack, on firm and even terrain?
4. List three emergency signals you could use when lost in the hills.
5. What is Naismith's rule?

Grading criteria

In order to pass this unit, the evidence that you present for assessment needs to demonstrate that you can meet all the learning outcomes for the unit. The criteria for a pass grade describe the level of achievement required to pass this unit.

To achieve a pass grade the evidence must show that you are able to:	To achieve a merit grade the evidence must show that, in addition to the pass criteria, you are able to:	To achieve a distinction grade the evidence must show that, in addition to the pass and merit criteria, you are able to:
P1 Describe four different types of expedition [IE2, IE3, IE4]	**M1** Compare and contrast four different types of expedition	
P2 Plan a one-day expedition, with tutor support [CT1, CT2, CT3, CT5, CT6, RL3, TW1, TW2, TW3, TW4, TW5, TW6, SM1, SM2, SM3, SM4, SM6, EP1, EP2, EP3]	**M2** Independently plan a one-day expedition	
P3 Plan a multi-day expedition, with tutor support [CT1, CT2, CT3, CT5, CT6, RL3, TW1, TW2, TW3, TW4, TW5, TW6, SM1, SM2, SM3, SM4, SM6, EP1, EP2, EP3]	**M3** Independently plan a multi-day expedition	

To achieve a pass grade the evidence must show that you are able to:	To achieve a merit grade the evidence must show that, in addition to the pass criteria, you are able to:	To achieve a distinction grade the evidence must show that, in addition to the pass and merit criteria, you are able to:
P4 Undertake two different expeditions demonstrating appropriate skills and techniques, with tutor support [RL3, TW1, TW3, TW5, SM1, SM2, SM4]	**M4** Independently undertake two different expeditions, demonstrating appropriate skills and techniques	**D1** Undertake two different expeditions, demonstrating advanced expedition skills and techniques
P5 Carry out a review of the planning and undertaking of expeditions, identifying strengths and areas for improvement [RL1, RL3, RL4, RL5, SM3, SM5]	**M5** Explain identified strengths and areas for improvement and relate them to suggestions made in personal development plan	**D2** Justify suggestions made in personal development plan
P6 Produce a personal development plan based on identified strengths and areas for improvement		

Unit 10
Skills for land-based outdoor and adventurous activities

Introduction

Land-based outdoor and adventurous activities provide an alternative to the traditional team and individual competitive sports which dominate an individual's thinking when considering physical activity. Participants compete not against each other but against the challenge of the environment and themselves. Most of the activities involve an element of risk, so it is very important that you examine the safety considerations that will need to be taken into account prior to and during participation. You also need to be aware of how to protect the environment while enjoying your activity, as it may have a tremendous effect on the biodiversity and ecological aspects of the great outdoors.

The aim of this unit is to develop and enhance your understanding of and

> **Key terms**
>
> **Skills** – practical ability; a craft requiring skill
> **Techniques** – methods of achieving a purpose; the manner of execution

abilities in land-based activity **skills** and **techniques**. You will begin by studying the variety of land-based outdoor and adventurous activities, and then the procedures regarding safety, the principles of good practice and environmental awareness. You then put your practical skills to the test in at least two different activities, describing the skills and techniques required and then showing how to put them into practice in the great outdoors. You will then have the opportunity to reflect upon your good practice in order to produce a development plan for future activities.

10.1 Know about different land-based outdoor and adventurous activities

Land-based outdoor and adventurous activities

Key terms

Aims – the aims of participants in adventurous activities might include recreation, skill development, team development and personal development – personal reasons to improve practical skills and techniques

Objectives – the objectives of participants in adventurous activities might be environmental, discovery, educational, a journey – the extrinsic factors that will develop and enhance the participant's ability in the activities

There are a number of activities that take place on land at all times of the year. These range from mountain walking and orienteering, through rock climbing, caving and mountain biking to skiing and snowboarding. Each one of these outdoor and adventurous pursuits requires particular skills and techniques to participate, while they all need their own specialist equipment in order for you to take part safely. The activities also have an element of risk, depending upon their location and their main **aims** and **objectives**. So why do people take part? Many of them like to set themselves aims and objectives to either become competent in one activity, or to try as many activities as possible to find which one interests them the most to pursue as a hobby.

Other factors to take into account include who will be providing the activity and where it will take place. There are a number of private organisations that will organise your activities either for the day or over several days in a residential setting. Although these organisations are extremely good at what they do, they tend to be quite expensive. There are public providers, usually run through the Local Authority, that arrange a number of outdoor and adventurous activities, and there are also voluntary groups that have qualified staff to lead you on your adventures. Some providers will target certain groups, such as children or young people, and others may offer activities for the disabled. What you decide to do, and where, will depend on what your aims and objectives are and whether you require a natural or manmade location.

The uniformed public services and public service organisations such as the Territorial Army and cadet schemes also run highly commendable outdoor and adventurous activities as part of their training, as do the Scout Association and the Duke of Edinburgh's Award Scheme. In most cases you are out overnight, or for a few nights, to get a real feel for the outdoor environment and all the different activities that you can participate in.

Compare and contrast two different land-based activities

Using the range of outdoor and adventurous activities listed previously, choose two activities that are very different from each other. You need to explain them in greater detail and compare and contrast them against each other. To compare them you need to outline the similarities between the two activities, and to contrast them you need to show the differences between them. You may look at the equipment used, distance covered, which uses most energy or a number of other factors, so the more different the activities are the easier it is to compare and contrast them.

If you are lucky, it may be possible to participate in more than two outdoor and adventurous activities, so this will give you a greater range from which to make your comparisons, and it will be easier to contrast the experiences. Explain why you chose the two activities from those that you took part in, and give reasons for each one before looking at the strengths and weaknesses of one activity against the other.

(g) Grading Tip!

When you compare and contrast the two activities, take into account the venue, the instruction, the cost, length of time you are active, health and safety factors, the fitness required and the skills and techniques learned. Write down your thoughts after each activity and gain feedback from others who were taking part, and from the leaders, on your performance to give you further information for the higher grade.

10.2 Be able to manage risks in land-based outdoor and adventurous activities

P2 P3 M2 D1

Risk assessments for activities

As with every physical activity, and even work that you participate in, the completion of a risk assessment is of paramount importance. It is even more important for outdoor and adventurous activities that ultimately carry more risks. If you are using a registered centre to deliver any of the outdoor activities, they will have already carried out risk assessments for each activity that they lead. However, if you plan to lead one yourself then it is your responsibility to complete the necessary paperwork and list all the risks of the environment, the participants, the equipment and the travel. You will have to assess the likelihood of any harm that could be caused, and its severity, in order to produce a risk rating (see opposite) and identify the **risk controls** that will be necessary to keep everyone safe.

Key term

Risk controls – controls that are already in place to prevent a hazard or the risk of the hazard causing harm, for example: trying a less risky option, preventing access or alternative work methods

A risk assessment is an important step in protecting everyone and is a legal requirement. It will help you to focus on the risks that have the potential to cause harm while taking part in an activity. You will not be able to eliminate all the risks – this would take all the enjoyment and exhilaration out of the activity – so you must prove that you have done everything that is 'reasonably practicable' to be as safe as is possible given the circumstances of the activities undertaken.

There are many types of risk assessment, depending upon the environment and activity, many of which are produced by the HSE, but as a general rule of thumb the following headings are usually used:

- What are the hazards?
- Who might be harmed and how?
- What action is necessary?
- Action carried out by whom?
- Action carried out by when?
- Date completed
- Review date

The advanced risk assessment will then rate the likelihood of an injury occurring, and the severity of harm if an injury does occur, to make calculations for the risk rating. Again there are a number of ratings used either

Ask Yourself!

What steps do you think need to be considered for a risk assessment?

According to the Health and Safety Executive (HSE), the five steps are:

1. **Identify the hazard.**
2. **Decide who might be harmed and how.**
3. **Evaluate the risks and decide on precautions.**
4. **Record your findings and implement them.**
5. **Review your risk assessment and update if necessary.**

Source: www.hse.gov.uk © Crown copyright material is reproduced with the permission of the Controller of HMSO and the Queen's Printer for Scotland

quantitative (numerical) or qualitative (low, medium or high). An example is shown in Table 10.1.

Extreme weather conditions could make it unsafe to undertake an activity. Weather forecasts can sometimes be unreliable, so you must be prepared to cancel any activity if the conditions do not allow you to take part safely. Participating regularly in an activity can improve your skills and will help to eliminate the risk of injury or potential accidents.

Skills and techniques required for land-based activities

Among the generic skills and knowledge that you will require while outdoors, such as interpreting weather forecasts, communication and the basics of navigation, you are also expected to understand about the

Table 10.1 Example of risk ratings

Likelihood	Severity		
	Slight L (1)	Serious M (2)	Major H (3)
Seldom L (1)	Low	Low	Medium
Occasionally M (2)	Low	Medium	High
Frequently H (3)	Medium	High	High
Key: (1) Trivial – no action required. (2) Acceptable – no further preventative action is necessary, but monitoring to ensure that the controls are maintained. (3–5) Moderate – try to reduce the risk within a reasonable time scale and considering the number of people exposed to the hazard. (6–8) Substantial – no activity can be carried out until the risk has been reduced, if it has already started the problem should be remedied as quickly as possible. (9+) Intolerable – no activity to be started or continued until the risk level has been reduced. Risk level: (1–2) L = Low, (3–5) M = Medium, (6–9) H = High			

conservation of energy and the planning of emergency procedures. Personal fitness is a fundamental requirement as you will need strength, stamina and flexibility, among other things, to carry out some of the activities. Technical skills will be particular to an activity and could include being able to use a compass, mending a puncture or the correct use of a rope and knots. However, the two most important skills to use are being secure and being safe.

Rock climbing

This is a complex sport with its own vocabulary and equipment. The idea is to climb from the bottom of a rock face to the top using hand and feet holds and, in many cases, placing safety equipment along the way. It is a sport with few rules, but it does have ethics, a code of practice and a climbing etiquette. It gives enjoyment, fulfilment and allows you to explore unknown territory. The main reason for taking part, however, is the element of risk. Important aspects include the personal

judgement you need to weigh up the degree of risk involved, the opportunity to learn new skills, the personal challenges of your physical ability and the level of risk acceptance.

A confident and competent rock climber needs to master many skills which could be physical, technical or mental.

Here is some of that specific vocabulary used by climbers to describe the movement and equipment used when rock climbing:

- Holds – sloper; off width; crimp; jugs; fingerholds; palming; pinch grip; side pulls; jams.
- Moves – dyno; Egyptian; layback; chimneying; mantelshelf.
- Equipment – harness; karabiner; quickdraws; belay devices; rock shoes.

There are different rock climbing styles:

- *Bouldering* is climbing at a low level to hone your skills for rock climbing at a higher level.

- *Sport climbing* has bolt protection, where you use bolts in the rock face to attach your rope and the focus is on physical and technical challenges.
- *Soloing* is climbing without ropes or any form of protection.
- *Traditional climbing* emphasises traditional values of climbing without pre-inspecting the route.
- *Free climbing* uses natural hand and foot holds, using rope and protection as a back up.

To climb a section of rock you need to look at it as a sequence of interlinked movements. You have to read the rock and look carefully at the availability of handholds and footholds to plan your moves in advance. You will need to practise the technique of good footwork using small steps and footholds as well as crossing your feet. Handholds come in all shapes and sizes and at all angles, so it is best to practise all the specific types of holds and remove rings and watches to avoid damaging them or yourself if they catch on the rock. Once you have mastered these skills and techniques it is necessary to start using a rope and harness as you begin to start climbing higher. These are explained in section 10.3.

Mountain biking

Mountain biking is an exhilarating activity and one of the best ways to have great fun on two wheels. It gives you the opportunity to discover parts of the great outdoors that most people never see, as you very rarely travel on roads and cannot ride on public footpaths. There is a strict code of conduct for mountain biking which you should always follow in order to protect the environment, show respect to others and consider the wildlife as well as following the Countryside Code at all times.

Ask Yourself!

Countryside Code

Five sections are dedicated to helping you to respect, protect and enjoy the countryside:

1. **Be safe, plan ahead and follow any signs.**
2. **Leave gates and property as you find them.**
3. **Protect plants and animals and take your litter home.**
4. **Keep dogs under close control.**
5. **Consider other people.**

   Source: www.naturalengland.org

Figure 10.1 Mountain biking is just one of the adventurous activities you can participate in

Think about it!

Mountain bike code of conduct – rights of way:

- Bridle ways (blue signs) – open to cyclists, but you must give way to walkers and horse riders
- Byways (red signs) – usually un-surfaced tracks open to cyclists. As well as walkers and horse riders, you may meet vehicles, which also have the right of access.
- Public footpaths (yellow signs) – no right to cycle exists.

Other access:

- Open land – on most upland, moorland and farmland, cyclists normally have no right of access without permission of the landowner.
- Towpaths – a British Waterways cycling permit is required for cyclists wishing to use canal towpaths.
- Pavements – cycling is not allowed on pavements.
- Designated cycle paths – can be found in urban areas, on Forestry Commission land, disused railway lines and other open spaces perfect for cyclists.

Finally – cyclists must adhere to the Highway Code.

The most important factors of mountain biking are: being able to ride the correct bike, being able to make small repairs, wearing the right clothing and footwear, being fit and safe. Being able to handle your mountain bike well on difficult terrain is an essential skill, as is navigating in unfamiliar territory. You must be able to read a map, use a compass in poor weather conditions and always be able to pinpoint your exact location. You must keep warm and dry and have the knowledge and skills to solve any simple breakdown such as a puncture.

Simple skills and techniques to master include pre-ride checks of the bike:

- Brakes – be able to adjust or alter front and back brakes and even change the brake blocks when they show signs of wear.
- Gears – front and rear derailleur cables may need adjusting as the cables stretch with use, and they need plenty of lubrication with oil.
- Handlebars – ensure they are at the correct height and securely fastened, as you need to pull up on them to raise the front wheel over an obstruction.
- Saddle – should be set at the correct height – legs slightly bent when the pedal is at the bottom of the crank – and set at the right level so that you are leaning down onto your handlebars.
- Tyre pressure – if the tyres are too hard you will bounce uncontrollably and if they are too soft they puncture quite easily so refer to your bike manual to check the correct pressure.
- Quick release bolts – check that the bolts on both wheels are secure and tighten the pedals if they are loose.

You are now ready to get on your bike and go exploring. Wear close-fitting, comfortable clothing (especially the specifically designed cycling shorts), a helmet, gloves and glasses. Ensure that you have waterproof protection, a repair kit, energy snacks and a drink, some money, a mobile phone and a small first aid kit all in a small backpack – and away you go.

Grading Tip!

For the Pass grade you will need to describe the skills and techniques required for two different land-based activities.

To upgrade to a Merit grade it is necessary for you to compare the two activities and explain their similarities as well as contrasting them, to show the differences and what makes them so individual and different.

The Distinction grade requires you to evaluate the skills and techniques of two, or more, different activities by looking at their strengths and weaknesses and the abilities required to successfully perform at a high level.

10.3 Be able to participate in land-based outdoor and adventurous activities

P4 **M3** **D2**

Demonstrating the skills and techniques in activities

A great many of the skills you will use are those which you use frequently and successfully every day – speaking, listening and calculating – however, you will now be putting them into a different context in an unfamiliar environment. Other skills will be specific to the activity you are taking part in.

Rock climbing

Skills you will need for rock climbing include:

- Fitting the harness – some harnesses are one size and you have to adjust them accordingly, whereas the more expensive ones are produced in different sizes and some have adjustable leg loops to fit over clothing. The harness uses a double-back system so when you thread the waist strap through the buckle and back again, it forms a 'C' which means it is safe and will not come undone. Leg loop buckles are doubled back like the waist belt, but do not adjust these before making sure that the waist belt is around your waist and not your hips.

- Attaching a rope – you have to use a 'figure of eight' knot and put the end of the rope through the front of the harness and back through the knot. As a fail-safe measure, the rope is then tied in a 'stopper' knot to prevent the rope from becoming undone.

- Belaying – a belayer 'takes in' and 'pays out' the rope while the climber moves up the rock face, and then lowers them back down again when they either reach the top or want to come down. The role of the belayer is crucial to the safety of the climber and they have to ensure they are competent in the use of the 'live' rope and the 'dead' rope. This is a good technique for any climbing situation and must follow the same procedure every time.

- Abseiling – a technique for descending a steep rock face after a climb has been completed. The rope is attached to a safe anchor at the top, and a belay device placed on the rope is attached to the front of the harness with a locking karabiner. You then lower yourself down backwards using one hand above the karabiner and one below in a controlled manner. Sometimes a belayer is also used as a safety back-up.

Mountain biking

There are a number of skills and techniques to learn which include how to stay in control of your bike, getting on and off correctly, carrying your bike, riding uphill and downhill, travelling through water and mud, and clearing obstacles.

- Pedalling technique – use your arms and legs to absorb the bumps and jolts as you ride over rough ground. Keep in your saddle to improve traction of the back wheel and stay in a low enough gear to maintain a good, quick pedalling rhythm. Off-road riding places particular strains on the body, so you must use the correct technique and style to maintain the maximum power from pedalling. The ideal pedalling rate is 90 revs (revolutions) per minute.
- Using the 21 gears efficiently – the gear shifters may be above or below the handlebar. The left hand controls the front derailleur, up and down the chain wheels. The right-hand lever controls the rear derailleur and takes you up and down each individual gear. On both the rear cogs and the front chain wheels, the lower the choice the harder it is to pedal.
- Riding uphill – adjust your body position to cope with the steepness: bend your elbows and put your head over the handlebar. Keep on the seat – do not be tempted to stand up in the pedals. Keep in a low gear. Try not to pull up on the handlebar, as the front wheel will lift. Pedal in a fluid motion.
- Riding downhill – keep your body well back in the saddle to move the centre of balance to the rear of the bike. Straighten your arms and use the back brake with care; try not to use the front brake. Descend slowly and in control without leaning forward.
- Carrying your bike – some terrain is impossible to cycle on and sometimes you may have to clamber over obstacles, so you will need to be able to dismount correctly. You can then lift the bike by holding the top tube and the handlebar, or a far easier technique is to shoulder the bike by putting your shoulder under the top tube and holding it from underneath, with the other hand on the handlebar.

Once these basic skills and techniques have been practised, you will feel more confident and be able to move onto terrain which is much more testing – water, mud, drops, uneven rocky ground, cambers and the like – and have the confidence to try bunny hops, pivots, sharp cornering and descending at speed.

Think about it!

You need to clearly demonstrate the skills and techniques for each activity in which you participate. Use the following checklist:

- Make the demonstration accurate by carrying it out correctly and clearly.
- Highlight the main points.
- Repeat if necessary.
- Ensure that you understand and remember the information.
- Keep movements simple and clear.
- Always emphasise the health and safety aspects.
- Explain any technical words.
- Give a reason why you are using a particular skill or technique.
- Accurate decision-making and judgement are vital.

Environmental issues

Because outdoor and adventurous activities take place in the natural environment, they have an impact on the surroundings.

Pollution is contamination of this natural environment and comes in many forms:

- With the increase of motor activities such as quad bikes, motorbikes and cars in the countryside, pollution from engines is rising and, therefore, so are greenhouse gasses.
- Pollution can come from the noise that we make and the lights that we use when outdoors.
- Soil and water pollution can come from rubbish left in the countryside. This is also harmful to livestock and cattle. You should always take all your rubbish away with you, and leave things as you found them.

Everyone should be made aware of the impact that activities will have on the countryside, and all National Governing Bodies of sport (NGBs) have codes of conduct related to the environment. You can help to preserve the environment so that other people can continue to enjoy it by keeping to paths and tracks, not climbing over dry stone walls and being aware of boundaries. The weather produces its own kind of erosion as the wind, rain and snow attack the natural environment, so it does not need man to speed up the process. The Countryside Agency is a government department that is regulated to improve and conserve the countryside and look at the social and economic impact of the people within it.

Safety Issues

An awareness of health and safety is an important skill. Safety checks prior to undertaking activities is essential, especially the checking of safety equipment and potential hazards. Outdoor and adventurous activities can be demanding, challenging and dangerous, so you must take suitable precautions at all times, and all activities must have been risk assessed. The Adventure Activities Licensing Authority (AALA) is an independent authority under the Health and Safety Executive that issues licences to providers of activities once they have been inspected. They look at the management of safety and ensure that providers follow proper procedures in delivering activities to young people.

National Governing Bodies of sport (NGBs) agree the rules and regulations and administer their particular activities. They have to follow health and safety guidelines and have policies and procedures in place to ensure good practice and so that you can participate safely.

Grading Tip!

For a Pass in this outcome you only have to participate in one outdoor and adventurous activity.

For the Merit, however, it will be necessary for you to acquire the practical skills and techniques for safe, efficient and personal independent development in two different activities.

To achieve the Distinction grade, the skills and techniques that you perform will need to be of an advanced nature, as laid down by the governing body, and will include a detailed understanding of safety and environmental awareness.

10.4 Be able to review own skills and development in land-based outdoor and adventurous activities

Own performance review in the demonstration of skills and techniques

By far the easiest and most efficient way to review your own performance is to keep a personal log or diary of all the activities you take part in, take photographs of your involvement and have all your notes to hand from the theory learnt in class with your group. Add to this the written feedback from your peers, leaders and any observers and you are well on your way to working out your strengths and areas for improvement. This way you do not have to delve far back in time and try and remember everything that you have taken part in, what the dates were, who was involved and your immediate feelings about your participation.

Your review has to lead to action, otherwise it is meaningless. The positive points will reinforce your good practice, which you can continue and develop, whereas the negative aspects should be actioned and improved.

Complete your diary entry immediately after each activity that you participate in and ask everyone else for their thoughts in order to gain an overall view. From this information you will easily be able to design a personal development plan.

When reviewing your performance in the application of the skills and techniques of two adventurous activities, identify what went well and what could be improved. Good performers will always try to improve what they do, even at the highest level – by thinking about and evaluating the activity they can learn more for the future. You may need to attend some training sessions, carry out more research in books and online, and listen to the feedback from others, especially the professionals in their chosen activities.

Personal development plan

Your personal development plan will enable you to set targets in order that you can maintain your strengths and improve the areas of the activities where you are less strong. The first task is to return to the aims and objectives that you set yourself at the beginning and match them to what you believe you have achieved. Then refer to your activities diary and write down all the areas that need maintaining and those that require some improvement. From this you can then devise a simple table, like the one in the example, and complete the areas you feel need to be mentioned.

Table 10.2 Example of a personal development plan

Activity	Strengths	Areas for improvement	How it can be improved – targets	Date to be completed
Rock climbing				
Mountain biking				

Once you have completed the table, list the targets and ensure that they are SMART. They can be short-, medium- or long-term targets, depending upon what resources you require to undertake your plan.

The public services use this method of planning to empower you in achieving your potential and in setting targets to plan further development for your own future.

SMART targets:

Specific – make sure the targets are not ambiguous but clearly set out.
Measurable – there has to be a way to measure how far you have got with your targets and know when you have completed them.
Achievable – you must be able to reach the targets, otherwise there is no point in setting them.
Realistic – be reasonable in what you want to achieve.
Time-bound – you cannot measure success if there is no time limit.

The development plan should have aims and objectives to achieve, and should list the resources required to get there. You will need to assess the barriers to the plan, such as injury or illness, the weather, costs or the lack of equipment or facilities. The plan has to be monitored and evaluated, and your performance assessed at regular intervals, as well as obtaining feedback from your peers, leaders or observers. You may need to include some training or coaching in some of the skills or techniques as part of the plan.

Take into account your previous and current experience and what level you have reached, what skills you have learnt and those that you want to learn. Consider your level of fitness and your commitment to training. Look at the access to equipment and facilities, and check your lifestyle and diet to ensure that they contribute positively to your development plan. Finally, as already mentioned, consider the barriers that you may face in trying to develop your skills in particular activities. Will the cost of equipment or travel be too much? Will all the training affect your studies or work? Are the venue or facilities easy to get to? Ensure that you cover all the possibilities, but do not give up too easily – if you want to do something badly enough, you must sometimes move out of your comfort zone to achieve it.

End-of-unit knowledge check

1. Why is it necessary to complete a risk assessment for every activity?
2. What is meant by the terms 'severity' and 'likelihood'?
3. Which organisation issues licences for people to run adventurous activities?
4. Define the terms 'skill' and 'technique'.
5. What are the five points of the Countryside Code?

Grading criteria

In order to pass this unit, the evidence that you present for assessment needs to demonstrate that you can meet all the learning outcomes for the unit. The criteria for a pass grade describe the level of achievement required to pass this unit.

To achieve a pass grade the evidence must show that you are able to:	To achieve a merit grade the evidence must show that, in addition to the pass criteria, you are able to:	To achieve a distinction grade the evidence must show that, in addition to the pass and merit criteria, you are able to:
P1 Describe four different land-based outdoor and adventurous activities	**M1** Compare and contrast four different land-based outdoor and adventurous activities	
P2 Carry out risk assessments for two different land-based outdoor and adventurous activities [IE1, IE2, IE3, IE4, IE5, IE6, CT1, CT2, CT4, CT5, CT6, SM3, SM4, EP2, EP3, EP4, EP5]		
P3 Describe the skills and techniques required for two different land-based outdoor and adventurous activities	**M2** Compare and contrast the skills and techniques required for two different land-based outdoor and adventurous activities	**D1** Evaluate the skills and techniques required to successfully perform in two different land-based outdoor and adventurous activities

To achieve a pass grade the evidence must show that you are able to:	To achieve a merit grade the evidence must show that, in addition to the pass criteria, you are able to:	To achieve a distinction grade the evidence must show that, in addition to the pass and merit criteria, you are able to:
P4 Demonstrate skills and techniques in two different land-based outdoor and adventurous activities, with tutor support [CT5, SM2, SM3, SM4, SM6, SM7, RL1, RL2, RL3, RL4, RL5]	**M3** Independently demonstrate skills and techniques in two different land-based outdoor and adventurous activities	**D2** Demonstrate advanced skills and techniques in two different land-based outdoor and adventurous activities
P5 Review own performance in the demonstration of skills and techniques in land-based outdoor and adventurous activities, identifying strengths and areas for improvement [IE1, IE3, IE4, IE6, CT2, CT4, SM2, SM6, SM7, RL1, RL2, RL3, RL4, RL5, EP4]	**M4** Review own performance in the demonstration of skills and techniques in land-based outdoor and adventurous activities, explaining strengths and areas for improvement	
P6 Produce a personal development plan, based on identified strengths and areas for improvement, for skills and techniques in land-based outdoor and adventurous activities [SM2, SM3, SM6, SM7, RL1, RL2, RL3, RL4, RL5, EP3, EP4]		

Unit 12
Crime and its effects on society

Introduction

This unit will help you to develop an understanding of the legislation in the UK that is relevant to crime and disorder, and how criminal justice agencies deal with those who have committed a crime. You will also consider how crime affects our society, and how society can help to reduce crime and support the victims of crime. Additionally, you will consider the reasons why some people believe the risk of becoming a victim of crime is greater than might be the case – the concept of 'fear of crime'.

Crime can be described as 'a violation of the law, a wicked or forbidden act'.

Some of the relatively low-level ('summary') crimes – which will be heard only at the Magistrates' Court, are often referred to as 'offences', and might include theft where property of little value has been stolen, assaults that involve little or no visible injury, and minor traffic offences.

You will also investigate how organisations work together to prevent crime, including intelligence-led policing and other local and national initiatives. The unit ends by researching how public services and other organisations support witnesses and victims through the court process.

Learning outcomes:

By the end of this unit, you should:

1. Know crime and disorder legislation, sentences and orders.

2. Know the effects of criminal behaviour on communities.

3. Understand approaches to reduce crime, disorder and anti-social behaviour.

4. Understand how the public services support victims and witnesses of crime.

12.1 Know crime and disorder legislation, sentences and orders

Since 1998 the main piece of legislation concerned with crime and disorder in the United Kingdom had been the Crime and Disorder Act of 1998. This Act made it compulsory for local authorities, police and other agencies to work together to develop and put in place schemes that would reduce incidences of crime and disorder in England and Wales. These liaisons are known as Crime and Disorder Reduction Partnerships; in Wales they are referred to as Community Safety Partnerships. There are many organisations involved in these partnerships, including statutory, community, voluntary and business groups.

At the end of 2009 a new piece of legislation, The Policing and Crime Act, came into force. This Act includes measures to protect the public, increase police accountability and tackle crime and disorder. Citizens will be given a voice in the policing of their local areas, and the Act brings in new powers to ensure that the police and local communities have the powers they need to deal with issues that matter to the public. Examples of these issues include alcohol-related disorder, gangs and violence and also prostitution.

The measures include a requirement that those who sell alcohol sign up to a code of practice, a new offence of paying for sex with a prostitute who has been pressurised into the profession, and police and local authorities can apply for an injunction against those involved in gang-related violence.

The Policing and Crime Act places a duty on police authorities to act upon the views of the public, and how the police carry out their activities in response to these views. Her Majesty's Inspector of Constabulary is required to assess the level of response when it carries out its inspection of police forces.

The (former) Home Secretary (Alan Johnson) welcomed the new legislation, saying:
'The public are at the heart of everything we do and they are our best weapon in fighting crime. The Policing and Crime Act gives police and local authorities new powers to tackle the issues of most concern to communities, like gang violence, alcohol-related crime and disorder, prostitution and lap-dancing clubs.'

With regard to protecting vulnerable groups, the Act increases police powers to close premises associated with prostitution offences for a set period of time. Sex offenders who are banned from travelling abroad are required to surrender their passport; the Vetting and Barring scheme, operated by the Independent Safeguarding Authority, will include extra sections to ensure that all vulnerable people are protected.

The Act makes amendments to the law on aviation, alcohol misuse, proceeds of crime and extradition. A small number of changes have been made to clarify the powers of Her Majesty's Revenue and Customs; it will be more straightforward to recover money, goods and other assets that have been obtained through criminal activity, and there should be more co-operation between the legal systems of the United Kingdom and other countries.

The Anti-Social Behaviour Act 2003 allows for groups of people under 16 years of age to be broken up and the individuals to be taken to their homes; this applies to groups of at least two young people, after 9pm. These new powers must be authorised by a police officer of high rank, and relate to a specific area; the officer (of at least Superintendent rank) must be satisfied that the area has suffered from persistent **anti-social behaviour**, and that the behaviour of groups in the area has caused harassment, alarm and distress to members of the public.

Key term

Anti-social behaviour – any aggressive, intimidating or destructive activity that damages or destroys another person's quality of life

So how can courts deal with the people who embark upon a criminal activity? A lot will depend on the offence that has been committed, whether it is a summary or indictable offence, and also the age of the offender. In an attempt to encourage young or first-time offenders to see the error of their ways and turn away from a life of crime, they might be given a reprimand and not have to appear in court. Reprimands and final warnings replace the cautions that were previously given to offenders under 18 years of age.

Typically a young person might receive a reprimand for the first offence, and this could be followed up with a final warning. However, if the crime is very serious, they will be given the warning immediately or they could be prosecuted. The final warning is given to the young person in the presence of their parent or other responsible adult and they are referred to the Youth Offending Team (YOT).

Every local authority in England and Wales has a YOT. These teams comprise members of a wide range of agencies including police, social services, probation, drugs and alcohol misuse charities, health service and housing officers. Every YOT has a manager, whose role is to ensure that the youth justice services are working together in an effective manner.

The offender is assessed according to a national standard. This means that their needs can be accurately identified and that a response can be made at an early stage, because of the wide range of representatives within the team. As a result a suitable programme or 'action plan' can be put into place.

The action plan order is a fixed-term method of dealing with offenders; it lasts just three months and is concentrated on addressing the behaviour that led to the crime. The action plan

order is carried out as a community sentence and is used for the more serious crimes.

Another measure that could be implemented to prevent young offenders committing further crime is the reparation order. The YOT meets with the victim before the offender is dealt with and their responses will influence the sentence given in court. Offenders could have the opportunity to apologise to the victim for their actions, or do something practical in an attempt to put right the damage they have caused.

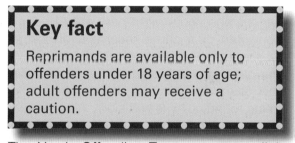

Key fact

Reprimands are available only to offenders under 18 years of age; adult offenders may receive a caution.

The Youth Offending Teams act as a link between all partner agencies and the courts, to ensure that all information regarding young offenders is available to the relevant agency at the right time.

Criminal courts are able to impose a range of punishments on those convicted of a criminal offence. These fall into four main categories: discharge, fine, community sentence, custody (prison sentence). Certain crimes carry an automatic prison sentence, but in some cases a sentence served in the community is deemed more suitable. One of the reasons is that, in addition to punishing the offender, community sentences often force the offender to consider the reasons why they committed the crime in the first place.

The sentence given by a court reflects the seriousness of the crime. Before deciding on the most suitable punishment, the court may ask probation staff to prepare a report on the offender. This will take into account any specific circumstances the court needs to be aware of; for example, if the offender is the sole carer of a child or adult, or whether it is a first offence, or if the offender has a history of committing crimes. Judges or magistrates will take this report into account when they impose the sentence. A first-time offender is likely to receive a lesser sentence that someone who has been convicted a number of times previously.

Key terms

Absolute discharge – means that no further action is taken
Conditional discharge – the offender receives no immediate punishment, but may do at a later date

On average about eight per cent of people convicted of a crime receive a discharge. This might be an **absolute discharge**, in the case of a very minor offence or when the court decides that the experience of being found guilty is sufficient. Alternatively, the offender might receive a **conditional discharge**. Although no actual punishment has been given at this time, if the offender commits another crime within a certain period, they can be punished for the original crime as well as the new one. Some people see this as the offender 'getting away with it', but they still get a criminal record.

Thirteen per cent of convicted people receive a community sentence. This could be in many forms, including carrying out compulsory (unpaid) work, curfew orders or not being allowed to take part in specified activities.

Activity

Carry out research into community sentencing and draw up a list of the many options available to the courts when using this punishment.

Almost three-quarters of those convicted of a crime receive a fine as their punishment; these will be the less serious crimes. Research has shown that this is not an 'easy option' – there is no evidence to suggest that offenders who receive a fine are more likely to re-offend than those who receive alternative sentences.

A very small percentage – just seven in every hundred – of offenders are given a prison sentence, and two-thirds of these sentences are for less than one year.

The Criminal Justice Act 2003 introduced measures intended to modernise many areas of the criminal justice system in England and Wales. Among the changes are laws relating to police powers, bail, **disclosure**, **double jeopardy**, release on licence and sentencing. In cases where it is feared a jury might be intimidated, the Act allows for a judge to sit alone, without the need for a jury.

Activity

Using a table similar to the one below, investigate the maximum sentence that could be imposed upon an offender convicted of each crime.

Crime	Legislation	Sentence
Theft	Theft Act 1968	7 years
Arson	Criminal Damage Act 1971	
Murder		Life imprisonment
Burglary	Theft Act 1968	
Common Assault		
Grievous Bodily Harm	Offences against the Person Act 1861	
Possession of Class B Drugs		

Key terms

Disclosure – a process in legal proceedings, whereby parties are required to inform others of any relevant documents

Double jeopardy – a legal principle which prevents someone from being tried for the same crime twice

This law came into force in April 2005 and the changes in this rule apply only to offences committed after this date; any earlier case will continue to be dealt with under the earlier (1991) Act.

Sometimes a prisoner will serve some of the sentence imposed by the courts, and then be released 'on licence'. This means that there are certain conditions imposed on the convicted person. The box below outlines the conditions that will apply to all offenders; in some cases additional ones will be added.

Release under licence is imposed on offenders who have committed serious crimes, and those who are considered by the court to pose a risk to the public if they are not monitored, as is the case on page 57.

During the month of January 2010 no fewer than 58 offenders were recalled to prison for breaking the terms of their licence; these included 28 whom it is alleged had committed further offences, 21 had failed to remain at the approved address, 13 had not kept in touch with the probation service and 4 were deemed to have behaved in an inappropriate manner.

Release on licence – conditions to be imposed

The prisoner will be subject to the following:
- Must maintain contact with their responsible officer, as and when directed.
- Must be visited by the responsible officer, as arranged.
- Must live at an address approved by the responsible officer, and obtain permission to stay away overnight.
- Must not make contact with named individuals.
- Will undertake any work only with the approval of the responsible officer.
- Must not travel outside the UK without permission.
- Must be on good behaviour.
- Must not commit any offence.

Grading Tip!

For P1, you will need to provide an outline of current legislation regarding crime and disorder. Although this does not need to go into great depth, you will be expected to include the main purpose of the Acts.

To achieve P2 you must identify the main sentences that can be imposed by the courts.

P3 requires a description of at least two theories of criminal behaviour, and the reasons why people commit crime.

To achieve M1 you must be able to *analyse the impact* of at least two pieces of crime and disorder legislation.

D1 calls for an *evaluation* of the impact of the legislation.

12.2 The effects of criminal behaviour on communities

Key terms

Psychological theories – look at the reasons why people adopt criminal behaviour

Sociological theories – focus on society as the primary cause of crime

Biological theories – relates to the role of genetics and hereditary factors

Theories of criminal behaviour

Many people have undertaken research into crime and the type of people who carry it out, resulting in a number of theories. These fall into three general areas – **sociological theories** and **psychological theories** and **biological theories**.

Sociological theories

Sociological theories claim that individuals commit crime because of social processes and pressures that are experienced by individuals and groups. As long ago as 1925, Park and Burgess put forward the 'social disorganisation theory'. This suggests that cities evolve in the same way as nature – with different types of people settling in certain areas. When these groups of people move about and new people come into the area, it causes disruption and deviant behaviour. This is borne out by other researchers such as Shaw and McKay (1942), who believed that crime was the natural outcome of ordinary people being put into a strange social setting. An even earlier theorist (Durkheim 1895) said, in his 'strain theory', that the main cause of crime is the difference between what society appears to offer people and what is actually delivered.

Another aspect of criminal behaviour that has sociological roots is that of 'labelling'. This is the process of giving someone a label, based solely on their behaviour. These labels can be either positive or negative, however, once the label is recognised it can significantly influence the way people are treated by others and how they behave.

Psychological theories

In contrast to sociological theories, the psychological theories consider the reasons why people commit crime. They do not pay any attention to societal influences and focus solely on the individual. The two major psychological theories are 'social learning theory' and 'psychoanalytical theory'.

The social learning theory attempts to explain crime by examining the ways in which people learn, in particular the way in which they learn criminal behaviour. It also argues that all behaviour is reinforced by rewards, or the promise of rewards.

Processes involved in social learning theory

1. Attention – the learner observes what is happening.
2. Retention – the learner remembers what happened.
3. Reproduction – the learner copies the action he observed.
4. Motivation – rewards and punishments that determine future actions.

As well as motivation, used to reinforce the learned behaviour, the social learning theory includes 'negative motivation'; these are punishments that result in discouraging the individual from repeating certain actions. If a person commits a crime, is found guilty and receives a sentence, the sentence is a punishment. Although this is seen as negative reinforcement in this theory, it could lead to low self-esteem and the criminal will continue to carry out crimes in an attempt to gain respect from others, who also have criminal tendencies.

Psychoanalytical theories fall within the realm of social learning. They are based on the teachings of Sigmund Freud, who believed that everyone has unruly and possibly criminal tendencies within their subconscious. In the majority of people these forces remain buried. Freud further stated that events in early childhood could destroy this balance and make people criminals.

Other theories of how and why people commit crime include the cognitive theories, which are based on learning theory, and behaviourist theory, which includes a belief that children go through three stages of moral development. These stages occur in early childhood, late childhood and during adolescence.

Key term

Morality – concerned with the goodness or badness of human behaviour (knowing right from wrong)

Who is affected by crime?

The individual

Some crimes, including theft of personal property, assault or damage to property belonging to an individual, will usually affect only the owner of the property or the person who has been assaulted.

Case Study

An office worker uses a pencil, highlighter pen or other small item, puts it in their pocket or bag and forgets about it. Some time later this person finds the item and uses it for their own purposes. When that person takes the conscious decision to use the item as their own and not return it to their workplace, they have stolen it (committed a theft).

This is just one small example but, if multiplied by all the staff in a company, on a weekly basis, it would result in the loss to that company of property worth a considerable amount. In this case the victim of

Figure 12.1 Stages of moral development in children

Age	Stage	Reasoning
Early childhood	Pre-conventional	Moral reasoning is based on fear and punishment.
Late childhood	Conventional	Moral reasoning is based on satisfying the expectations of family and friends.
Adolescence	Post-conventional	Beginning to question **morality** – may lead to deeper understanding or to abandonment of morality. Will show itself in criminal behaviour.

Source: Kohlberg, L (1964) *Development of Moral Character and Moral Ideology*

the crime is the company that owned the property that was stolen; this company will suffer financially because the property will need to be replaced.

The community

On some occasions the effects of certain crimes are experienced by more than the direct victim. An example of this is when harm is inflicted upon a child – at the very least the family of the child will feel the effect of this crime.

State

Occasionally such a horrendous crime occurs that it has an effect upon society which is far removed geographically from where it happened.

Case Study

In September 2009 Vanessa George, a nursery worker from the South West of England, pleaded guilty to sexual assaults on children in her care. Throughout her trial, and even when she was sentenced, George refused to name the children whom she had abused. This means that the families of all the children attending the nursery do not know if their child was subjected to the abuse. In this way the actions of one person will have had an effect on the entire community.

Case Study

On 22 August 2007 11-year-old Rhys Jones from Liverpool was returning home from football practice when he was hit in the neck by a bullet, resulting in his death. Very soon after the killing, police arrested four teenagers, who were all later released on bail. More than 300 officers were involved in the hunt for Rhys's killer and by April 2008 11 people aged 17 to 25 had been questioned. In December 2008 18-year-old Sean Mercer was convicted of murder and sentenced to life imprisonment.

Activity

Using a table similar to the one below, enter in the first column things that you consider to be crimes. In the second column provide an example of this crime. In the final column explain the effect this crime has on society, on an individual or on other victim(s).

Example of crimes, and their effects

Crime	Details	Effect on victim(s)
Burglary	Broke ground floor window, stole money and iPod	Loss of property; cost of repair and replacement

Many people fear that they will become a victim of crime at some point. Part of the reason for this is what they have read or heard in the media, or they might feel particularly vulnerable because of the nature of their work.

The Department of Health employs more than 30,000 people who work alone in the community, for example health visitors or support workers. In an attempt to prevent its staff becoming victims of crime, the NHS is piloting the use of mobile alarms that staff can use in an emergency.

Case Study

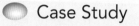

The Telford NHS Trust has issued staff working in the community with devices they can use to raise the alarm if they are confronted with an emergency; this could be a physical attack or being faced with abusive behaviour. More than 300 staff in the Trust will carry the devices, which can be activated to alert staff at a call centre. Staff will then be able to monitor and record the incident, essential as evidence if the incident leads to a prosecution.

The device uses Location Based Service technology to help locate the user; an automated alarm is activated if the device is forcibly removed from the user.

The Department of Health intends to make this device available to all its staff who work in isolated situations, to improve their safety and security.

12.3 Crime reduction and anti-social behaviour

Many organisations, including the public services, are involved in a great number of strategies across all of England and Wales that seek to reduce levels of crime in the community. As discussed at the beginning of this chapter, the Crime and Disorder Act 1998 places a duty on local authorities, police forces and other agencies to work together to develop strategies to reduce crime. Many charities have also become involved in these initiatives.

These initiatives target specific types of offenders, including repeat and prolific offenders and those who have been released from custody and might need assistance to lead a decent lifestyle away from crime. A proportion of crime is committed by people who are dependant on drugs and other stimulants; for this reason many of the initiatives involve working with those who are addicted to drugs and other substances. These programmes might include treatment for the addicts in the hope that when they are 'clean' they will stop committing crimes to pay for more drugs. The organisations that deliver crime reduction initiatives rely on support from volunteers to be able to deliver their services.

Activity

Working in pairs, select one of the organisations identified below and find out how they are involved in crime reduction initiatives.

Police

Community Support Officers

Community Wardens

Church Groups

Youth Offending Team

Neighbourhood Watch

Community Beat Officers

Community Action teams

Probation Service

One term often used to describe the ways in which some individuals or groups go about their daily lives is 'anti-social behaviour'. This type of behaviour is extremely upsetting for individuals, and it can cause them great distress. Very occasionally the effects of this type of activity can have devastating results, as in the case of a mother and daughter in Leicestershire.

Crimes vary greatly in their severity, and this is reflected in the penalties associated with them. For every crime that is committed, there will be a victim, or victims. Some people believe that some of the less serious crimes do not involve anyone else, and that there is no real victim; read the case study opposite, and see what you think!

Anti-social behaviour does not just upset individuals in the community, it can prevent areas developing into places people want to be, and creates 'no-go' areas, where crime can easily escalate.

The examples you have given above might include rowdy or noisy behaviour, fly-tipping, begging, drinking on the street or setting off fireworks late at night. There are ways in which this type of behaviour can be discouraged, and hopefully stopped before it goes too far. These include police visits and warning letters – often this is enough for the offenders to stop what they are doing. If not, further ways of tackling the problem might include contracts and agreements involving juveniles and families, parenting orders, anti-social behaviour orders (ASBOs), arrest and custodial sentences.

Case Study

Fiona Pilkington and her family had suffered many months of harassment, including damage to property, name-calling and threats, by a group of 16 youths. She reported these incidents to the local police, but the incidents did not stop.

In desperation, and with her daughter Francesca at her side, on 23 October 2007 Mrs Pilkington drove her car to a lay-by and set it alight. Both women perished in the blaze.

At the inquest into the deaths the police superintendent said that police officers were allowed only to issue warnings to young troublemakers (unless their behaviour was judged to be serious), and he agreed that the criminal justice system was set up 'to avoid sending juveniles to prison'.

He also added that low-level anti-social behaviour is mainly the responsibility of the council.

Source: www. telegraph.co.uk
© Telegraph Media Group Limited

1. Working in pairs, jot down as many examples as you can of activities that could be described as anti-social. What is it about the activity that you believe makes it unacceptable to most people?

An acceptable behaviour contract (ABC) is a method that can be used, and is designed to allow the individual to recognise their behaviour and how it affects others. An ABC is usually put in place for young people, but can also be used for adults. They usually last for six months, but can be renewed if needed.

Anti-social behaviour orders are orders issued by the court that forbid certain threatening or intimidating actions. This might include preventing someone from spending time with a group of friends or visiting certain areas. ASBOs are in place for at least two years and can be longer. If someone breaks the conditions of an ASBO, they have committed a criminal offence and could be fined or go to prison.

In order for there to be a reduction in crime and anti-social behaviour in our communities, a great deal of effort needs to be invested, by individuals, organisations and the community itself. The case study below describes how this is being achieved in North Wales. The North Wales Police 'Federation Community Service Award' is presented to the officer who has, on his or her own initiative, made an unselfish contribution to community relations in the previous 12 months. PC Mike Smith, who is the Community Beat Manager (CBM) for Penmaenmawr, was the winner of the most recent award.

Case Study

Focus – Link (magazine of North Wales Police) Spring 2010
PC Mike Smith was presented with this award at an event attended by the Chief Police Officer, members of the Police Authority, Members of Parliament and Members of the Welsh Assembly. He was recognised for his efforts in running a number of policing initiatives across his beat; this involved working with a Police Community Support Officer (PCSO) and local partnership agencies.

Schemes that were introduced over a short period of time, and which are ongoing, include Truancy Watch, Penmaenmawr Train Station project, Adopt a Street, Clean-up Day and a Community Football Tournament. Penmaenmawr is a small town on the North Wales coast and it attracts a high number of holidaymakers during the summer months. With this in mind, one of the initiatives introduced by PC Smith was 'Caravan Watch'.

In his nomination, PC Smith's sergeant described the officer thus:

'Having a fresh approach to the role and always keen to try out new projects and ideas. He is full of new and innovative ideas that will promote NWP in a very positive light, both locally and nationally.'

In addition to receiving a trophy and certificate, PC Smith accepted a bursary of £1,500, which will be used for a number of local projects; these include the Bluelight Summer Scheme and the Conwy Neighbourhood Police Alder Hey and Conwy Youth Club Appeal.

12.4 Support for victims and witnesses of crime

Victims of crime are those people who are affected by the criminal act. Everyone reacts differently to crime and this will depend upon many different factors. Some of the things that influence the way we react to a situation will relate to the incident itself, some to the individual and the experiences they may have encountered previously. The effects will also stay with individuals for different lengths of time – some people will be able to get on with their lives straight away, while for others it may take weeks, months or even longer. Some people never fully recover from the ways in which the crime has affected them.

Responses to being a victim of crime differ greatly also; the majority of victims feel angry, upset or afraid immediately following the crime, but often these feelings diminish over time.

Victims often have great difficulty coming to terms with the effects that a crime has had on them. In the past there was no support for these people, but over recent years the situation has developed to provide support and assistance for victims of crime.

Many people who become victims of crime will suffer physically, or they might relive the event for a long time after it has occurred. It is at this time that advice and support are essential if the victim is to recover from the experience.

Victims of crime are entitled to free, confidential advice from a charity called Victim Support. This is an independent national charity and staff and volunteers are trained to provide emotional support and practical assistance. Victim Support aims to get in touch with the victim within four days of them reporting a crime. If the victim agrees,

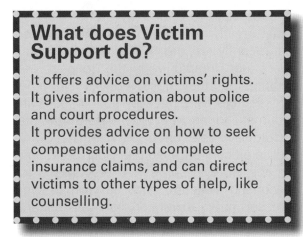

What does Victim Support do?

It offers advice on victims' rights.
It gives information about police and court procedures.
It provides advice on how to seek compensation and complete insurance claims, and can direct victims to other types of help, like counselling.

the police provide Victim Support with their details.

Anyone affected by crime can contact Victim Support for help, even if they have not reported the crime to the police. It does not matter, either, how long ago the crime took place.

Right to privacy

On occasions, if it might help with their investigation, the police will release details of a crime to the media. They will normally ask permission from the victim before doing this. One reason for this action is that media coverage might uncover more evidence, such as eyewitnesses coming forward. However, in the case of sexual assault or rape, it is a criminal offence for *anyone* to publish the name, photograph or other details which may identify the victim. A victim's right to privacy and the media's right to freedom of expression are both set out in the Human Rights Act 1998.

Society

As discussed earlier in this chapter, some crimes affect a single victim, while others affect many people. The reasons for a crime affecting many people can be the severity of the crime itself, or the attention it has received from media such as newspapers or television reports.

When a crime has been committed, there are many ways in which the public services, victims and society may work together towards an acceptable outcome. One of these measures is the use of the restorative justice scheme.

Restorative justice brings victims, offenders and communities together to decide on a response to a particular crime. It's about putting victims' needs at the centre of the criminal justice system and finding positive solutions to crime by encouraging offenders to face up to their actions.

This approach can be used for a wide range of crimes, ranging from incidents described as anti-social behaviour, such as graffiti or name-calling, to serious crimes such as robbery or burglary. For restorative justice to be used, the offender must have admitted responsibility for the crime and the effect it has had on their victim.

The ways in which offenders and victims might be brought together include:

- direct mediation – where victim, offender, facilitator and possibly supporters for each party meet face-to-face
- indirect mediation – where victim and offender communicate through letters
- conferencing – involving supporters for both victim and offender.

A victim might ask for a restorative justice outcome to make the offender realise how their life has been affected by the crime. They might also discover some information that will help them to put the experience behind them. It might be possible for the victim to forgive the offender through this approach.

There are benefits to the use of this approach, including the victim being able to make choices, receiving an explanation of why they were targeted and making the offender take responsibility for their actions.

Evidence gathered from those involved in the restorative justice approach suggest that dealing with the aftermath of crime in this way can reduce post-traumatic stress disorder (PTSD) in victims. In some cases, offenders have been so moved by the experience of confronting their victim that they have changed their ways and moved away from crime.

Examples of possible outcomes of restorative justice include making offenders remove graffiti or repair property they have damaged, or writing a letter of apology to their victim.

Interagency support

The UK government has announced a partnership with Victim Support, with the introduction of the National Victims Service. This new service will cost £8 million in the first year, focusing initially on those victims affected by the death of loved ones.

This initiative seeks to provide emotional support more quickly to those most in need. In January 2010 Gillian Guy, Chief Executive of Victim Support, described the partnership as 'really good news for all victims'. She went on to explain how, by building upon 35 years of experience helping victims of crime, and the expertise that has been gained from supporting over 1.5 million people annually, the charity will be able to make an even bigger difference to the lives of victims.

The initiative will involve being able to utilise the services of 'specialist victim' groups, and it will put Victim Support in a stronger position to encourage other public services to help victims and tackle a wider range of needs.

The services provided by Victim Support differ greatly from the situation that existed as recently as the 1990s, when victims were not treated with the respect and dignity that they deserved. At that time, prosecutors were not allowed to speak with victims and an interview before the trial would have been out of the question. Some police officers believed that victims of some crimes were in some way responsible for becoming a victim, such as women who dressed provocatively or drank alcohol and later reported they had been raped. This treatment of victims was a direct example of prejudice and discrimination based on assumption. The main purpose of the police service at that time was to investigate the crime, arrest the suspect and see the case through to conviction; the focus was weighted towards the offender, and the needs of the victim were not taken into consideration.

Grading Tip!

To achieve P6 you need to select a range of public and third sector organisations and outline their role in supporting victims and witnesses of crime. This should include practical, emotional and financial support. The third sector comprises a diverse range of organisations, including voluntary groups, community, residents and faith groups. It might also include co-operatives and social enterprises, where profits are used for the benefit of the community the group serves.

End-of-unit knowledge check

1. Taking account of the theories of why people commit crime, do you believe individuals are really responsible for the crimes committed? Give reasons for your answers.
2. Identify three sentences that the court may impose on a person under the age of 18 years.
3. Describe ways in which victims of crime may be supported by at least three public service organisations.
4. Outline current crime and disorder legislation.
5. Describe one psychological and one sociological theory of crime.

Grading criteria

In order to pass this unit, the evidence you present for assessment needs to demonstrate that you can meet all the learning outcomes for the unit. The criteria for a pass grade describe the level of achievement required to pass this unit.

To achieve a pass grade the evidence must show that you are able to:	To achieve a merit grade the evidence must show that, in addition to the pass criteria, you are able to:	To achieve a distinction grade the evidence must show that, in addition to the pass and merit criteria, you are able to:
P1 Outline current crime and disorder legislation	M1 Analyse the impact of two pieces of crime and disorder legislation.	D1 Evaluate the impact of one piece of crime and disorder legislation.
P2 State the main sentences and orders criminal courts can impose		
P3 Describe two theories of criminal behaviour and the factors that contribute to these		
P4 Describe the effects crime has on communities and the individual	M2 Analyse the effects of crime on communities and individuals	D2 Evaluate a local public service initiative designed to address crime and its impact on the community
P5 Identify approaches used by public services to reduce crime, disorder and anti-social behaviour	M3 Analyse how the strategies used by the local community public services, work to reduce crime, disorder and anti-social behaviour	
P6 Outline how public and third sector organisations support witnesses and victims of crime		

Unit 13
Command and control in the uniformed public services

Introduction

Command and control is fundamental to the way in which the uniformed public services operate. This unit will explore the command and control structures of the various uniformed public services. The unit will examine the rank structures in the different services, how different ranks generate different levels of authority and how rank is reflected in the chains of command in these services.

The people who exercise command and control in the public services need to possess specific skills and attributes. These qualities are also explored, in addition to tasks and problem-solving techniques used to exercise command and control. Finally, in this unit you will be able to demonstrate your own command and control skills by carrying out different command tasks.

Key term

Command and control – the term used for situations where objectives are achieved by the giving and receiving of instructions

Learning outcomes:

By the end of this unit, you should:

1. Know how the principles of rank, responsibility and the chain of command relate to the command structures of the uniformed public services.

2. Understand the skills and personal qualities required for command and control.

3. Understand how an individual can exercise command and control.

4. Be able to demonstrate command and control skills through command tasks

13.1 Know how the principles of rank, responsibility and the chain of command relate to the command structures of the uniformed public services

P1   P2   M1   D1

Rank structures

All uniformed public services have a clear rank structure. Rank structures in the armed forces are usually more clearly defined than in other uniformed services. A rank is a position in the **hierarchical structure** of an organisation, and the higher the rank, the greater the responsibility and authority are.

Key term

Hierarchical structure – an organisational structure, commonly depicted as a pyramid structure, where the head of the organisation, with the most power, is shown at the top of the pyramid and those with the least power are shown at the bottom of the pyramid

The following tables show the rank structures of some of the uniformed public services:

Army
Field Marshall
General
Lieutenant-General
Major-General
Brigadier
Colonel
Lieutenant-Colonel
Major
Captain
Lieutenant
Second Lieutenant
Warrant Officer Class 1
Warrant Officer Class 2
Colour Sergeant, RM
Sergeant
Corporal Bombardier
Lance Corporal
Lance Bombardier
Private

Fire and Rescue Service
Brigade Manager
Area Manager
Group Manager
Station Manager
Watch Manager
Crew Manager
Firefighter

Police
Chief Constable – the ultimate commanding officer of a Police Service
Deputy Chief Constable – Deputy to the Chief Constable
Assistant Chief Constable
Chief Superintendent
Superintendent
Chief Inspector
Inspector
Sergeant
Police Constable

Prison Service
Senior Manager A
Senior Manager B
Senior Manager C
Senior Manager D
Manager E
Manager F
Manager G
Principal Officer
Senior Officer
Prison Officer
Operational Support Grade
Night Patrol
Storeman
Assistant Storeman
Prison Auxiliary

Royal Air Force
Air Force Marshal
Air Chief Marshal
Air Marshal
Air Vice-Marshal
Air Commodore
Group Captain
Wing Commander
Squadron Leader
Flight Lieutenant
Flying Officer
Pilot Officer
Warrant Officer Master Aircrew
Flight Sergeant Chief Technician
Sergeant
Corporal
Junior Technician

Rank badges

In any uniformed public service people of different ranks wear different badges to represent their rank. People of higher ranks have the 'power' or authority to command people of lower ranks, and the lower ranks are expected to have respect for the higher ranks and to acknowledge that rank, even if they do not know the person who carries the rank. People of lower ranks will salute the wearer of a badge of higher rank – this is one way in which discipline is instilled in new recruits to the armed services. All the uniformed services have a very formal rank structure but the ranks and titles, and the responsibility of each rank, are different in each service.

Figure 13.1 British army officer rank insignia

Responsibilities

All ranks carry a degree of responsibility – the higher the rank, the greater the responsibility.

For example, in the police service, a constable is responsible for carrying out the duties assigned to him, such as routine patrols, investigating crime, attending road traffic incidents, etc. A police sergeant is responsible for the welfare and development of all police constables under his command, and needs to maintain discipline and ensure that they carry out their duties. A police inspector is responsible for ensuring that the sergeants under his command are carrying out their duties effectively, and is also ultimately responsible for ensuring that the police constables are working effectively also. Similarly, the Chief Inspector and Superintendent are responsible for all the officers below their ranks. The Chief Superintendent is the head of the division, so his chain of command goes from the top to the bottom, and he will be responsible for several hundred officers in the division.

The ranks above Chief Superintendent are usually based at Divisional Headquarters and are non-**operational**. This means that they are not involved in everyday police work, but are responsible for **strategic** planning, for implementing government policies and for achieving the targets set by central government.

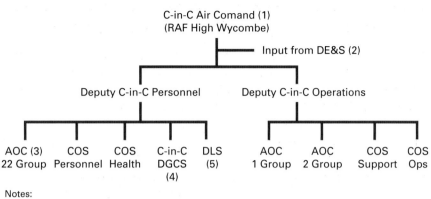

Notes:
(1) C-in-C – Commander-in-Chief
(2) DE&S – Defence Equipment and Support
(3) AOC – Air Officer Commanding; COS – Chief of Staff
(4) DGCS relates to a modular system of mobile, deployable and fixed
     assets that are designed to task, receive, process, exploit all source
     intelligence from national and alliance collection assets
(5) DLS – Director Legal Services

Figure 13.2 RAF Air Command structure

Key terms

Operational – this is the part of the operation where the plan is actually implemented

Strategic – planning something in a considered, calculated and deliberate manner to take all the factors involved into account

Uniformed services frequently work together. In major emergency situations such as the London bombings of 2005, all the emergency services need to combine very quickly, and it is important that someone is in overall command of the situation. Similarly, in situations such as Afghanistan all our armed forces need to work together, and often with services from other countries. The chain of command needs to be very clear in order to avoid any confusion, and it may be that the commander of a service may not be the overall commander of a particular operation.

Chain of command

Police

There are 43 police services throughout England and Wales, and the structure of all these services is very similar. Each service will be divided into divisions and will have a central divisional headquarters where the main administrative and personnel services are based. Criminal Records Bureau checks are usually carried out here, and also other services such as Scenes of Crime, and other specialist units could be based here. Each division will have its own divisional headquarters, which will be commanded by a Chief Superintendent, and some outlying areas, or sub-divisions, will have a smaller police station. Some rural areas may have a section station, which is not always staffed 24 hours a day.

Army

The Army, Royal Navy and RAF have similar, although not identical, command structures. They all need to be prepared to deploy and operate anywhere in the world at short notice. All the organisations need to be clearly divided into separate, but linked, units to enable them to do this.

The British Army consists of five divisions, two fighting divisions and three support divisions. Each fighting division consists of three or four brigades.

Case Study

On 7 July 2005 three bombs exploded on three trains almost simultaneously on the London Underground during the morning rush hour. A fourth bomb exploded on a London bus almost an hour later.

Fifty-six people died in this incident and 700 people were injured. A number of different emergency services were involved in dealing with this major incident. London's transport system was closed down for the whole day, the large number of casualties needed to be transported to nearby hospitals, temporary mortuaries had to be set up and relatives of the deceased and injured needed to be informed. This was a very good example of how command and control were implemented swiftly and efficiently in an emergency situation.

According to the Strategic Emergency Plan, a document published by a government body called the London Resilience Partnership, the capital's response to a major incident is a matter of strict hierarchy. Upon being alerted to 'an event or situation which threatens serious damage to human welfare', senior figures in the emergency services, the NHS, the military, the government and transport are summoned to New Scotland Yard, behind St James's Park tube station. (They are then transferred to a secret location, which becomes known as the Strategic Command Centre.) Once in place, they form the Gold Coordinating Committee, which devises a response to the crisis, their commands cascading down the levels of seniority to the police officers, ambulance crews and firefighters on the ground.

Source: www.guardian.co.uk/society/2005/jul/21/attackonlondon.terrorism2
Copyright Guardian News & Media Ltd 2005

A brigade contains three or four battalion-sized units, around 5,000 personnel, and is commanded by a one-star officer, a brigadier. The brigade will contain a wide range of military disciplines, allowing it to carry out a variety of military tasks.

The brigade would be required to deploy up to three separate battlegroups, the main **tactical** formation used in the British Army. The battlegroup is a mixed formation around the core of one unit, an armoured regiment or infantry battalion, with sub-units providing artillery, engineers, logistics, aviation, etc., as required.

Key term

Tactical – the methods used to implement a formulated plan

Relative levels of control

All the uniformed public services are comprised of units. This 'unit' could be a regiment, a battalion or platoon in the army, a squadron in the RAF or a division in the police or fire services. Every 'unit' will have a commander.

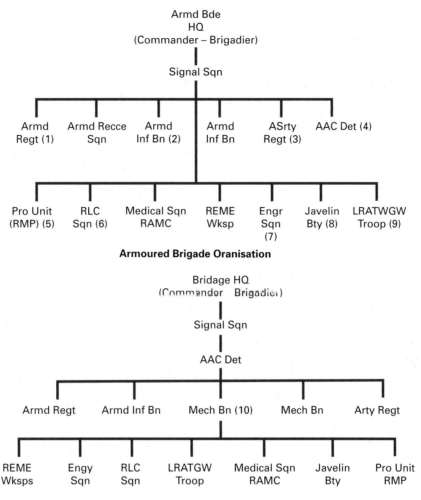

Figure 13.3 Organisation chart of a brigade

Control of the public services by non-uniformed organisations

As explained, all uniformed services have a hierarchical structure with a strict chain of command from the bottom to the top. Every service is also accountable to and governed by a higher authority.

The emergency services are controlled by the Home Office, which is a department in central government. The Home Secretary is the head of this department, which is responsible for maintaining law and order in the UK and providing us with a safe environment. The Home Office provides the funding of the Police and Fire Services via taxation.

All of the armed services are governed by a separate government department, the Ministry of Defence (MOD), which is headed by the Secretary of State for Defence. The person in this role is responsible for implementing the defence policy for the UK in order to defend our interests both at home and abroad, but does not interfere with the day-to-day running of the army or other armed services.

Grading Tip!

For P1 you should show the structure of two contrasting uniformed public services – one emergency service and one armed service.

P2 requires a closer examination of one of these public services, describing the chain of command, which will allow the relationship between post and rank to be explored in detail. This will identify the chain of command and how both post and rank interrelate.

To achieve M1, you will need to be able to analyse the importance and use of, command and control within a uniformed public service and analyse the situations or activities that require command and control. Examples of both good and poor command and control should be examined in detail. Much can be learned from examples of poor command and control.

To achieve a D1, you should be able to evaluate the importance and use of command and control within the uniformed public services, and evaluate its uses, using examples from a uniformed public service.

13.2 Understand the skills and personal qualities required for command and control

Figure 13.4 Army commander

Personal qualities are the natural characteristics of a person. These are different from personal skills, which are things that have to be learnt and developed, e.g. communication skills.

'Unit 2 Leadership and teamwork' looks at the skills and qualities of a good leader. A commander will possess similar qualities in order to be successful and effective, but may also need additional qualities, as listed below:

- Role model – a role model is someone who sets a good example for others to follow. A good leader is one who leads by example and sets a standard that others will wish to emulate (copy).
- Courage – a quality that demonstrates a lack of fear, even in the face of great adversity (difficulty) or danger.
- Tenacity – the ability to persevere to see a job through to completion.

- Confidence – boldness when decisions need to be made and actions need to be taken.
- Integrity – honesty and high moral standards.
- Determination – a real commitment to carry out whatever tasks are required.
- Decisiveness – the ability to make decisions quickly and effectively and to stand by these decisions.
- Mental agility – the ability to think quickly, to assess a problem and to provide a solution.
- The ability to keep calm – essential in conflict or emergency situations.
- Strength of character – this is a quality which may be difficult to define but which is required by commanders, who are often faced with difficult or dangerous situations and who have to make decisions which could put the lives of others in danger.
- Sense of humour – this can help to lift team morale when necessary.
- Objectivity – commanders need to be objective in order to be able to make decisions.

Qualities instilled by a good commander

The qualities listed above are those which good commanders should possess. In order to be effective as leaders they also need to be able to instil certain qualities in those who are under their command. These qualities include the following.

Trust

Any commander needs to have the trust of those under his or her command. This means that those they command will know that they can totally rely on the commander to make decisions which are in their best interests, and which have been made from a position of knowledge and understanding of the situation. Trust should be mutual and reciprocal (go both ways) for successful command and control.

Loyalty

Members of the uniformed services will demonstrate loyalty to their commander by having the faith and commitment in the tasks they are asked to carry out, even if this means putting their own lives in danger.

Discipline

Discipline is obviously essential in all the uniformed public services. A good commander instils and maintains discipline throughout the organisation. Command and control systems would disintegrate if there was no discipline.

Respect

Most people would agree that respect has to be earned. However, as mentioned earlier, in the uniformed services respect needs to be shown to higher ranks, irrespective of whether the person carrying that rank has personally earned your respect or not. There is an assumption that in order to gain a higher rank the person concerned must have performed well enough to deserve it.

A lack of respect for the higher ranks could lead to low morale and poor motivation and performance by those in the lower ranks.

Morale

Morale is a state of mind that can affect how a person performs and deals with certain situations. It is essential that a high level of morale is maintained in the uniformed services. If morale is low, the performance of the whole team can be affected. A good commander will recognise when morale needs to be raised and will ensure that this is addressed when necessary.

Key term

Repatriated – when someone is sent back to the country where they are from

Ask Yourself!

What effect on morale do you think the following would have on soldiers serving in Afghanistan?

1. **Demonstrations against the war in Afghanistan have taken place in the UK by members of the public.**

2. **Food at the camp is poor and there is a shortage of much-needed equipment.**

3. **Soldiers see reports of the town of Wootton Bassett, where hundreds of residents have lined the streets to pay their respects as the bodies of three soldiers killed in action are repatriated.**

Motivation

Motivation is what drives a person to perform well. If a person is not well motivated this can have an adverse effect on the performance of the whole team. A good commander will recognise when a person, or a team, is not motivated and will take steps to address reasons for the low motivation.

Motivational strategies

A good commander recognises that if morale and motivation are high then it will be easier to maintain command. Although an authoritarian style of discipline exists within the uniformed public services, a good leader will recognise that loyalty and obedience cannot be enforced in this way. When morale and motivation are low, lower ranks can start to feel devalued and rebel against authority. Good leaders will address the situation by recognising and appreciating the individual talents and skills of the lower ranks and enabling them to feel valued. This, in turn, will help to improve performance and to achieve the organisation's objectives.

Maintenance of authority

The rank structure that exists in the uniformed public services gives higher ranks the authority to give orders to the lower ranks, who should then carry out these orders unquestioningly. If orders are not obeyed then the rank structure will be undermined and the hierarchical structure could collapse. If a corporal in the armed forces orders a private to carry out 50 press-ups, and the private refuses, then the chain of command and control has broken down as the rank carries no authority.

Failing to comply with an order from someone in a position of authority is considered to be a very serious offence in the uniformed services. Orders are given for good reason – and disobeying those orders could mean putting the life of a colleague, or member of the public, in danger. General disobedience to orders is bad for discipline and could undermine morale and team spirit. The main purpose of each uniformed service can only be fulfilled if orders are given and carried out correctly, in accordance with the hierarchy of authority.

Course of action if orders are not obeyed

In the uniformed services, failing to carry out an order given by a higher-ranking officer amounts to an act of misconduct. This would lead to an investigation being carried out by a senior officer, who will then decide if a disciplinary hearing is required. A commanding officer would normally conduct this type of hearing. In the armed services, serious cases would be taken to a court martial, which would be conducted along similar lines to a court hearing, and a military judge would preside over these proceedings. The accused person would have access to legal representation. If convicted, there are a range of penalties which could be applied, including cautions, fines, demotion, reduction in salary, imprisonment and/or, for certain offences, dismissal from the service. This would be known as a dishonourable discharge.

> ## Ask Yourself!
> **Why is it important that orders are clearly communicated?**

Credibility as a commander

As with all good leaders, a commanding officer must be seen to act fairly at all times. Commanders may need to make very difficult decisions in certain situations, in order to carry out the main purpose of the service. A commander is also ultimately responsible for the welfare and discipline of colleagues. Although orders must be given and obeyed by everyone concerned, there are often personal issues and circumstances which need to be considered. For example, if someone has a relative who is very ill, or has suffered a bereavement, or is dealing with other personal problems, this may affect their performance in the service. In such circumstances a commander may approve an application for compassionate leave from the service. This decision will need to take account of the requirements of the service and also the personal circumstances of the individual. Every case will need to be looked at on its own merit and all decisions made will need to be seen to be fair. This could mean that different decisions are sometimes made in what appear to be a similar set of circumstances. So long as the commander can explain the reasons for the decision, and can demonstrate that favouritism or other personal feelings have not contributed to the decision, this should avoid any resentment or lowering of morale within the ranks.

It is also important that a commander demonstrates equal opportunities in line with the Equal Opportunities Policy that each service operates. This would normally mean that all individuals should be given the same fair treatment, regardless of colour, gender or religion. Any promotion of an individual should reflect this, and should be based on merit, and how they have carried out their duties, and should not be given for any other reason.

> ## Case Study
>
> 1. Petty Officer Robinson applied for leave to attend his friend's stag night.
> 2. Petty Officer Brown applied for compassionate leave as her grandmother had been admitted to hospital for an emergency operation and she was really worried about her.
>
> The commander decided to refuse both requests as he felt he could not approve one request and not the other. Was this a fair decision?

Know the strengths and weaknesses of direct reports and managers

Commanders should know the strengths and weaknesses of those who report directly to them and of others who are under their command. This should allow strategies and operations to be planned taking these into account to ensure that those who are going to carry out the plans are those most suited to the task.

Commanders should also understand the role or function of the group as a whole in order to ensure that the group is used to best effect. In the uniformed services different groups often operate like a small piece of a large jigsaw, with each group playing an important part in a larger operation. A good commander will understand the role and function of each group within that bigger plan.

Demonstrate confidence

It is vital for commanders to demonstrate confidence at all times in order to maintain the morale and trust of those under their command. In the uniformed services, it is essential, when about to embark on a difficult operation, that commanders show that they have every confidence in their colleagues. They must demonstrate that they are confident of success in the proposed operation to raise the spirits and morale of the group.

Ensure that information is shared and orders disseminated

Success of the chain of command and control depends on orders being passed promptly and accurately down the chain's structure. Where an operation involves various different units, it is essential that orders are communicated accurately across these units. It is very important that other information is also passed down the lines of command and control, so that those at the base of the hierarchical structure are kept informed and up to date with developments, particularly regarding the success of any operations they may be involved in. This is important to ensure that everyone feels valued. There may, however, be instances when commanders will need to decide whether to withhold certain information knowing that the morale of the team could be adversely affected.

Case Study

Briefing before Operation Moshtarak

On the eve of the major battle last night, Lieutenant Colonel Matt Bazeley, commander of the British Engineer Regiment, told his men at Camp Bastion: 'We are going into the heart of darkness.'

'You will be tested. If things go wrong, no sad moments, no pauses, we regather, recock, and go again.

'It is bloody dangerous out there,' but, he added, 'this is what you have been trained for. I repeat: much of this operation rests on us.'

Source: www.dailymail.co.uk.

1. What was the message the commander was giving to his troops?
2. How do you think the men felt after this briefing?

Grading Tip!

To achieve P3, you should explain how an individual can exercise command and control. This is a fairly straightforward task where you should give an explanation of the skills and qualities discussed above.

For M2, you should be able to identify the specific skills required for given practical scenarios. You should demonstrate, through practical activities, an ability to relate your own performance to identified skills.

13.3 Understand how an individual can exercise command and control

P4

Command and control

Individuals can exercise command and control by using:

- information and intelligence concerning operations
- strategy from senior officers
- leadership skills
- communication skills
- planning skills
- knowledge of available resources
- sequence of events.

In the uniformed public services, the chain of command and control is established by rank and status within the hierarchy of each service. There are, however, occasions when this may not be quite so clear, and there is then a need for command and control to be established. For example, when the emergency services are called to the scene of a road traffic accident, the first police officer to arrive at the scene will take control of the incident, regardless of rank.

Who is responsible for assuming control and how they would do it

The Emergency Procedures Manual, published by the Association of Chief Police Officers, states that the police will take overall command of major emergency incidents where different services are involved.

The first police officer on the scene assumes the role of initial police incident officer and will contact the police control room where the incident will be coordinated from. This officer will assess the situation and generally maintain overall control, regulating the flow of traffic, cordoning off the accident scene, making the area safe and coordinating other emergency services, such as the paramedics and fire and rescue services, when they arrive at the scene. When a more senior police officer arrives at the scene, he or she will then assume overall command of the whole operation. This action will not be a cause for discussion; just as the first officer would not hesitate to take control of the scene regardless of rank, so there will be an automatic assumption that the senior officer will then take over the command and control.

The first police vehicle on the scene becomes the command and control vehicle for the police service until a specially designated command and control vehicle arrives. The first fire and rescue vehicle to arrive on the scene will act as the control vehicle for that service, and a red flashing beacon will identify this. Similarly, the first ambulance to arrive will become the control vehicle for the ambulance and paramedic teams and this will be identified by a green flashing light.

All the control vehicles will park alongside each other, easily identifiable by their coloured flashing lights. An overall chain of command is then established by dividing the incident into sectors or levels of command. These sectors are:

- strategic
- tactical
- operational.

Each of the sectors will have a sector commander and a team of emergency service personnel. These levels of command are explained more fully below.

If an emergency involves a fire or hazardous materials then the Fire and Rescue Services would take overall control, as they are the specialists in such situations. If there are

fatalities then Her Majesty's Coroner needs to be informed before any bodies can be removed from the scene.

A coroner is someone who determines:

- the identity of a dead person
- when, where and how the person died
- the cause of death.

A formal identification must be carried out by a police officer, who acts on behalf of the coroner. In such a situation, this officer, who will usually be a police constable, will assume control of the scene, above officers of a higher rank.

All of the emergency services use similar methods of command and control, as discussed above, so that when all services are involved in a major incident, a clear process and chain of command immediately comes into effect and the operation is not hindered by any confusion over who is in control.

There is a standard procedure for the first emergency service officers to attend an incident such as a major accident. This uses the mnemonic CHALETS.

Table 13.1 CHALETS

Casualties	Approximate number of casualties – fatal, injured and not injured
Hazards	Present and potential
Access	Best routes for emergency vehicles and suitable provisional RVP (rendezvous point)
Location	Exact location (road junction or map reference) to pinpoint the scene
Emergency services	Emergency services present and required
Types and timescales	Type of incident, with details of types and numbers of vehicles involved
Safety	Safety of self and others involved

Comparison of the methods used by the services

The armed forces use different methods of command and control, so that one service takes overall command depending on the type of conflict, as discussed above. Command and control in the armed forces is often carried out in dangerous, unstable conditions, such as on the front line. To deal with these situations, commanding officers give orders to the troops about what needs to be done and why they need to do it, but they then delegate the tactical decisions to people lower down the chain of command.

When the armed forces are involved in large, combined operations, such as the Iraq war and the Afghanistan conflict, a decision will be made by the service commanders and the Ministry of Defence as to who will take overall command. This will depend on the type of conflict and where it is taking place. If the conflict is mainly on land then the army will be in overall command, whereas if the conflict is mainly at sea then the Royal Navy would be in full command.

Levels of command and control

The three levels of command and control mentioned briefly above are strategic, tactical and operational. Each level signifies a function of command and control, and the commander of each function would be at the same level of the command control hierarchical structure. Let's look at these in more detail.

Strategic command (gold command)

Strategic planning means making plans or strategies to achieve certain objectives. These objectives could include dealing with a major incident, reducing crime or planning for a war.

Strategic command usually takes place away from the major incident, either at a police headquarters in the case of a major emergency incident, or at the Ministry of Defence in London in the case of the armed forces.

Strategic command would normally be undertaken by the lead commander of each uniformed service. The Police and Ambulance Services refer to this as 'gold command'. A plan will be formulated by the different heads of service to find the best way forward to deal with the particular situation.

Tactical command (silver command)

When a plan has been formulated by strategic command, it then becomes the task of the tactical commander to implement the plan. Tactical command develops the strategic plan and decides how, when and by whom the plan should be carried out. Tactical commanders will not be directly involved at the scene of an operation or incident. This tactical role could be compared to that of a control centre, where models and tabletop activities assimilating the particular set of circumstances can be used to consider different strategies. In a major incident, tactical command would be known as 'silver command' by the Police and Ambulance Services.

Operational command (bronze command)

This command takes place on the 'battle-field' or at the scene of an emergency incident. This is where the operational commanders would control the resources of each service to implement the plan to best effect. The strategic plans put in place by their strategic commander would be implemented by the operational commanders, using the tactics set by tactical command. This would be known as 'bronze command' in an emergency incident situation.

Planning

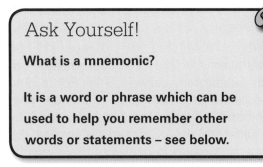

Key term

Briefing – a meeting where relevant information and instructions are given, usually by a senior officer, before any operation or mission

Activity

Set yourself a set of SMART objectives to help you to complete your course.

One example of a suitable SMART objective could be:

I will complete all the pass grades for my Command and Control unit by 30 April.

This objective is SMART as it clearly spells out what you need to do (specific) and the date you are going to do it by (timed). The objective is measurable, as you can clearly see the number of pass grades you are required to achieve, and it is also achievable and realistic. By setting yourself a target of completing the pass grades only, you are not setting your standards too high, and you can then set yourself a further target to achieve the merit grades.

In order to achieve any goal or aim it is necessary to have clear objectives (or steps). One popular model for setting clear objectives uses the mnemonic SMART. This model is used in the uniformed services and also in private organisations. It enables individuals to have the control to develop themselves to their full potential. SMART objectives are:

- **S**pecific – setting clear and specific targets will help you to be clear about the steps you need to take.
- **M**easurable – objectives must be measurable, which means you will know when you have completed them.
- **A**chievable – it is important that your objectives can actually be achieved and that you are not striving for something which may not be achievable.
- **R**ealistic – you should ensure that your objectives are realistic and that you are not setting targets for yourself which are too high, which could be demoralising and demotivating.
- **T**imed – you should set yourself a time limit in which to achieve your objectives, otherwise you may never achieve them.

Briefing

This subject is covered in much greater detail in 'Unit 2 Leadership and teamwork'. Simply, a **briefing** is a meeting where all relevant information about a forthcoming mission or operation is given to the officers involved in the operation. This briefing meeting is usually led by the senior officer in charge of the operation. It is a very important meeting where the information given out needs to communicated in a very clear manner, so that there is no misunderstanding. Lives could be put at risk if this is not done correctly.

Effective control

Anyone who has played the game 'Chinese Whispers' will know how messages can be distorted when they are passed from person to person. Giving orders clearly and with authority demands a good knowledge and understanding of the reasons, strategy and background to the orders. People who give orders must know what detail to put in and what to leave out to make the order most effective.

The most effective way of giving instructions or orders is obviously to give them directly from one person to another. This is not always possible, however, particularly in a major emergency or conflict situation. In the immediate aftermath of the London bombings in 2005 there was a major communication breakdown when landlines and mobile networks crashed due to the increased usage. On the front line in a conflict situation, 'runners' may be utilised to relay orders and instructions. External factors such as noise, stress, hunger and fatigue can all affect a person's hearing or perception. For this reason, wherever possible, a commander should give and receive orders directly.

Good commanders will constantly monitor the teams under their command. They will then be assured that the teams are performing well and fulfilling their objectives, but there is also another aspect to this. Maintaining a physical presence can have two benefits for a commander. Teams will feel supported if they see that a commander is taking an interest in their progress and development. They could start to feel neglected if a commander appears to show no interest. A good commander will want to be seen to be hands-on, especially when the rest of the team are experiencing difficult conditions. There is a difference, though, between monitoring teams as a way of providing support and monitoring as a means of 'checking up' to see that someone is doing their job properly – this will lower the morale of the team.

Maintaining a strong presence

Maintaining a strong command presence means demonstrating command by use of body language and tone of voice, instilling confidence and trust in others. Strong commanders usually have a quality called charisma, which is difficult to define but is a quality which is possessed by many great leaders.

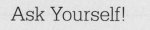

Ask Yourself!

Can you think of a leader who has a strong presence and charisma?

Delegation

Good commanders will know when to delegate tasks. This means handing down responsibility and authority to someone of a lower rank. This can empower teams and individuals and can improve motivation and morale.

Functional command methods

Functional command methods ensure that commands are carried out effectively. Command tasks can be broken down into manageable steps, which can be remembered by the mnemonic PICSIE:

- **P**lan – this plan or strategy sets out the aims and objectives for achieving a mission.

- **I**nitiate – this is the first stage in carrying out the plan – the briefing stage.
- **C**ontrol – the plan is carried out with monitoring and control by the leader.
- **S**upport – the leader will support the team by praising and encouraging members and also encouraging them to support each other.
- **I**nform – the leader should ensure that all relevant information is shared within the team.
- **E**valuate – the leader assesses the team's progress and performance.

Grading Tip!

To achieve P4 you should provide an explanation of the personal skills and qualities, discussed above, that are needed for command and control within a uniformed public service.

13.4 Be able to demonstrate command and control skills through command task activities

P5   M3   D2

Command and control skills and qualities

We have already identified the personal qualities required for command and control earlier in this section. Good leaders should understand these skills and qualities, but they should also be able to demonstrate them by using command task activities.

Effective communication can be described as a means of sending the right message to the right person at the right time. This may mean using good speaking and listening skills, effective use of body language such as using eye contact and good body posture. A leader needs to convey many different kinds of information – good and bad news, instructions and orders, reprimands and praise and encouragement. Good leaders will appreciate the importance of good communication skills when doing this.

Types of command task activities

The following are situations where command and control are exercised.

Combat

Combat situations involve fighting. This type of activity is where a commander must use many skills and qualities in order to defeat the 'enemy'. In combat, command tasks should be carried out to:

- surprise the enemy
- upset the tempo of the enemy's activities
- disrupt enemy communications and strategy
- weaken enemy capabilities by killing people and destroying equipment and infrastructure.

Rescue

All of the uniformed services take part in rescues. Rescue operations usually have to be carried out quickly and in dangerous conditions, e.g. from a burning building or crash situations. Rescues are command tasks because:

- There is a mission that needs to be carried out.
- Teamwork is involved.
- The task needs to be done quickly.
- There is a problem to be solved.
- Improvisation and initiative may be needed.

Containment

The emergency services are sometimes called to incidents such as a major fire or chemical spillage where the services must prevent the hazard from spreading further. A commander will need various skills to protect other members of the services and the public.

Situation control

Uniformed services sometimes need to control situations. This could involve the armed services keeping the peace in countries such as Afghanistan, prison officers curtailing a prison riot or the police controlling large crowds. In such situations there is always the risk that things can flare up and escalate at any time. The commander will need to put all of his skills and qualities to good use in order to protect everyone involved.

Accident

The kind of tasks carried out at accidents are command task activities. These include:

- rescue activities
- blocking off roads
- safeguarding property at the scene
- taking photographs at the scene
- informing relatives.

Recovery

The emergency services not only have to deal with emergencies such as road accidents, fires and floods, they also have to restore the scene back to normal, as far as possible. This is to ensure that businesses and individuals can return to some normality as quickly as possible. In the case of flooding, this could take a number of months, and requires good command and control.

Problem-solving techniques

Problem-solving techniques are used by many commanders in many situations. Although the various problems may be very different, they can all be tackled by using a particular plan, as follows:

- Define the problem.
- Gather all the relevant information.
- List the possible solutions.
- Test the possible solutions.
- Select the best solution.

Grading Tip!

To achieve P5 you need to demonstrate a number of command and control skills in different situations. You can ask your tutor for support when doing this.

For M3 you will have to be able to demonstrate that you have an effective level of competence in the practical activities. This is an opportunity for you not only to demonstrate the practical skills that you have learned, but to show that you can achieve the outcomes of the activities effectively.

For D2 you should evaluate how well you performed the command control activities and think about how you could improve on these for your own personal development.

End-of-unit knowledge check

1. Who is the commander of a police service?
2. Name three qualities that a good leader should possess.
3. Name three qualities that a good leader should instil in others.
4. Give three examples of body language.
5. Identify three elements of effective control.

Grading criteria

In order to pass this unit, the evidence that you present for assessment needs to demonstrate that they can meet all the learning outcomes for the unit. The criteria for a pass grade describe the level of achievement required to pass this unit.

To achieve a pass grade the evidence must show that you are able to:	To achieve a merit grade the evidence must show that, in addition to the pass criteria, you are able to:	To achieve a distinction grade the evidence must show that, in addition to the pass and merit criteria, you are able to:
P1 Identify the rank structure in two contrasting uniformed public services including responsibilities [IE1]		
P2 Describe the chain of command for one public service, including its uniform structure [C16]	**M1** Analyse the importance and use of command and control within a uniformed public service	**D1** Evaluate the importance and use of command and control within the uniformed public services
P3 Explain the skills and personal qualities required for command and control [IE4]	**M2** Assess the skills required for given practical command and control scenarios and compare these to own performance	

To achieve a pass grade the evidence must show that you are able to:	To achieve a merit grade the evidence must show that, in addition to the pass criteria, you are able to:	To achieve a distinction grade the evidence must show that, in addition to the pass and merit criteria, you are able to:
P4 Explain how an individual can exercise command and control [EP3]		
P5 Demonstrate with support the use of command and control skills in different situations [TW1, SM2]	**M3** Demonstrate practical command and control in different situations within uniformed public services	**D2** Evaluate own performance in command and control situations, identifying areas of personal development

Introduction

Local authorities and public services in the United Kingdom use the term **'major incident'** to describe any incident that requires special arrangements by one or more of the emergency services, the National Health Service or local authority. In this unit you will learn about different types of major incident and investigate ways in which public services manage them. You will also consider the ways in which major incidents affect individuals, communities and the wider environment.

You will explore UK legislation in respect of managing major incidents. The Civil Contingencies Act 2004 sets out the requirements of the emergency services, National Health Service (NHS), Health and Safety Executive (HSE), Armed Forces, transport and utilities companies, as well as aid agencies to be in a 'state of preparedness'.

You will investigate the ways in which these organisations work together to prepare for a major incident, and you will be involved in tabletop scenarios of such incidents, so that you can better understand the interdependency of these organisations when responding to a major incident.

Key term

Major incident – any emergency that requires special arrangements by one or all of the emergency services

Learning outcomes:

By the end of this unit, you should:

1. Know the effects of recent major incidents.

2. Know the type of work carried out by the public services during major incidents.

3. Understand the considerations for emergency planning and preparation for possible major incidents.

4. Be able to prepare for a particular major incident by using tabletop scenarios.

15.1 Know the effects of recent major incidents

Causes of major incidents

The likelihood of being involved in a major incident is, thankfully, extremely small for most of us. However, rarely a year passes without a major incident occurring in the United Kingdom. It is for this reason that all public services must be ready to cope with such an event.

Causes of major incidents can be classified in two main ways: natural and manmade. Within these categories there are further sub-divisions.

Now you have some idea of how incidents can be classified and the ways in which they occur, you will need to investigate further some specific major incidents and provide information about them. Note that to achieve P2 and M1 you must refer to *at least three* recent incidents (from the last five years) and one of these must have occurred in the United Kingdom. The reason for this is that you will need to refer to UK public services when you provide evidence for some of the criteria in this unit.

(g) Grading Tip!

To achieve P1 you will need to provide a definition of the term 'major incident'. This definition must take into account the terms used by the UK emergency services.

For P2 you will begin to look into different types of major incidents. You must describe at least three and state the cause of each. (Remember that these will have occurred in the last five years.)

M2 needs a more thorough investigation of the incidents – and at least one of your incidents will have happened in the UK.

Activity

Using the examples provided below, carry out research into each type of major incident. Using this information, produce a poster to display in your classroom. You should include dates (the more recent the better) and brief details of each incident.

Natural causes of major incidents:

- severe weather, e.g. heatwave, blizzard
- epidemic
- landslide
- earthquake
- flooding
- hurricane

Manmade causes:

- air, road, rail, waterway accident
- terrorist
- crowd-related (e.g. crush)
- building collapse
- explosion
- pollution; chemical, oil
- fire (including arson)
- technology failure

Effects of recent major incidents

When people think of major incidents it is natural that they consider the number of people who have been killed. In some incidents, such as earthquakes, tsunamis or air traffic accidents, it is very likely that some deaths will occur. However, to return to the definition of a major incident being an incident that 'requires special arrangements by one or more of the emergency services, the National Health Service or local authority', it is the incident itself (and subsequent necessary actions) that is important.

This account (shown in the Case Study opposite) of the storm and casualties on the island of Madeira is what made the initial headlines in newspaper, television and radio reports. A short while later, information on the wider issues began to emerge, including the loss of communication systems, closure of the airport and destruction of roadways and bridges. A local man told how he had seen his family swept away by the floodwaters, while a manager of one of the island's hotels described it as the worst storm in almost 20 years. He added that he had seen a BMW car floating past his hotel.

It soon became clear that the landslides which occurred high up in the mountains, and which brought rivers of mud through the city, would inevitably have an impact on the island and its people. Although the death toll was thought to be 43, it was feared that rescue workers would find more victims under rubble and mud in isolated villages. Many residents had been left homeless. Temporary shelters for the homeless were provided by the local government.

The Portuguese Prime Minister promised that his government would provide help to make sure that recovery work could begin as soon as possible, and would make an application for funds to the European Union. A naval frigate containing medical equipment, and a helicopter to assist in recovery, were

Case Study

Flood and mudslides in Madeira

On 20 February 2010 extreme weather conditions affected the Portuguese island of Madeira (population fewer than 250,000) in the North Atlantic Ocean. More than 10 cm of rain fell within five hours – the average rainfall for the whole of February is just 88 mm. The storm that led to the flooding was one in a series that affected Spain, mainland Portugal, Morocco and the Canary Islands.

Damage was limited to the south of the island; landslides damaged much of the city of Funchal; at least 43 people died and a further 100 were injured.

Figure 15.1 A street in the centre of Funchal, Madeira's capital, is covered with rocks following landslides caused by the severe storms which hit the island

sent to Madeira. Three days of national mourning for the victims was announced; the Portuguese government also considered declaring a state of emergency in the region.

The battle to return to some form of normality was set in motion almost immediately. On the day the floods happened, many trucks and heavy machinery went to Funchal and other affected sites, to begin removing mud, rocks and other debris that had passed through the area. Within a few days several hundred vehicles and staff were involved in the major clean up; all services in the capital were accessible.

It is estimated that a full return to normality for the surrounding area, including roadways, bridges and other affected aspects of the infrastructure, could take a few years at an estimated cost of 1,4 billion euros.

Case Study

Chilean earthquake

On 27 February 2010 a massive earthquake, lasting approximately 3 minutes, struck the Maule region of Chile. The earthquake measured 8.8 on the Richter scale, and tremors were felt as far north as Peru. Initial reports of deaths were in the region of 700, although this was later reduced to an estimated 250, with many more unaccounted for.

The epicentre of the earthquake was about 100 miles from Concepcion, Chile's second-largest city. As a result of the earthquake, tsunami warnings were issued in more than 50 countries and it also caused abnormal waves at Lake Pontchartrain, north of New Orleans, some 5,000 miles away.

As with the previous example, this major incident caused damage to the environment and a substantial amount of effort and money will be needed before things return to anything like the situation before the event. However, the behaviour of some individuals in these situations can cause further distress to many and can divert the attention of public services to deal with this.

With almost half of the regions in Chile pronounced 'catastrophe zones', and chaos everywhere, some individuals began a campaign of looting and other types of public disorder. Supermarkets in the city of Concepcion were attacked and items stolen. This might be understandable if it was limited to food, as many services were unavailable and people would soon become hungry. However, in addition to food and other necessities for survival, electronic goods and other valuable items were also stolen.

In an attempt to control this vandalism, a special force of *carabineros* (police) was drafted into the area; this included national police, local police and military police. Among the tactics employed by the police were tear gas and water cannon. In spite of these measures, the stealing continued and, within two days, more than 160 people were arrested.

The behaviour demonstrated in Concepcion was repeated in other areas hit by the earthquake. In Santiago police shot into the air in an attempt to make looters move away; in at least one case, a supermarket was set ablaze by the mobs.

The after-effects of major incidents can have devastating effects on individuals, communities and the environment for a long time after the situation is apparently over. Examples include people who have survived the event but have received injuries that will change their lives forever, or those whose loved ones have perished.

Members of the public services that deal with the incident witness some truly dreadful scenes, which can lead to them reliving the situation, and might result in post-traumatic stress disorder (PTSD). This is now a recognised illness; it can affect anyone who has undergone events that were so shocking that they suffer 'flashbacks' of the scene. They might also display angry outbursts or avoid close emotional situations entirely.

Almost a century ago, during the First World War, soldiers displaying similar symptoms were said to be suffering from 'shell-shock'. However, with proper treatment many people suffering from PTSD can be cured.

Where there is lack of fresh water following a major incident, the risk of disease increases. This can include diarrhoea and cholera, both of which can be exacerbated by lack of proper sanitation.

On occasions there will be a need to examine a major incident. Reasons for the investigation might include an unusually high number of deaths occurring, or if obvious reasons for damage to property or loss of life are not evident. Similarly, the emergency services might be faced with a situation for which, initially, there was no obvious cause. The investigation takes the form of a review, and the purpose of this is to collate (bring together) all relevant information about the event from all those involved. It should also enable an improved response in the event of a similar incident in the future.

incident, the review will take the form of a public inquiry; this is similar to a review but is carried out in a formal manner, and is chaired by an impartial expert.

Public inquiry

This is an investigation into all aspects of a major incident. It is initiated by a government minister and announced in Parliament. There is no restriction on who can be present at the sessions; typically the media will attend and publish reports on television, in newspapers and in radio bulletins. The inquiry itself will usually not be broadcast directly through any form of media. This method of investigation aims to be as free and fair as possible. It will be chaired by a judge or panel, and assessors are allowed to assist, if needed.

Evidence presented at the inquiry might be on oath. This decision rests with the chairperson. The purpose of an inquiry is to identify causes and seek solutions; it is not designed to lead to prosecutions, although this could happen. After the conclusion of an inquiry, a report is published. This could lead to action by the government, possibly resulting in a change in legislation.

Review of a major incident

A review usually comprises the following elements:
- facts of the incident
- cause of the incident
- response of emergency services
- assessment of the effectiveness of the response
- reflection on who might be at fault.

The actual composition of the review will depend on a number of factors, including the nature of the incident, who is presiding over the review and whether it is in the public interest to publish the results.

Where there is clearly a case for the public to be informed of the response to a major

Grading Tip!

To achieve P3 you will return to the incidents you began to research for P2 and describe the effects of these incidents on communities and the environment. You should include short- and long-term effects. Where the incidents are very recent, you will need to base your evidence on reliable sources of information.

For M2 you need to *explain* these effects; that means you should go into more detail and not rely on the first report you find on the subject.

15.2 Public services involvement in major incidents

Whenever a major incident occurs in the UK there is a need for involvement from many different organisations, each with their own area of expertise. These will include statutory and non-statutory agencies, for example the police, fire and rescue service, health service, charities, armed forces, local authority organisations and many more.

All agencies will need to co-operate fully to achieve a successful outcome. This could mean that agencies will be working together on the same task, or independently, even though they may be in the same vicinity. For this reason it is essential that major incidents are planned for, and that all agencies involved train together.

While each organisation will have its own area of expertise, the main objectives of all remain the same: the first duty of every agency is to save life, and the final involvement will be to contribute to the debriefing process, after threats posed by the incident have passed.

The table below identifies the main duties of the three emergency services; these are not listed in any particular order.

In the vast majority of cases, the first service to arrive at the scene of a major incident will be the police. This could be because the police are the first point of call for anyone who finds themselves in an emergency situation. Each emergency service is fully aware of the roles of the others in emergency situations; they will also have a good understanding of the ways in which other agencies work to achieve a

Activity

Using the information in the table as a starting point, carry out your own investigation into other tasks that the emergency services are required to perform at the scene of a major incident. Draw up a list of all other agencies you can think of that might also be involved.

Table 15.1 The main duties of the three emergency services

Police	Ambulance	Fire Service
Cordon off the area	Provide emergency aid	Fight any fires
Obtain statements	Resuscitate if needed	Minimise risk of fire
Coordinate all agencies	Set up casualty point	Search for casualties
Investigate the cause	Transport casualties	Identify hazardous substances
Ensure access and egress (exit)		Inform of any substances
Update control room		Set up decontamination units
Identify any dead		

successful outcome. For this reason they will be well equipped to make an initial assessment of the situation and use this information to determine which services might need to be involved. It is absolutely essential that the information that is transmitted to the control room is accurate, as the lives of many might depend upon it.

If the incident is very serious, and support is required from a number of agencies, the mnemonic CHALETS is adopted when relaying information.

> **C**asualties – number or estimate (including severity of injuries)
> **H**azards – present or potential (nature of hazard)
> **A**ccess – routes in and out, for emergency vehicles and other services (no one else)
> **L**ocation – *exact* location of incident (essential so no time is wasted)
> **E**mergency services – what and how many are needed
> **T**ype of incident – e.g. traffic accident, fire, chemical, railway
> **S**afety – of self and others involved

Police Service

Soon after a major incident occurs, a casualty bureau will be set up. This is where the police gather all information relating to the incident. Outside information may also help the police to determine who may be involved in the incident. As soon as practicable a designated telephone number will be supplied through the media; the first priority is to establish whether anyone is missing and to identify survivors and casualties.

Survivor reception centres may also be established. Those who were not seriously injured might be interviewed at this location, so that their version of events may be recorded as soon as possible after the event.

Family liaison officers are police officers who support families that have lost loved ones. They provide help and guidance while investigations are carried out and will remain the named person for that family to contact if they need any information afterwards.

Local authorities

Local authorities are heavily involved in major incidents in the UK. Once they receive initial information from the emergency service that was first on the scene, their emergency planning unit will set up the first response. This could include reception centres (for relatives of casualties) and might also include organising emergency transport. In the event that people might be unable to return to their homes, it is the job of the district council to provide temporary accommodation. Up to the point when suitable links with other organisations are established, the county council is responsible for coordinating the response from the district; they then perform more of a supporting role. Both the district and county councils then work together towards resuming normal services.

Military aid

Military assistance is sometimes needed in large-scale emergencies. This is referred to as Military Assistance to Civil Authorities (MACA). This assistance can be requested from local authorities, for example in providing relief in flood situations. The police might also ask the military to assist in tasks relating to law and order or security.

Activity

Investigate the role played by the army in restoring transport links following the floods in Cockermouth in November 2009.

In all emergency situations that are classed as major incidents there must be an integrated response to ensure that the common objectives of all agencies are met to the highest level possible. These objectives fall under the following general headings:

- Save lives – this will involve rescues, evacuation and providing safety advice.
- Prevention – avoid escalation, e.g. by setting up cordons, controlling traffic and public.
- Protection – of environment, e.g. by limiting pollution from smoke, oil or chemical.
- Preservation – of scene, for investigation by police or fire service.
- Investigation – by police or fire service.
- Restoration – clean up; remove debris; reconstruction of buildings.
- Debriefing – to learn from response, to plan for future.

Think about it!

If a member of your family was involved in a major incident you would probably want to receive information as soon as possible. The British Red Cross has established a number of help lines following UK major incidents. Visit their website to find out more about what other support they can offer: www.redcross.org.uk

A framework for emergency response and planning for major incidents is enshrined in a relatively recent piece of legislation, the Civil Contingencies Act 2004. This Act covers the requirements for the ways in which agencies respond at local and at national level. The legislation that was in force before this Act was unable to cope with the outbreak of foot and mouth disease in 2001 and the widespread flooding in 2000. In both these instances the response was uncoordinated and led to accusations that the agencies involved did not appear to have a laid-down role to carry out.

The first part of the Act sets out who needs to be involved in responding to major incidents, and these agencies are placed into two groups. Category 1 responders include the police, fire, ambulance, local authorities and health protection agency. Organisations not directly involved in planning, but which nevertheless play an essential role in responding to incidents, are known as category 2 responders, and will include providers of telephones, gas, water and electricity, health and safety organisations and transport operators.

All those organisations in category 1 must meet together at least twice a year to review their emergency plans, and it is recommended that those in category 2 should co-operate and share information that would result in an effective plan being in place.

The Act requires a risk assessment to be undertaken, which is then recorded and forms the basis of the emergency planning process. The purpose of this risk assessment is to ensure that the plans which are developed are proportionate to the risk from the major incident.

Many organisations are involved in emergency planning, including local authorities, the National Health Service, church groups, Coroner, Salvation Army and many others. There are also different types of emergency planning guides that are employed by all these agencies; the type of plan will depend upon the level of the perceived emergency.

Chains of command

Although all agencies are required to work together towards a successful outcome, in any major incident situation there must be an understanding by all those involved of the way in which authority is undertaken. Within all the public services there is a 'chain of command' that operates at three levels.

The first of these links in the chain is known as 'bronze' or operational command. At this level the central function is to deal with immediate events, at the scene. This might include rescue of trapped people, fighting fire and administering first aid. It is essential that an inner cordon is in place around the incident to prevent contamination of the scene. The operational staff involved at this level will include the emergency services, local authority and any other agency deemed necessary.

Grading Tip!

To achieve P4 you will need to identify which agencies were involved in each of the major incidents you have investigated and described in P2.

For P5 you will describe the type of work that UK agencies (statutory and other) undertake in a major incident; this will include their legal duties. Returning to your chosen incidents you will need to explain how these agencies worked together in the aftermath of one of the UK incidents.

To achieve D1 you will need to analyse the importance of emergency planning by all agencies.

The tactical command (also known as 'silver') comprises one member from each of the emergency services. These take charge of the situation and each will generate tactics for his or her staff to follow. At this level the staff are not directly involved at the scene of the incident.

If the incident is very severe and cannot be dealt with by the silver command alone, a higher level – strategic or 'gold' command will be utilised. This level involves senior officers from the emergency services and other agencies. The gold command is likely to be housed within a police station or council building.

Most often the police will be in charge of coordinating major incident response, however, there will be times when specialist knowledge is required and another service will take the lead.

15.3 Participate in a tabletop scenario

P6 P7 M4 M5 D2

As outlined in the previous section, the Civil Contingencies Act places a duty on all agencies to prepare for major incidents and have in place a plan to deal with such an event. There are many ways in which the agencies carry out their planning, including staging a 'mock incident' where it might be necessary to close roads or train stations. Alternatively, the planning might take place indoors; regardless of the nature of this exercise, it is usually referred to as a tabletop exercise. The purpose of regular planning sessions is to allow those involved to work through proposed responses to a given situation.

The tabletop exercise will require a realistic scenario, which will take the form of an outline of a major incident, and everyone involved will be given a specific role. They will be encouraged to act out their roles and endeavour to plan their response to the incident provided in the scenario.

Any individual agency may carry out its own scenario. This will assist that agency in perfecting its role in a given situation, but the scenarios with the highest chance of creating an effective outcome will involve personnel from many agencies. These situations better reflect real-life conditions, where a coordinated response is required.

Many different situations might be considered for tabletop scenarios, including flood, chemical incident, pandemic, aeroplane crash, pollution and many more. When you carry out your own scenario it is essential that you are able to become involved, and gain a good understanding of how agencies work together.

An important consideration in any major incident is the resources needed to resolve it. These will include emergency lighting if the incident occurs when it is dark, or extends over a period when it is dark. If a building has partially collapsed, there will be a need for props, or a bulldozer to complete the demolition. All major incidents will also require technological resources, such as telephones and computers and, of course, human resources too.

Following the involvement of the emergency services at a major incident, other organisations might still be involved. The Health and Safety Executive might carry out an inquiry into the cause of the incident. In the case of air incidents, the Aviation Authority will be looking for answers, and the Environment Agency will be responsible for examining the after-effects of pollution.

The ultimate task of those agencies involved in planning is to evaluate, debrief and review the response to the given situation. In this way they will be able to identify the strengths of those involved, and make arrangements for improvements to performance to be implemented.

 Grading Tip!

To achieve P6 you will need to explain the main considerations that organisations involved in planning need to consider when they are preparing for major incidents.

You will be awarded P7 if you take an active part in a tabletop scenario. This might be planned by your tutor or you might be given the opportunity to prepare your own.

For M4 you will need to assess the role undertaken by each of the identified organisations.

To achieve M5 you will provide an analysis of the tabletop scenario.

Remember, it might not have worked out as you had hoped – just ensure that the analysis reflects the experience, and remember to identify anything that you would change on a future occasion.

Finally, to be awarded D2 you will need to evaluate the process. This will include an in-depth examination of what went right (and not-so-right) and suggestions of how you might respond differently in another situation.

End-of-unit knowledge check

1. Define the term 'major incident'.
2. Explain why an investigation might be necessary following a major incident.
3. Identify at least six of the agencies involved in responding to a specified major incident.
4. Identify the common objective of all agencies involved in an integrated response to a major incident.
5. Why is it important that 'tabletop scenarios' in relation to major incidents are undertaken by all relevant agencies?

Grading criteria

In order to pass this unit, the evidence you present for assessment needs to demonstrate that you can meet all the learning outcomes for the unit. The criteria for a pass grade describe the level of achievement required to pass this unit.

To achieve a pass grade the evidence must show that you are able to:	To achieve a merit grade the evidence must show that, in addition to the pass criteria, you are able to:	To achieve a distinction grade the evidence must show that, in addition to the pass and merit criteria, you are able to:
P1 Define the term major incident		
P2 Describe different types of major incident and the cause of each	**M1** Investigate recent major incidents and identify their cause	
P3 Outline the effects of the major incidents on people, communities and the environment	**M2** Explain the short- and long-term effects of the major incidents on people, communities, environment and the wider impacts they may have had	
P4 Identify the agencies that were involved different major incidents	**M3** Explain how UK agencies involved in a specific major incident worked together in accordance with their legal duties	
P5 Describe the work of agencies at UK incidents and their legal duties		

To achieve a pass grade the evidence must show that you are able to:	To achieve a merit grade the evidence must show that, in addition to the pass criteria, you are able to:	To achieve a distinction grade the evidence must show that, in addition to the pass and merit criteria, you are able to:
P6 Explain the main considerations when planning and preparing for major incidents	**M3** Explain the role of the organisations involved in planning for major incidents	**D1** Analyse the importance of inter-agency emergency planning for major incidents
P7 Carry out a tabletop scenario of a major incident	**M4** Analyse the tabletop scenario	**D3** Evaluate the tabletop scenario

Unit 16
Career planning for the public services

Introduction

In spite of public spending cuts and some **privatisation** of services, public services will always be required, and the public service sector is the largest employer in this country.

Some jobs in the uniformed public services may be seen as glamorous, exciting jobs that appeal to many young people. The recruitment and selection processes are usually competitive and lengthy. It is important that applicants are fully prepared before applying for a job, to give them the best possible chance to succeed. If you are intending to apply for employment in this area, this unit will help you.

In this unit you will examine the entry requirements and different routes of entry for different careers, which may then give you several options to consider for your future, such as going on to higher education, or gaining relevant voluntary or paid work experience, before applying to enter your chosen service.

Figure 16.1 A prison officer

Public services employees may need to have particular skills and qualities, qualifications and training, which enable them to deal with the different situations they may encounter. Some public services require certain levels of fitness and stamina to carry out the physical work involved.

You will investigate these requirements and carry out a personal evaluation of your own skills and qualities. You can then produce a personal action plan to enable you to improve on any weak areas. Remember, the entry requirements given are the *minimum* that you should have. Having more than the minimum entry requirements will give your application a better chance of being successful.

You will also look at the different application processes. Completing this career planning unit should help to give you the best possible chance to get through the required processes when applying to the public services for employment.

Learning outcomes:

By the end of this unit, you should:

1. Know the application and selection process for public service employment.

2. Know the skills and qualities required for a job in the public services.

3. Be able to complete an application for a role in a chosen public service.

16.1 Application and selection processes for different careers in the public services

P1 P2 M1 D1

As competition for most jobs has risen, more emphasis has been placed on the application and recruitment processes. Many employers now demand that job applicants should attend multiple interviews and that they should also, in many cases, complete various tests and possibly also give a presentation to the interviewing panel.

Wherever possible, public service employers should seek to ensure that the workforce they are recruiting is as diverse as possible. This means that they should encourage applications from a wide range of people, including people with different ethnic backgrounds and people with disabilities (if this doesn't interfere with their ability to do the job), and ensuring that both men and women are recruited in equal numbers, where possible.

We will now look at the different entry requirements for several public services.

Entry requirements

Army

You can enter the army as a regular soldier, as an officer or as a member of the volunteer Territorial Army. You have different entry options:

- Further education in the army – three army colleges provide further education opportunities for teenagers considering a military career, and joining one means you commit to the army for a certain period of time.
- Army Technical Foundation College – this college, in Winchester, runs a 24-week course teaching core military and vocational skills for a variety of regiments and corps.
- The Army Foundation College – this college, in Harrogate, offers a 42-week school-leavers' course for both technical and non-technical recruits.
- Welbeck Defence Sixth Form College – this is the Ministry of Defence's residential sixth-form college offering a two-year A-Level education, after which students go on to university.

Officer entry requirements

The Royal Military Academy Sandhurst in Surrey is where all officers in the British Army are trained to take on the responsibilities of leading soldiers.

More than 80% of Officer Cadets are university graduates, but some arrive with A-levels or equivalent. Others are serving soldiers who have been selected for officer training, and some come from overseas, having been chosen by their own armies to train at this world-famous academy.

Ask Yourself!

How can public service employers ensure that they recruit a diverse workforce?

Assignment tip

Remember not to cut and paste or copy work from other sources into your assignments. This is known as plagiarism – which is stealing someone else's words or ideas! Read the text, then write about the subject in your own words.

Regular soldier entry requirements

Age	16–33
Qualifications	No formal qualifications are required, but a good standard of literacy and numeracy is required.
Health	Successful completion of a GP questionnaire and a full army medical check-up.
Nationality	Must be a British citizen, citizen of a Commonwealth country or have British Overseas Territories Citizenship.
Criminal record	You *must* declare all criminal convictions – having a criminal record will not necessarily prevent you from joining the army.

Officer entry requirements

Age	17–28
Qualifications	A minimum of 35 ALIS points for the best subjects at GCSE or equivalent. A minimum of 35 ALIS points for the best 7 subjects at GCSE or equivalent, which must include English Language, Mathematics and either a science subject or a foreign language at grade C or better. Plus 180 UCAS tariff points acquired in separate subjects at AS and A-Level equivalent, to include a minimum of two passes at A-Level at grades A–E or equivalent. (ALIS is the A-Level Information Service database. It contains hundreds of thousands of AS/A Level results and provides information about how students' average GCSE scores relate to the grades they are likely to get at AS or A-Level in particular subjects.) (The UCAS Points System is a means of differentiating students based on grades from various post-GCSE qualifications. It is used as a means of giving students places at UK universities.)
Medical and physical	Successful completion of a GP questionnaire and a full army medical check-up.

Figure 16.2 A Corporal of the Royal Military Police

The Police Service

There are 43 different police forces in this country but they generally all have very similar selection and recruitment processes. Every police force handles its own recruitment, but there are national entrance tests. In England and Wales this is the 'Police Initial Recruitment Test' or 'PIRT'.

A police career is a well-paid, varied career, which is why the police recruitment process is thorough. You will be up against strong competition when you come to apply.

Police entry requirements

Age	You can apply at 18 years but cannot be appointed until you are 18½.
Height	There is no minimum or maximum height requirement.
Fitness	You will be required to undergo a fitness test. Expect to be tested on two key fitness requirements: • Dynamic strength – involves performing five seated chest pushes and five seated back pulls on the dyno machine to measure your strength. • Endurance – you will be asked to run to and fro along a 15-metre track in time with a series of bleeps, which become increasingly fast.
Qualifications	The police service does not require any formal qualifications, but a good standard of literacy and numeracy will be required.
Health	You will undergo a physical examination, so you should be in a good state of health. Applicants may be rejected if they are obese, diabetic, asthmatic, or have mental health problems
Tattoos	You should not have tattoos which could cause offence. Tattoos are not acceptable if they are particularly prominent, garish, offensive or undermine the dignity and authority of your role.
Eyesight	A good level of vision is required – glasses or lenses may be worn.
Financial status	Applicants will have their financial status checked. These checks are carried out because police officers have access to privileged information, which may make them vulnerable to corruption.
Nationality	You must be a British citizen, a member of the Commonwealth or EU.
Criminal convictions	A number of crimes will mean a definite or likely rejection of your application. Anyone who has received a formal caution in the last five years, committed a violent crime or public order offence can expect to be rejected.

Proper preparation will give you the best chance of securing a police career. This section explains the process, including information on the Police Initial Recruitment Test (PIRT).

Spending some time thinking about it now will play a key part in making your police application successful. Once you are accepted into a police force and have completed your training period, you will then have a wide range of different jobs to choose from.

It is understood that a Graduate Entry Scheme to the Police Service is to be reinstated at some point in the near future.

UK firefighter

Figure 16.3 A firefighter

Each fire service handles its own recruitment, but they all follow National Fire Service recruitment procedures. You should contact the personnel or recruitment department of the Fire and Rescue Service to which you intend to apply, or search online for their website.

If you wish to join the Fire and Rescue Service as a firefighter, you will need to complete and pass the following stages shown below, all of which are explained in more detail throughout the recruitment section.

Firefighter entry requirements

Age	You must be at least 18 years old.
Qualifications	Formal qualifications are not necessary, but a good standard of literacy and numeracy are required. Personal qualities and physical attributes are more important than academic qualifications. The Fire Service will look for the following qualities in applicants: • willingness to adapt to shift work • the ability to operate effectively in a close team • initiative • flexibility • honesty • the ability to take orders • good communication skills to deal with people who are injured, in shock or under stress • sound judgement, courage, decisiveness, quick reactions and the ability to stay calm in difficult circumstances • an interest in promoting community safety, education and risk prevention.
Height	There is no minimum or maximum height requirement.
Fitness	You will be expected to pass the following tests: • enclosed space to check for claustrophobia • ladder climb • casualty evacuation • ladder lift • equipment assembly • equipment carry.
Psychological tests	Working with numbers. Understanding information. Situation awareness and problem-solving.
Health	You will undergo a physical examination, so you should be in a good state of health. You will be asked to complete a questionnaire covering your medical history and will then have to take a series of tests.
Eyesight	A good level of vision is required and you will be tested for this.
Hearing	A good level of hearing is required and you will be tested for this.
Criminal record	You *must* declare all criminal convictions – having a criminal record will not necessarily prevent you from becoming a firefighter.

Activity

Find out exactly what the fitness tests and the psychological tests for the Fire Service involve.

Social services

Social worker entry requirements

Qualifications	Undergraduate entry via UCAS (Universities and Colleges Admissions Service). Most universities ask for 2 A-Levels or equivalent qualifications, and experience of working with people as a volunteer or employee in social care. All students must have at least the equivalent of Key Skills Level 2 in English and Maths and be able to communicate clearly in spoken and written English.
Criminal record	You must disclose any previous criminal convictions, but this would not necessarily prevent you from becoming a social worker

Education

Teacher entry requirements

Qualifications	Undergraduate entry via UCAS. 4 GCSEs including Maths and English. Bachelor of Education degree or BA plus one year Post Graduate Certificate in Education (PGCE).
Criminal record	A CRB (Criminal Records Bureau) check will be required.

Figure 16.4 A primary school teacher

Grading Tip!

To meet the P1 grade you should describe the entry requirements for two different public service careers. One of these careers should preferably be one that you are interested in, whereas the other could be a service that you have not thought about previously.

The application process

Most jobs need to be applied for. All public service jobs have strict application processes which must be followed correctly. Practically all public service jobs ask for an application form to be completed, some of which are lengthier than others. All job application forms must be completed accurately and neatly. This is your one chance to get through to the next stage – don't blow it! Many public services use a 'paper sift', which means that any form which is not completed correctly gets thrown straight into the bin.

Application forms are designed to screen you out rather than to get you in. Because of this you need to put a lot of thought and effort into answering each question, to be competitive in your application. Remember, this is the only chance you have of getting to the next stage, so take your time and do the best you can. The tips given here will make it easier.

Some services, such as the police, will ask you to talk about your own experiences in dealing with certain situations. You should think very carefully how to answer such questions. You may feel you have not experienced the situation you are being asked to describe, but you should try to relate this back to any situation, either at home, in college, school or at work, or when socialising.

You may also be asked to describe how and when you have demonstrated good communication skills or good team skills. Always be prepared and have some suitable answers ready for such questions.

Activity

Answer the following question, which is an example of something you may be asked on a police application form:

Explain a situation when you have demonstrated good communication skills.

Personal statements

You will often be asked to provide a personal statement or other supporting information as

Tips for completing your application form

- Make photocopies of the application form to practise on. Keep the original form for your final draft.
- Read through the form carefully, making sure you understand all the instructions and questions.
- Draft your answers in rough first. Think carefully about how you are going to convey your skills and abilities through the questions asked and bear in mind the research you have done on the organisation.
- Write using capital letters only if required. The form will include instructions on how to fill in the form: block capitals, handwriting, ink colour, etc. People often write or type without using capital letters in the correct places.
- Do not leave any blank spaces – many services will fail you for forgetting to put a postcode in the right box if they have asked you to supply it.
- Check spelling and punctuation and get a friend or colleague to double-check it for you.
- Once you have done all the checks, you can complete the original form neatly in the required ink colour. The importance of correct ink colour cannot be stressed enough. Many applications are sifted out at a glance if completed in blue ink when black was specified.

part of your application. This is an extremely important part of your application and is your opportunity to make sure your application is better than the many others that will be submitted. You should give details of any past experience that is relevant to the job you are applying for.

Curriculum vitae

At some point you will probably be asked to provide a **curriculum vitae** (or CV), where you give specific details about yourself. A CV may be the one chance you are given to sell yourself to a future employer. If your CV does not meet the required standard, you will not be given a chance to attend for an interview.

There are many ways to compose and structure a CV and there is no single correct way. You will find many different examples of these online, but the following tips may be helpful.

> ### Key term
>
> Curriculum vitae – life story

Personal details

Normally these would include your name, address, date of birth (although, with age discrimination laws now in force, this isn't essential), telephone number and email.

Education and qualifications

Your degree subject and university, plus A-Levels and GCSEs or equivalents. Mention grades unless they are poor!

Work experience

- Use action words such as developed, planned and organised.
- Even work in a shop, bar or restaurant will involve working in a team, providing a quality service to customers, and dealing tactfully with complaints. Don't mention the routine, non-people tasks (cleaning the tables) unless you are applying for a casual summer job in a restaurant or similar.
- Try to relate the skills to the job. A finance job will involve numeracy, analytical and problem-solving skills, so focus on these. However, for a marketing role you would place a bit more emphasis on persuading and negotiating skills.

Interests and achievements

- Keep this section short and to the point. As you grow older, your employment record will take precedence and interests will typically diminish greatly in length and importance.
- Bullets can be used to separate interests into different types: sporting, creative etc.
- Don't use the old boring clichés here: 'socialising with friends'.
- Don't put many passive, solitary hobbies (reading, watching TV, stamp collecting) or you may be perceived as lacking people skills.
- Show a range of interests to avoid coming across as narrow: if everything centres around sport they may wonder if you could hold a conversation with a client who wasn't interested in sport.
- Hobbies that are a little out of the ordinary can help you to stand out from the crowd: skydiving or mountaineering can show a sense of wanting to stretch yourself and an ability to rely on yourself in demanding situations.
- Any interests relevant to the job are worth mentioning: current affairs if you wish to be a journalist; a fantasy share portfolio such as Bullbearings if you want to work in finance.

- Any evidence of leadership is important to mention: captain or coach of a sports team, Course Representative, Chair of a student society, scout leader.
- Anything showing evidence of **employability skills** such as teamworking, organising, planning, persuading, negotiating etc.

Key term

Employability skills – skills that future employers will find valuable

Skills

- The usual ones to mention are languages (good conversational French, basic Spanish), computing (e.g. 'good working knowledge of MS Access and Excel, plus basic web page design skills') and driving ('full, current, clean driving licence').
- If you are a mature candidate or have lots of relevant skills to offer, a skills-based CV may work for you.

Referees

Normally two **referees** are sufficient: one academic (perhaps your tutor or a project supervisor) and one from an employer (perhaps your last part-time or summer job).

Source: www.kent.ac.uk/careers/cv.htm

Key term

Referee – someone who is asked to provide a reference and comment on the character or qualifications of another person who is applying for a job

A CV should be produced accurately and neatly and saved to disk so that it can be updated regularly.

Tip: Use a sensible email address on your CV.
Here are some, slightly changed, inappropriate student email addresses:
demented_bovine@...
so_kiss_me@...
platypus_mcdandruff...
busty-beth@...
flockynockyhillipilification@...
virgin_on_the_ridiculous@...
original_madcow_jane@...
circle-of-despair@...
deathwish@...
sexylikewoaaaah@...

Activity

Produce a draft CV using the guidelines above.

The selection process
Local authority jobs

Step 1 Application

Vacancies for **local authority** positions such as teachers, social workers, planning officers, administration workers, librarians etc. can usually all be found on the websites of local councils. The websites will give the general details of the advertised vacancies and will also normally include an online application form, or details of how to request an application form. The websites should provide the job description and details of all the required skills and qualities for the

Key term

Local authority – local council

job. You will be given a closing date for the receipt of completed application forms.

Step 2 Interview

If your application form meets the required standard, you may be invited to attend an interview. This will usually take place before a panel. You may be asked to carry out a presentation or some other activity, such as a psychometric test or a simulation activity, which you will be given details of before the interview date. If you get through this stage you may be asked to attend a second interview.

Step 3 Job offer

After the interview process you will be notified, either by telephone or by letter, whether you are being offered the job or not. You will then need to decide whether to accept the job offer. It is wise to wait for written confirmation of any job offer before resigning from any previous job.

Police Service

Step 1

Check that you meet the basic entry requirements for entry to the UK Police Service.

Go online and find out which forces in the area that you would like to work in are recruiting. You should then request an application pack, either by telephone, by post or online.

Step 2

On receiving your application form, the force that you have applied to will check that you are eligible and they will mark your answers to the questions. Your application form *must* be completed very neatly and accurately. Sixty per cent of candidates do not complete the form correctly and so are rejected at this stage. If your application is

successful, you will be invited to attend an assessment centre.

Step 3 The assessment centre

Two weeks before attending the assessment centre you will be sent material for it. At the centre you will be tested on your written English skills, verbal reasoning, oral skills and your mathematical skills. This test is called the 'Police Initial Recruitment Test' (PIRT).

There will also be an interview, role-plays and written tests. During the interview you will be asked questions about five 'competencies'. These competencies are:

- community and customer focus
- resilience
- teamworking
- respect for race and diversity
- oral communication.

Step 4 Health and fitness

You will need to pass the police fitness test, plus an eyesight test and a thorough medical. (Refer to the PoliceCouldYou website for full details of these.)

Step 5 Security checks

Before you can be accepted as a police officer you will be required to undergo rigorous security checks and background checks.

The above process can take several months (could be up to 18 months) from start to finish. It is recommended that you seek alternative employment while waiting for your application to progress. This will enable you to gain some valuable life skills, which the Police Service look for in applicants.

You should refer to the PoliceCouldYou website (www.policecouldyou.co.uk) where you will find lots of helpful tips and information about all of the recruitment tests and processes.

Example of a verbal reasoning test

Scenario
Some time on the night of October 1st, the Copacabana Club was burnt to the ground. The police are treating the fire as suspicious. The only facts known at this stage are:
- The club was insured for more than its real value.
- The club belonged to John Hodges.
- Les Braithwaite was known to dislike John Hodges.
- Between October 1st and October 2nd, Les Braithwaite was away from home on a business trip.

There were no fatalities.
A plan of the club was found in Les Braithwaite's flat.

1 A member of John Hodges' family died in the blaze.
True
False
Impossible to say

2 If the insurance company pays out in full, John Hodges stands to profit from the fire.
True
False
Impossible to say

3 The flat where the plan was found is close to the club.
True
False
Impossible to say

4 John Hodges could have been at the club when the fire took place.
True
False
Impossible to say

5 There are definite grounds to arrest John Hodges for arson.
True
False
Impossible to say

Example of a numeracy skills test

1 A purse was found containing one £5 note, four 20p coins and five 2p coins. How much did the purse contain altogether?
£5.10
£5.22
£5.82
£5.85
£5.90

2 A car park has space for 220 cars per floor. How many can fit on 3 floors?
440
460
640
660
680

3 A work shift begins at 14.15 and lasts for six hours. What time does it end?
20.15
16.15
20.45
22.30
19.45

4 If there is an average of 30 accidents per month, how many would you expect there to be in 12 months
420
380
360
300
120

5 What percentage of £40 is £8?
5%
20%
22%
25%
48%

Source: www.policecouldyou.co.uk © Crown copyright material is reproduced with the permission of the Controller of HMSO and the Queen's Printer for Scotland

Tests

Psychometric tests

Psychometric tests are structured tests, taken in exam-like conditions, which aim to measure a person's ability, or certain aspects of their personality.

Most psychometric tests are devised by occupational psychologists. Their aim is to provide employers with a reliable method of selecting the best applicants, and to design tests carefully so that they are fair to all applicants.

All psychometric tests, except for personality tests, are strictly timed.

Simulations

Simulation exercises are designed to imitate particular work-place tasks, behaviour or skills. The most common types of simulation exercises include:

- group exercises/case studies
- presentations
- fact-finding exercises
- role-plays
- in-tray priority exercises.

Competency assessment

The box on page 202 shows an example of a competency assessment question which a person who has applied to be a Police Community Support Officer may be asked, along with a suitable answer.

Interviews

Most people will need to go for a job interview at some point in their careers. There are several different types of interview.

- Informal interview – these are more relaxed than formal interviews and may consist of a chat with one or more people. You must not be too relaxed, however, as you are still 'on trial'.
- Formal interview – this is a more structured interview, usually taking place in front of a panel of people, who will ask you some 'set' questions. You may

also be asked to prepare and deliver a presentation to the panel.
- Full day interview – this can consist of several different parts. You may be asked to give a presentation to the panel, take part in one or more interviews and may be asked to meet and interact with other candidates or existing employees. For certain jobs, you may be asked to do a task. For example, if applying for a teaching job, applicants may be asked to deliver a short lesson while being observed. Basically, you will be constantly assessed throughout the day so may feel quite exhausted by the end of it.

So, you have passed the application stage and been invited to attend for an interview. This is now your chance to really sell yourself and prove that you are the right person for the post. It can't be stressed enough just how important it is to prepare for your interview. You will usually be competing with many other applicants and you need to make sure that you stand out – for the right reasons! There are many ways you can prepare for an interview that will help you to be successful.

Research

Make sure that you research the public service you are applying to. Try to find out about any new developments or how the service has changed in recent years. If you are applying to an armed service, read up about any current deployments that they are involved in. Carry out research to find any organisational reports and to learn about the structure of the organisation. Take a look at the website for the service – you will probably find samples of the questions you could be asked. Think how you will answer these.

Take part in any mock interviews which are arranged at your school or college to give you an idea of what to expect.

Plan

Make sure you know where and when the interview is to take place. If it is somewhere you have never visited before, carry out

Example of a competency assessment question and answer

Question: PCSOs need to be prepared to take responsibility for making difficult decisions. Think of a situation when you have had to make a difficult decision that might have upset other people and when you have had to then tell them what you have decided. What was the decision you had to make?

Answer: I had been invited to a close friend's wedding and asked to help with the arrangements. The wedding was arranged at quite short notice and the date conflicted with a holiday with my parents and sister. We had already booked the holiday and I had paid a large deposit on it. My friend made it clear how important it was to her for me to be at her wedding, and when I told my family they made it clear that they felt I should go on holiday with them as it had been booked for a long time and could not be rearranged at this late date. I had to decide whether to go on the holiday and upset my friend, or cancel my holiday, lose my deposit and upset my family.

Question: What did you take into account when making the decision?

Answer: I took into account the fact that she was a very old and close friend who, in the past, had gone out of her way to be with me at events which had been special for me (for example birthday parties and when I got my exam results). However, my family deserved and had been looking forward to the holiday with me and had chosen the hotel and the resort to suit me. I would also lose my deposit. I considered the option of joining my parents at the holiday location a few days later than anticipated, but this fell within a peak holiday season and when I checked with the travel agent there were no flights available.

Question: What decision did you make?

Answer: I decided to go to the wedding and cancel the holiday.

Question: Tell us exactly how you went about telling the other person or people.

Answer: I told my sister first, as soon as I had made the decision, as she was likely to know how my parents would react. I then waited until my parents were both at home and had eaten their evening meal and were more relaxed. I turned the TV down and said that Jayne (my friend) had been very good to me over the years and that I really wanted to be there for her wedding. I said that I had decided to go to the wedding and cancel my place on the holiday with them. I said that I knew they would be disappointed but that we would have future holidays together whereas Jayne would only have one wedding like this.

Source: www.policecouldyou. co.uk © Crown copyright material is reproduced with the permission of the Controller of HMSO and the Queen's Printer for Scotland

a 'practice' journey before the day of the interview, at a similar time so you know what to expect regarding volume of traffic, roadworks, bus and train times, parking and so on. Don't underestimate the time it will take you to reach the interview venue. Park up, or walk from the bus stop or train station, and find the actual room or building where the interview is taking place.

Plan your outfit and appearance for the interview. Public service interviews are always quite formal so a smart appearance is required. This is probably not the time to show what a trendy dresser you are! You should not dress for an interview in the same way as you would for a night out. Tone down any distinctive hair colours and remove any facial piercings. Make sure your clothes are clean, pressed and ready before the day.

On the day

The more you have prepared for the interview, the less nervous you are likely to be. Nerves are perfectly natural, however, and most interviewers will make allowance for this. Do not 'over-compensate' for nerves by appearing too confident or 'cocky'. Most public service interviewers are looking for someone who can work well within a team and not be too domineering.

Some public service interviews will involve interaction with the other candidates, when you could be observed. How you react in such a situation could indicate whether you are a good team player or have the necessary social skills required for a public service job.

Be aware of your body language during the interview. Sit up straight and maintain good eye contact with the panel. Try not to fidget! Listen carefully to the questions asked – if you don't understand the question, ask the interviewer to repeat it or clarify it. If it's something you think you may know the answer to but are not sure, then say what you know – it may be correct! If you really

don't know the answer, however, simply apologise and say so. Don't waffle on for ages about something you know absolutely nothing about!

Always tell the truth during an interview. Most public service interviewers will be well-experienced in judging whether a person is being honest or not. Also, checks will certainly be carried out where any 'untrue stories' will be discovered.

Figure 16.5 Confident body language is important during an interview

Interview questions

Certain questions can crop up regularly in interviews. The following is a selection of these:
- What is your greatest strength?
- What are your weaknesses?
- How do you handle pressure?
- Why are you applying for this role?
- What skills can you bring to this role?
- Do you prefer to work independently or within a team?

Activity

Write down your answers to the questions listed on page 203.

Case Study

Sarah has an interview for a job she has always wanted. She has checked the letter, which tells her the time and place of the interview. She knows where the building is and guesses that it will take her about half an hour to drive there.

On the day of the interview Sarah feels well prepared. She is dressed and ready and leaves home allowing herself 45 minutes for the journey. Unfortunately, she encounters road works en route, which puts an extra 10 minutes on the journey. On arrival near the interview venue, Sarah has problems finding somewhere to park. She finally finds a space in the car park but then realises she has no change for the ticket machine. She manages to obtain some, then starts to panic as she realises she is already in danger of being late. She starts to run towards the building, eventually finds the reception and asks the way to the interview room. She is directed to a room in another part of the building. When she finally arrives at the place of the interview she is late, breathless and feeling very hot and bedraggled! This is not how she wanted to appear!

1. List three things that Sarah could have done differently.
2. What impression of Sarah would the interviewer have in the above scenario?

Grading Tip!

To meet the P2 criteria you should choose a service and outline the different stages a candidate has to go through when applying to join the service, and give a short explanation of what each stage involves.

16.2 Skills required in the public services

Most public services, uniformed or non-uniformed, require a range of different skills and qualities.

Skills

Some of the skills are specifically required for certain jobs, but others are more 'generic' and are needed in most public service jobs. We will now take a look at some of these skills.

Teamwork

Teamwork plays a very large part in the public services. Being part of a team means looking out for others and sharing the workload. All public service jobs involve working in teams of one sort or another. The British Army has several different regiments, the Fire Service has different watches, while the Police Service has different teams such as CID, Traffic Section, Drugs Squads etc.

Leadership

Many public services employees are required to have leadership skills. Leaders need skills which allow them to direct others in a way they will respond to. This can mean being assertive without being domineering, being fair but firm, and being positive and enthusiastic even if others are not. Good leaders are able to motivate others and to know when to delegate or 'pass down' certain tasks or responsibilities.

Communication

Good communication skills are essential for public service employees. Speaking, listening, reading and writing are skills which they will use every day in their working life. Dealing with the public will be a main role, and the way in which public service members do this is extremely important. It does not matter if you are a police officer, a social worker or a local planning officer – the way you speak to members of the public can make a very real difference, and this requires skills which should be developed wherever possible. Non-verbal communication skills (or body language) are also very important. Potentially aggressive situations can often be defused if dealt with in a calm, controlled manner. It is therefore important that you are aware of your body language and the message it sends out.

Activity

Jot down as many examples that you can think of where different public service workers need to use good communication skills.

Time management

Punctuality is an absolute 'must have' in the public services! Public service workers must be able to manage their time effectively, whatever their role. This usually means being organised, looking ahead and 'planning' your time effectively. Using a diary or wall planner is a good way of doing this, and inputting all your assignment hand-in dates will help you to ensure that these are handed in on time.

Problem-solving

Public service workers often have to deal with a very wide range of problems and situations. Problem-solving is a skill which can be practised and developed in order to deal with such situations.

Qualities required

Qualities are slightly different from skills. Qualities are the things that make us the people we are, and are usually things we are born with. However, some qualities can be acquired as we mature and develop (e.g. punctuality, positive attitude to work, concern for others). Think about the following qualities and whether you have them:

- Honesty – it goes without saying that public services employees should be honest and law-abiding. The public needs to know that they can trust and respect members of the public services.
- Integrity – if a person has integrity it means that they have good morals, know what is right and wrong, and are of good character.
- Commitment, or dedication – this is required by all public service employees. Most public services jobs are not '9 to 5' jobs. Many employees work many more hours than they are supposed to in order to do the work that is required. They are generally willing to do this for the benefit of other people who are relying on them. Being committed usually means doing whatever needs to be done and not letting people down.
- Reliability – being reliable means doing what you have said you will do when people are depending on you, and this is an essential quality for public service employees.

Specific skills and qualities

The skills and qualities listed above are 'generic' skills, which means that they are general skills which would be needed for most public services. There are also other skills which would be needed for specific jobs. For example, anyone who is thinking of joining the army to train as a soldier would be seen as possessing bravery and courage; similarly, firefighters can sometimes find themselves in dangerous situations and most people would consider that entering a burning building to save someone requires a certain amount of courage.

Social workers, nurses and most other public service workers would need to be caring people, often trying to improve the lives of others.

 Grading Tip!

To achieve P3 you need to identify the different skills and qualities required by a public service worker and explain a little about them.

16.3 Completing an application for a role in a chosen public service

P4 **M1** **D1**

You have already learnt a lot about applying for a job in the public services in the earlier sections of this chapter. In addition to what has already been discussed, there are a few other issues to consider.

Skills audit

It is most important to know what skills and qualities you already possess. Many of us are often unaware of these until we actually sit down and think about them. It can be quite difficult to look at yourself and see how you measure up.

When you are asked to rate yourself in a particular skill, think carefully and answer the question truthfully. Think about your strengths and weaknesses and how you may compare yourself with others. For instance, you may have noticed that you are more likely to speak up in class than others, which indicates that you have good communication skills. Do you listen to others when they tell you about their own problems? Are you good at finding solutions to problems? When asked about your time management, consider whether you arrive at school, college or work on time, or are you frequently late? Are you good at handing in assignments by the deadline date?

Activity

Complete the table on page 207 and rate yourself accordingly:

1. I have no experience of using this skill.

2. I have some experience but feel I need to improve further.

3. I have experience of using this skill but still need to improve in certain aspects.

4. I am an expert and feel that this is not a priority for my development.

	1	2	3	4
Teamwork				
Leadership				
Time management				
Problem-solving				
Communication – reading				
Communication – speaking				
Communication – writing				
Communication – listening				
Communication – body language				

Action planning

Once you have carried out your skills audit you will then need to think about how to improve the skills that you have identified as needing to be developed. To meet the P6 criteria you should draw up an action plan to outline how you and when you are going to develop your skills.

Action planning model

There are many different models of action planning, but following the points in the bullet list below is good starting point. Action planning needs to be flexible – you may change your goals as you progress, and you must be prepared to revise your plan as circumstances dictate. The stages are as follows:

- *Where am I now?* This is where you review your achievements and progress, and undertake self-assessment.
- *Where do I want to be?* This is where you decide your goals.
- *How do I get there?* This is where you define the strategy you will use to achieve your goals and break down your goal into the smaller steps you will need to take to achieve your target. (See SMART targets below.)
- *Taking action.* This is the nitty gritty, where you implement your plan!

Make sure that your action plan is SMART!

An action plan should be:

- **S**pecific – stating clear objectives will help you to be clear about what action to take.
- **M**easurable – being able to measure your progress will help you to set further objectives.
- **A**chievable – setting small, achievable tasks will encourage you to make progress towards your long-term goals.
- **R**ealistic – be realistic about what you can achieve. Do not set yourself goals which you can never achieve.
- **T**imed – set yourself realistic deadlines for completing your objectives.

You may already be demonstrating some of the skills listed above, even if you're not aware of it! Think about the classes you take part in at college, e.g. Team Building, Team Development, Outdoor Activities. What skills are you using? Think about the jobs that you may do in your part-time work, or even when you're at home. Do you look after younger brothers and sisters? What skills or qualities are needed to do this?

In order to achieve the P4 grade you need to carry out an audit of your own skills which would be required for a job in your chosen public service. Think about the tasks you have carried out in any paid work or any work experience you have undertaken. Have you worked as a member of a team? Think about the activities you have carried out in your Team Development and Team Leadership units. You could have evidence of how these skills have been demonstrated. This will mean keeping a record which could be in the form of a logbook or a diary, with signatures from others who have witnessed the evidence. The evidence could also include photographs or video recordings.

You have now completed this chapter. By putting the above theory into practice you should give yourself the best chance possible when you come to apply for a job in your chosen public service.

Grading Tip!

For P5 you should complete an application for a role in a specific public service.

In order to achieve M1 you should provide some analysis of how your identified skills compare with those required for a public service job.

For D1 you need to evaluate how your skills compare with those required for a public service job.

End-of-unit knowledge check

1. What do the initials CV stand for?
2. Name two different types of interview.
3. Identify three different skills required by public service workers.
4. Name three different types of communication skills.
5. Think of three SMART targets which would help you to complete your qualification.

Grading criteria

In order to pass this unit, the evidence you present for assessment needs to demonstrate that you can meet all the learning outcomes for the unit. The criteria for a pass grade describe the level of achievement required to pass this unit.

To achieve a pass grade the evidence must show that you are able to:	To achieve a merit grade the evidence must show that, in addition to the pass criteria, you are able to:	To achieve a distinction grade the evidence must show that, in addition to the pass and merit criteria, you are able to:
P1 Describe the current entry requirements for two public service jobs [IE3]		
P2 Describe the application and selection process for two public service jobs [IE3]		
P3 Identify the different skills required in a given public service role [IE3]	**M1** Analyse your skills against a given public service role	**D1** Evaluate your skills against a given public service role
P4 Carry out a skills audit for a given public service role		
P5 Complete an application for a role in a specific public service		

Unit 22
Aspects of the legal system and law-making process

Introduction

The United Kingdom does not have a single legal system in force; when the Treaty of Union (in 1707) led to the creation of the United Kingdom, Scotland was allowed to keep its law-making system separate from the other UK countries. Today there are three systems in operation: Scotland, Northern Ireland, and England and Wales.

English law (which applies in England and Wales) and Northern Ireland law have their basis in the principles of Common Law; that means it is developed by judges in court, examining the facts that are put before them. More detail on these aspects will be covered later in the chapter.

Jurisdiction, which means *to speak the law*, refers to the power of a court over a person or a claim. This system shares out cases to relevant courts, in both the civil and criminal system. Jurisdiction has its origins in common law.

By studying this unit you will gain an understanding of the courts that operate in the United Kingdom, especially in England and Wales. You will study the civil and criminal process, and explore the personnel of the courts and also how cases are heard.

Learning outcomes:

By the end of this unit, you should:

1. Know the hierarchy of the courts system.

2. Know the role undertaken by the personnel of the courts.

3. Know how legal rules are created by precedent.

4. Understand how the criminal trial process works.

22.1 Know the hierarchy of the courts system

P1

To achieve P1 in this unit you need to understand the *hierarchy* of the courts; this means what they are called, their functions and how they fit into the whole justice system. There are two types of law that need to be investigated: civil law and criminal law.

Civil law

Civil law enables individuals or organisations to take action against another, in order to settle a dispute. This action usually results in a legally binding settlement that might include payment by the person found to be at fault, in the form of compensation, or a division of responsibilities or assets. The most common forms of civil law involve **slander**, **libel** and divorce. In civil law, cases must be proved by 'the balance of probabilities'. This means that the decision reached is what would be expected of any 'man in the street' if he was given the same facts.

Key terms

Libel – a published false statement damaging to a person's reputation
Slander – a malicious and false statement spoken about a person

The courts that deal with civil cases include Family Courts and County Courts. Although primarily concerned with criminal cases, Magistrates' courts also grant drinks licences and carry out some family work. Employment tribunals are not strictly part of the courts system but they hear civil law cases involving mistreatment of employees at work, including claims of discrimination and unfair dismissal.

Many of the smaller civil cases are dealt with in a County Court, through a process known as 'small claims'. The purpose of small claims courts is to deal with cases brought by individuals or organisations that usually involve money. This court can deal with claims for personal injury, as long as the amount of compensation sought is not more than £1,000. In all other small claims cases the sums of money involved must not be above £5,000.

The police have no involvement in civil cases; the individual or organisation on each side of the case is referred to as a 'party'. The party making the complaint is called the complainant, and the party against whom the complaint is being made is the defendant – this side is attempting to defend itself against the claim.

There is a lot of procedure involved in civil cases, with many forms to complete and documents to be provided before permission is given to attend court. The vast majority of cases are settled out of court; either the defendant agrees to pay compensation to the complainant, or the complainant ceases to pursue the claim. Those cases that do proceed to a final hearing are ruled over by a judge, who makes their decision based on the facts of the case.

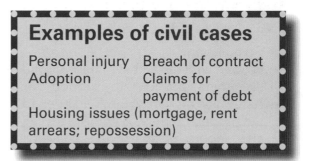

Examples of civil cases

Personal injury	Breach of contract
Adoption	Claims for payment of debt
Housing issues (mortgage, rent arrears; repossession)	

Criminal law

The main characteristics of criminal law are that the laws are passed by an Act of Parliament; all actions that contravene the criminal laws are crimes, regardless of how minor they might seem to some people. This includes some incidences of anti-social behaviour, although many people believe that those who are involved in it are just 'larking about'. When the term 'anti-social behaviour' was first introduced it was used to apply to such actions as dropping litter or making too much noise in the street. It now seems to include vandalism (criminal damage), burglary, threatening behaviour, serious bullying and other forms of criminal activity. All too often the consequences of this type of crime are devastating for those who are targeted.

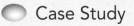 Case Study

David Askew – a human tragedy and national scandal

A 64-year-old man with a mental age of 10 was subjected to years of bullying and harassment by local youths until the moment he died of a heart attack. David Askew, 64, collapsed and died outside his house minutes after CCTV cameras recorded two teenagers approaching the house.

Greater Manchester police confirmed that an 18-year-old man had been arrested on suspicion of manslaughter; adding that the case had been referred to the Independent Police Complaints Commission.

Police insisted they had done everything possible to support Mr Askew and his family; they had been to the property ten times in the last year, after reports of anti-social behaviour. Neighbours claimed that too little had been done to resolve the situation that led to the death of Mr Askew.

Source: Mark Hughes, *Independent*, 12 March 2010 © The Independent 12/03/2010

Time will tell whether the youth identified in this case will be charged with a criminal offence, or if he will be given an 'anti-social behaviour order'.

Criminal courts

Magistrates' Court

The court that hears minor criminal cases is the Magistrates' Court. The personnel of this court include either a bench of lay magistrates (at least three) or a legally trained district judge, who sits alone. It is the magistrate or district judge who decides whether an accused person is guilty; there is no jury in a Magistrates' Court. As previously described, magistrates also deal with licensing applications.

Youth courts cater for offenders between the ages of 10 and 17, and proceedings are similar to those in a Magistrates' Court. Specially trained magistrates preside over a youth court and they have a broader range of sentences to use when dealing with those found guilty. This takes into account the age of the offender, and what punishment best fits the severity of the offence.

Crown Court

The Crown Court is part of the senior courts of England and Wales. Criminal trials that are heard in Crown Courts usually involve a judge and jury. There are approximately 90 Crown Courts in England and Wales, divided into seven regions, which are governed by Her Majesty's Courts Service. The Central Criminal Court at the Old Bailey in London is part of the Crown Court system; many of the most serious criminal cases are heard at this venue.

The roles undertaken by Crown Court are many: it hears appeals from decisions at the Magistrates' Court and it imposes sentences on defendants committed from Magistrates' Courts; it carries out trial by jury and it also sentences those convicted at Crown Court.

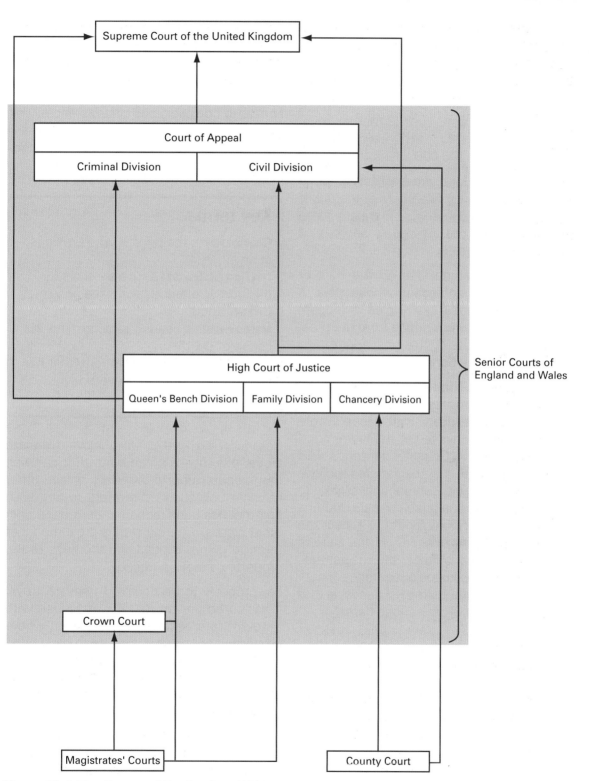

Figure 22.1 The Courts of England and Wales

Defendants attending Crown Court may be brought into custody or appear on bail. The average time before a case is heard at Crown Court is in excess of three months.

The Crown Court also deals with the most serious criminal cases such as murder, rape, robbery and burglary. Each year this Court deals with about 100,000 cases.

Trials at Crown Court are heard by a judge and a 12-person jury. Members of the public are selected for jury service. There are some people who are not allowed to serve on a jury in a criminal case.

It is the jury that decides on the guilt or innocence of a defendant whose plea is 'not guilty'; where a guilty plea is lodged, the judge hears the evidence from the prosecution and decides on the most appropriate sentence for the offender.

As well as trial of **indictable offences** and hearing appeals from the Magistrates' Court, the Crown Court deals with cases where the offender is convicted at the lower court and sent to Crown Court for sentence. This is often because the magistrates believe that the maximum sentence available to them – six months in prison or a £5,000 fine – is not sufficient punishment to reflect the seriousness of the offences. In the case of a violent or sexual offence, the magistrates might feel that a custodial sentence longer than their powers permit is necessary to protect the public from serious harm.

Coroner's Court

When someone dies unexpectedly, or in unusual circumstances, the death(s) will need to be investigated at an **inquest** to determine the cause. This takes place in a Coroner's Court, and will involve evidence being given by a number of people. The **coroner** will hear the evidence and might determine the cause of death independently or, in certain circumstances, it will fall to a coroner's jury to determine the cause of

death. A coroner in England or Wales must have been a solicitor, barrister or a doctor for at least five years. Additional instances that will require an inquest to be held include where a death occurs abroad, where there appear to be suspicious circumstances, or if the death occurred while the person was in the care of central authority (e.g. in a police cell).

Key terms

Coroner – the person who presides at an inquest

Indictable offences – trials for this sort of offence take place only in Crown Court

Inquest – a hearing to determine the cause of death

Treasure trove – property that had been hidden and is discovered when no heirs can be traced

Coroners also have jurisdiction over **treasure trove**; this means an amount of gold, silver, gemstones, money, jewellery or any other valuable collection. This refers to any such find that has been hidden underground or in other places, where it can be presumed that the true owner is dead and the heirs to the property cannot be traced.

For property to be declared treasure trove, it has to be proved that it was hidden with a view to later recovery by its owner; where property is found that appears to have been lost or thrown away – e.g. on the surface of the ground – it either belongs to the person who found it or the landowner on whose ground it was discovered.

Courts of Appeal

As the title suggests, Courts of Appeal hear petitions against a decision that was made at a lower court. The Court of Appeal has two divisions, the Civil Division and the Criminal

Division. The Civil Division hears appeals concerning civil law and family cases; it also hears appeals from tribunals and certain cases from the County Courts. The Criminal Division hears appeals from the Crown Court.

Anyone who has been convicted of a crime at Magistrates' Court may appeal to the Crown Court against the sentence imposed. If the person pleaded not guilty they may also appeal against the conviction. Notice of appeal must be lodged within 21 days of conviction. When an appeal has been lodged the offender might be allowed bail until the case is heard at the higher court. The appeal to Crown Court takes the form of a retrial, where all the evidence is heard for a second time. Any new evidence may also be heard, but the Crown Court may not make any changes to the evidence upon which the conviction and/or sentence was taken.

The purpose of this appeal is to decide whether the decision taken at Magistrates' Court was correct. The options available to Crown Court are to uphold the decision, to reverse it or to vary the decision. Appeals are usually heard by a Crown Court judge and two lay justices, who must not have been involved in the original trial. Decisions on law will be made by the judge, but the justices may be involved in deciding the facts. The judge will provide reasons for the decision and publish the judgment on whether the appeal is allowed or refused.

The highest court of appeal in the UK is the Supreme Court. This court came into being in October 2009, replacing the House of Lords, and is separate from both Government and Parliament.

The Supreme Court hears appeals involving points of law in civil cases for the whole of the UK, and for criminal cases in England, Wales and Northern Ireland only. The High Court of Judiciary remains the highest criminal court in Scotland. The Supreme Court also decides on matters concerning devolution, and will decide whether the legislative powers in Scotland, Wales and Northern Ireland have acted within their duty.

22.2 Court personnel

P2 M1 D1

Almost 250,000 people are employed within the courts system of England and Wales; this includes professional and non-legal personnel. The type of people involved with proceedings differs between the various courts; the section that follows outlines some of the responsibilities of these people.

Barristers

Barristers are professional lawyers who deal with criminal law, and who work mainly in the Crown Court and other higher courts. They will be appointed either to prosecute or defend the accused person. As well as requiring knowledge of criminal law, they also need to possess the skills necessary to persuade a jury, by their submissions, of the guilt or innocence of the defendant. There is a lot of training involved before a barrister is able to practise in court.

Solicitors

Solicitors are also qualified lawyers. In a Magistrates' Court it is far more usual for a solicitor to take on the role carried out by a barrister at the higher courts. Solicitors can deal with all aspects of the criminal process and they might also represent the prosecution or defence in the case in the same way as barristers do in the higher courts. Those solicitors involved in prosecuting a case work for the Crown Prosecution Service (CPS). They prepare the prosecution case, using the evidence gathered by the police. Solicitors also undertake a great number of the legal duties of the barrister in the Crown Court, providing the information that the barristers require to adequately present the case.

For every barrister in the UK there are approximately ten solicitors. The majority of solicitors work in the civil division, and their work will include small claims, conveyance and divorce proceedings.

Legal executives and paralegals

Solicitors are supported in their work by legal executives or support workers. There are more than 230,000 legal executives in the UK; they are non-graduate lawyers, who undertake a wide variety of legal work. The legal executives liaise with the public, whether in small claims cases, debt collection or other legal maters. On some occasions, when the facts are straightforward, legal executives will appear at a Magistrates' Court in place of a solicitor. Other personnel who carry out the same role as a legal executive are paralegals. A paralegal does not need to have the same training as a legal executive, but it is usually essential that their knowledge of the law is sufficient for them to be able to undertake this work in a competent manner.

The judiciary

In addition to those roles already identified, the criminal process would not be complete without the personnel who preside over the events that are brought before the courts. These individuals are referred to as the judiciary, and their role is to make decisions, based upon the facts put before the courts.

The main players in the judiciary are the judges and magistrates, whose role is to interpret the law in relation to the cases they hear. In certain cases these will be assisted by a jury. This is a group of people selected to listen to the evidence put forward in a Crown Court case and decide upon the guilt or otherwise of the accused person(s). In addition to hearing the evidence submitted, the jury will be supported by the judge's 'summing-up' of a case.

Circuit judges

Circuit judges wear bands over a violet robe and a short wig.

When hearing criminal cases, a red tippet (sash) is worn over the left shoulder.

When dealing with civil business, circuit judges dress as in criminal cases, but with a lilac tippet and without a wig or bands, wing collar or collarette.

On some occasions – when dealing with certain types of High Court business, or when sitting at the Central Criminal Court (Old Bailey) in London – circuit judges wear a short wig and black silk gown over a court coat and/or waistcoat.

Those who wish to be considered for selection as a judge must have been practising as a solicitor or barrister for a minimum length of time. The application process is very strict, and will involve an extended application form, eligibility and character check (and that is just the first part!). In many ways this application is as extensive as the process involved in police recruitment.

In both civil and criminal cases, the role of the judge includes preparing and managing the case, hearing evidence, deciding on legal issues, directing the jury (in criminal cases), summing-up and sentencing (in the case of a guilty verdict).

Lay people

An essential aspect of the legal process in the UK is that involving lay people. These are people who have not received formal legal training to the same extent as qualified personnel.

A very important principle of law is that it acts in the name of the people, and that we are all 'equal before the law'. The law exists in the public interest and serves the public, it follows therefore that a vital aspect of this process is that the public should be involved in the law.

By tradition there are two types of magistrate: lay magistrates, who work on a voluntary, unpaid basis, and those who are paid for carrying out their role. The paid magistrates are also known as District Judges. In cases involving lay magistrates, there will usually be three magistrates on the bench, whereas a District Judge will often sit alone to hear a case.

Think about it!

Can you think of any reasons why three magistrates sit together to decide on guilt of an accused?

Lay magistrates are recruited from the general public; they must be between 18 and 65 years of age on appointment, and sit for a minimum of 35 half-days per year. Magistrates undergo some training before they hear a case, which includes understanding their role, observing court cases and visiting a prison, youth offender institution and facility within the probation service. They also receive updates on a regular basis. Those magistrates involved in the work of youth courts will receive additional training specific to that role.

Activity

Explore the stages involved in training to become:

- a paralegal
- a legal executive
- a magistrate
- a solicitor
- a barrister.

Crown Court trials and some civil cases require a jury to be selected to listen to the evidence and consider its verdict. In a Crown Court trial the jury comprises 12 citizens aged between 18 and 70, who are called to pass judgement on the accused person(s).

Prospective jurors are selected at random from the electoral role (so if an individual does not register with their local authority they will not be able to undertake this duty).

Unless there is a very good reason why they may be excused, anyone selected is required to undertake the role of juror when they have been identified. Jurors are sent a summons (a letter that sets out the time, date and place of the hearing); they are required to take an unbiased approach in the case they will hear. The role of the jury is to listen to the evidence presented and the judge's summing-up. Following the process that is conducted in the courtroom, the jury retires to consider its verdict. To do this, all 12 go into a private room to discuss whether they believe the case has been proved and whether the defendant is guilty or not guilty. A leader (spokesperson) is appointed, and this person delivers the jury's verdict to the judge.

Grading Tip!

To achieve P1 you will present an introduction to the courts, identify the role of each one and be able to demonstrate the way in which they are ordered.

For P2 you need to explain the diverse roles undertaken by both professional and lay personnel involved in the criminal justice system, particularly in relation to criminal courts.

M1 requires a *comparison* of the roles undertaken by paid and lay court personnel, their functions and the part they play in the court process.

To achieve D1 you will need to *critically analyse* the role of lay personnel in the court process in England and Wales. This will involve an objective review of the role of lay magistrates and juries and reaching a conclusion as to the benefits or limitations of the court process.

22.3 Legal rules and precedent

Legal rules

At the beginning of this chapter you read that some of our present-day laws have their origins in common law. Within the legal system there are also statutory rules. Unlike common law, which has existed without the need to be written down, statute law is devised by government and passes through all the processes necessary before receiving Royal Assent.

The majority of legal rules are statutory laws; these comprise Acts of Parliament and Statutory Instruments, often referred to as Regulations. Acts of Parliament cover the whole law and are sometimes general in their nature; Regulations are smaller and more specific. Often a Regulation will be introduced to support a particular part of an Act; an example of this is the Management of Health and Safety at Work Regulations (1999), which was introduced to support the need for risk assessment and other practices described in the Health and Safety at Work Act (1974).

In Unit 1 Government, policies and the public services, you were provided with a brief outline of how laws are made in the UK. These might be as the result of a Public or Private Members' Bill. A Public Bill is introduced by the government. The process of consultation about the Bill before it becomes an Act is often quite lengthy, and involves much discussion by Members of Parliament (MPs) and the Lords. More than 90 per cent of Bills that are passed by Parliament and become Acts are Public Bills. Because they are Public Bills, the government is able to put a lot of pressure on its MPs to support them and, as the government has more MPs than all the other parties, the Bills are very likely to become law.

Private Members' Bills are introduced by the MP themselves, and can be proposed by a member of any political party in the UK. The only exception to this rule (at the time of writing) is MPs belonging to the Sinn Fein party, who are not allowed to sit in the House of Commons because, although they are elected representatives within Parliament, they have refused to swear allegiance to the Queen.

Members can introduce a Private Bill in one of four ways:

- After a ballot of MPs, where sufficient support is achieved
- Through the '10-minute' rule
- By peers (members of the House of Lords)
- Through 'ordinary presentation'.

The rules surrounding Private Members' Bills are quite complex; the vast majority of these Bills do not make it onto the Statute Book. This is partly because not enough time is available to properly debate them, and there are many opportunities during the process to slow down the process or halt it altogether. Despite a Bill not progressing at the first attempt, if the idea is worthy of further consideration the government might adopt it and include it within a future Public Bill.

Activity

Carry out research into 'the 10 minute rule' and 'ordinary presentation'

Prepare a short report to explain to your classmates what you have discovered

Precedent

Precedent is derived from the Latin word meaning 'what comes before'; in the legal sense it refers to previous decisions made in court, of which the current judge needs to take notice. Judicial precedent is the way that decisions made in previous cases guide present-day judges. It could be thought of as a form of quality control, because it assists in keeping decisions fair and consistent across different courts and over a period of time.

Precedent originates from the ancient system of Common Law and continued to be the main form of reaching decisions until the end of the 17th century. The purpose of this was to ensure that a person convicted of a crime received a sentence that was relevant to the crime, regardless of where he/she lived and regardless of the judge in the case. Precedent is also referred to as case law, as it depends on studying the judgements laid down in old cases. Lawyers refer to these records when they attempt to persuade a jury or judge of the merit of accepting a particular view in a case.

In certain cases a judge may decide that it is not appropriate to follow a precedent. The most common reason cited for adopting this stance is that, in the view of the judge, although many similarities exist between the previous case law and the current case, there are also sufficient differences to allow a new approach to be taken.

g Grading Tip!

To achieve P3 you will need to describe how legal rules are created by precedent, and explain relevant terminology.

22.4 Criminal trial process in England and Wales

Criminal law covers the most serious crimes, including murder, robbery, violence and rape. These laws are enforced by the police and the courts, and anyone found guilty of breaking the law can be prosecuted in court. As outlined earlier in the chapter, sentences can range from fines to community sentences, or a custodial sentence might be imposed if it is deemed appropriate.

The body that decides whether a criminal charge (prosecution) is to be brought against an individual is the Crown Prosecution Service (CPS). As over 95 per cent of criminal cases are heard in the Magistrates' Court, this is where the majority of decisions are made; however, it is usually the high-profile cases that receive media attention. The prosecution and defence attempt to convince the magistrates (or district judge) that they are right and they try to prove to the court that the other side is wrong. In UK law an individual is presumed innocent until proven guilty, and it is the role of the prosecution to prove 'beyond reasonable doubt' that the defendant is indeed guilty of the offence with which he or she is charged.

In the Magistrates' Court the magistrate(s) will hear a 'summary of facts' and decide on the outcome; in the Crown Court this role is undertaken by the jury. In the Crown Court the case will be heard by a circuit judge, and very serious cases, such as rape and murder, may be heard by a High Court judge. Both magistrates and judges have the authority to deliver a custodial sentence, if they believe the crime is sufficiently serious to warrant such a sentence.

Although punishment is one of the main considerations when sentencing, the magistrate or judge will also be mindful of how a particular sentence might reduce the likelihood of the offender being involved in criminal activity in the future.

The seriousness of the alleged crime will normally determine the court where the trial will take place. For an adult (someone 17 years of age and over) **summary trial** takes place in a Magistrates' court; trial for indictable offences are heard in the Crown Court. The third category of crime is referred to as **either-way offences**.

> ## Key terms
>
> **Summary trial** – takes place only in a Magistrates' Court
>
> **Either-way offences** – can be dealt with in either the Magistrates' or Crown Court

Most criminal cases in England and Wales begin in one of the 400 Magistrates' Courts. Summary offences will be dealt with in this court, and triable either-way offences, for example theft or criminal damage involving low-level property, may be tried either summarily or by judge and jury in the Crown Court. If the magistrates consider that an either-way offence is too serious for them to deal with, they may decline jurisdiction and the defendant will be sent to the Crown Court for trial. In such cases the defendant also has the right to demand that he or she is tried in the Crown Court. Defendants under 18 years of age do not have this right; they must be tried in a Youth Court. The exception to this rule is where the alleged offence is very serious, for example, murder.

A Magistrates' Court hearing

Defendants brought before a Magistrates' Court are either brought in custody, on bail or by summons. A summons is an order directing a person to appear before a specific court, at a stated time on the date in the summons.

When a defendant pleads not guilty, the magistrate(s) will hear evidence from all involved in the case; this might include victims, police, others who have relevant information and the defendant themselves. All these people are referred to as witnesses.

The process begins with the prosecution calling its first witness, who is shown into the court and led to the witness box. Before the witness begins to give their evidence, they will be asked by the usher to swear to tell the truth. In the case of a witness who follows a religion, the oath is taken while holding the holy book of that religion, and the words printed on a card are read. Those who do not have a religious faith will be asked to 'affirm' – to promise to tell the truth. This process is known a being sworn in. From this moment they are 'on oath' and anything they say must be the truth – lying on oath is a very serious matter, and the witness can be in trouble if they do so.

Figure 22.2 A Magistrates' Court hearing

Once the first witness has been sworn in, the solicitor or barrister for the prosecution will ask some questions. The purpose of these questions is to elicit the same information from the witness as they gave previously, in their statement to the police. This is known as 'evidence-in-chief'.

When a witness has answered all the questions put to them, the lawyer from the defence may ask some questions. The purpose of this cross-examination is to put doubt in the mind of the magistrate or jurors of the validity of the evidence provided by the witness. The lawyer will often ask leading questions; witnesses should try their best not to change their story from the evidence they have already provided.

On some occasions there may be a re-examination of a witness. This is where the first lawyer will ask some more questions, to clarify anything that was said in cross-examination. They cannot introduce questions on a new matter at this point, as there is no opportunity for the opposing side to react. Occasionally the magistrate or judge may also ask a question of the witness.

When all the prosecution witnesses have given evidence the process is repeated with defence witnesses; this time the lawyers for the defence are involved in the examination-in-chief and any re-examination, while the role of the prosecution lawyers is confined to cross-examining the witness.

Tips for witnesses in court

- Listen carefully to all questions.
- Make sure you understand the question – if not, ask for it to be repeated.
- Answer only what is being asked for (do not stray away from the point).
- Speak slowly and clearly.
- Do *not* argue with the lawyer.

Crown Court

The more serious indictment. This is clearly the accus person. As in the CPS that instigate be tried at Crown Court. the evidence gathered by the police, the CPS will decide whether a *prima facie* case exists – in other words, whether there is a case to be answered. If the elements of this first stage are satisfied, the case will be dealt with by a magistrate, who will be provided with documentary evidence by the CPS. If the case proceeds it will be heard in the Crown Court. This trial will (with very few exceptions) be before a judge and jury.

The judge controls the trial by endeavouring to ensure transparency and fairness. The judge also considers legal issues that occur during the trial, and he or she instructs the jury about the exact view of the law relevant to the case. The jury decides on the facts they have heard; this means they decide on guilt or innocence based on whether the prosecution's or defence's story is more believable. They must also take any instructions from the judge into consideration when they make their decision. As stated earlier, in criminal cases, the standard of proof is heavy; guilt must be proven beyond reasonable doubt.

In both Magistrates' and Crown Court, if the defendant pleads guilty there is no need for witnesses to give evidence; the magistrate or judge will simply be provided with a summary of the case and decide upon a suitable sentence. This will take into account the seriousness of the crime and previous history of the offender.

Rights of the defendant

Legal assistance is available to people who face criminal charges. This includes advice and the right to be represented by a

or their representative. Everyone is
[entitl]ed to advice and assistance if they are
[qu]estioned by police, even if they have not
been arrested. At the police station a duty
solicitor is available for all, free of charge.
This person is not employed by the police
and acts in total independence from them.
If a suspect requests legal advice the police
are not allowed to interview that person
until they have spoken with their representative. In exceptional circumstances a senior
police officer may remove this right, but it
has to be justified.

Under the Police and Criminal Evidence
Act 1984 (PACE) police may release on bail
a person who has not been charged. This
means they will be required to attend a court
or return to the police station at a future
date, to answer any charge or be released.
After a person has been charged they will
normally be released, on bail or without bail.
Exceptions to this include instances when
the charge is particularly serious, or where it
is believed that the suspect will be a danger
if released.

Protecting witnesses

Sometimes witnesses in a criminal trial
will feel worried at the thought of giving
evidence in court; it is a very serious
criminal offence if someone threatens or
attempts to influence a witness. In cases
where it is felt that witnesses might be
at risk of harm, they may be placed on
a witness protection programme. Without
the evidence of witnesses many criminals
would not be convicted, and it is essential
that support is provided, where necessary,
to allow this process to take place.

In extreme cases, where there is perceived
to be a significant danger to jurors who hear
a criminal trial, there is the possibility that a
case may be heard by a judge sitting alone.
The Criminal Justice Act 2003 (which came
into force in July 2007) allows for trial by a
judge sitting alone, in certain circumstances.

This process was permitted for the first time
in June 2009. See the Case Study opposite.

Estimated costs to bring these men to
justice are in excess of £25 million; this is
far greater than the amount that was stolen
in the robbery. Portia Ragnauth, chief prose-
cutor for Surrey CPS, described the case as
a 'benchmark prosecution'. She added that
our jury trial system should not be undermined by any suspected intimidation and
jury tampering.

Sentencing powers of the courts

Sentences (punishments) issued by courts to
convicted criminals vary in type and severity,
depending on the crime, the court in which
the criminal is convicted and also the circumstances of the criminal. There are restrictions
placed on the sentences that can be given for
each offence, and by each court.

- *Magistrates* can enforce a custodial
  sentence of maximum six months'
  duration. The maximum fine given by
  magistrates is £5,000 for an adult, £1,000
  for a person under 18 years old and £250
  for a person under 14 years old.
- *Judges* in Crown Court may hand down
  sentences up to and including life
  imprisonment (if the crime warrants it).
  For major crimes they can also impose
  unlimited fines. However, fines may *not*
  be given for crimes of murder.

Murder caries a compulsory life sentence;
the judge has no leeway in this matter.
However, he or she may suggest a minimum
length of time before the convicted criminal
is considered for release on licence.

The courts have a wide range of sentences
at their disposal; these could include
custody, fines or a combination of the two.
Most crimes have a maximum sentence
attached to them – for example, theft carries
a maximum of 7 years' imprisonment; if

Case Study

Judge rules in favour of no-jury trial

Lord Chief Justice (Lord Judge) declared that the trial of four [men?] at Heathrow Airport in 2004 should be heard by a judge sit[ting?] reasons for allowing this ground-breaking event, Lord Judge said that jury tampering was a very significant danger in this case. He also stated that the cost of measures to protect the jurors from influence was too high (and that they may not be wholly effective). Additionally he felt that individual jurors should not be expected to carry the burden of these measures.

The case involving four accused men, aged between 41 and 61, had been brought to trial on three previous occasions, and concerned 'very serious criminal activity'; this included possession of a firearm with intent to endanger life, possession of a firearm with intent to commit robbery and conspiracy to rob. Although the gang planned to steal over £10 million, along with foreign currency, the actual amount gained was £1.75 million; most of this was not recovered during the ensuing police investigation. Isabella Sankey, director of policy at Liberty, claimed Lord Judge was setting a dangerous precedent; she claimed that the right to trial by jury is a practice that ensures one class of people does not sit in judgement over another.

While this is a new procedure in England and Wales, no-jury trials have featured in other parts of the UK for many years; Diplock courts have been used in Northern Ireland since 1973, to combat intimidation of potential jurors by paramilitary groups. The subsequent trial of the accused men concluded on 30 March 2010; all four were convicted of the charges and received sentences ranging from 15 years to life imprisonment. Two other suspected robbers have never been brought to justice.

the case is dealt with at a Magistrates' Court the maximum sentence would be six months in prison or £5,000 fine. However, as this is an either-way offence, if dealt with at Crown Court the maximum 7 years could be imposed, with a much greater fine.

The courts personnel are provided with guidelines for sentencing criminals. These involve taking into account the intention of the criminal and the harm caused to the victim of the crime. These are referred to as aggravating and mitigating factors and should be considered by the magistrates and judges when deciding on a suitable punishment.

Types of sentences include:

- conditional discharge
- community sentence
- suspended prison sentence
- binding over
- fine
- absolute discharge
- prison sentence
- compensation order
- disqualification (driving offences)
- compensation order.

Grading Tip!

To achieve P4 you will need to outline the rights of the defendant in criminal proceedings. This will include the right to representation, the right to bail (where appropriate), and the right to a fair trial.

P5 requires a description of the criminal trial process, for both summary and indictable offences.

For P6 you will need to outline the powers of the courts in sentencing in both summary and indictable offences.

For M2 you will need to compare the trial process in both Magistrates' and Crown Courts, using a summary, either-way and indictable offence.

To achieve M3 you must explain the grounds for appeal from the Magistrates' Court to Crown Court.

End-of-unit knowledge check

1. Outline the role of the jury at a Crown Court trial.
2. What is the role of the duty solicitor?
3. Describe the ways in which laws are made.
4. What is the difference between examination-in-chief, cross-examination and re-examination?
5. Explain the term 'precedent'.

Grading criteria

In order to pass this unit, the evidence you present for assessment needs to demonstrate that you can meet all the learning outcomes for the unit. The criteria for a pass grade describe the level of achievement required to pass this unit.

To achieve a pass grade the evidence must show that you are able to:	To achieve a merit grade the evidence must show that, in addition to the pass criteria, you are able to:	To achieve a distinction grade the evidence must show that, in addition to the pass and merit criteria, you are able to:
P1 Outline the hierarchies of the civil and criminal courts in England and Wales		
P2 Describe the roles of judges, lawyers and lay people in criminal trials, in England and Wales	**M1** Compare the roles and functions of paid and lay personnel within the court system of England and Wales	**D1** Critically analyse the role of lay personnel within the court system of England and Wales
P3 Describe how legal rules are created by precedent		
P4 Outline the rights of the defendant to legal representation and bail		
P5 Describe how the criminal trial process works for both a summary and an indictable offence	**M2** Compare the trial process in the magistrates' and crown court, using a summary, either-way and indictable offence	
P6 Outline the powers of the courts in sentencing offenders, using one example of a summary offence and one indictable offence	**M3** Explain the grounds for appeal from the Magistrates' Court and the Crown Court in England and Wales	

Unit 23
Extended research in public services

Introduction

What do you understand by the term 'research?' Research is being carried out all the time, by many organisations, employing many diverse methods. You might even have been involved in a research project, either as a willing participant or without realising it.

If you have been approached by someone in the street who asks for 'just a few minutes of your time' you have been involved in market research. You have probably completed and returned a registration card (with your new phone, for example); if you were asked to tick boxes on the form your answers will have been included in data for research.

While at college some people take part in trials, for example, to test the effect of sleep deprivation on completing maths tests – this too is a form of research.

There are many reasons for undertaking research, such as examining current issues relating to the subject under scrutiny, extending knowledge and understanding of the topic, identifying needs, evaluating services (and therefore identifying any gaps). In some cases progress following the outcome of research will be observed, and it could lead to improvements in service, policy and practice.

The focus of this unit is carrying out research into one aspect of the public services. You will need to develop the skills to design a research project, carry it out and present your findings. You will improve your skills of research and investigation and, while you will be able to rely on support

Activity

Can you think of any instances when you have been involved in research? Discuss this with others in the class. From the information you have gathered can you identify the methods that were used in these examples? Now try to determine what you believe to be the purpose of research.

and guidance from your tutor, you will be expected to demonstrate that you have undertaken the research independently. Once you have completed the practical aspects of the project, you will need to work with the information you have gathered and disseminate (make known) the results to others.

As with other areas of study, there are many terms associated with research that can seem alien when you first encounter them. To assist with this you will find a key terms feature at the end of this chapter. Think of this as a dictionary – and remember to look up the meanings whenever you need to. In no time at all you will become familiar with these new ideas and be able to use them to support your research project.

You will also realise that each learning outcome builds upon the previous one: you will need to *design* the project (LO 1), then *implement* it and *interpret the results* (LO 2). You will then *review the results* (LO 3) before you are able to finally *present the project* (LO 4). Think of this as a flight of stairs – you cannot get to the top until you have climbed the ones below.

Key fact

Every learning outcome in this unit begins with 'be able to' – this means you must demonstrate your ability to carry it out (be actively involved in the process, from start to finish).

Learning outcomes:

By the end of this unit, you should:

1. Be able to design a research project.

2. Be able to implement and interpret the research results.

3. Be able to review the results of the research project.

4. Be able to present the research project.

23.1 Designing and implementing your research project and interpreting the results

P1 P2 M1 M2 D1 D2

The research proposal

You are probably thinking, 'Where will I start?' Don't worry, even experienced researchers find the thought of a new project rather daunting, until they 'get a feel' for what they need to do. It is probable that you will either be looking forward to the idea of exploring an area of your choice and one that you already know something about, or that it feels like a huge chore and you might feel a bit out of your depth. In fact your task is relatively straightforward, because you are being given some guidance in your choice

Activity

- **Discuss with other members of your class which public service each of you wishes to explore.**

- **For the next part of the task it would be helpful to work in groups where each member's interest is in the same service.**

- **Within your new group consider what is happening within your chosen public service and what you would like to investigate.**

- **For each service that the class is going to research, display a poster that identifies each class member and their area of research.**

of subject – you will focus on some aspect of the public services.

First steps to research

Find out as much as you can about what the current topics are in your chosen service. Examples might include the reasons behind falling numbers in the British Armed Forces or the suggested lack of adequate equipment available to soldiers on the frontline in Afghanistan. You might be more interested in the ways in which the Fire and Rescue Service or the Police Service administer their pension schemes.

Further examples of research possibilities might include:

- the role of the Prison Service
- craft of the Royal Air Force
- the history of the Royal Navy
- what does the National Health Service do?
- do we really need a Police Service?

It is essential that you discuss your area of interest with your tutor. Together, you will be able to avoid any misconceptions that might later on prove to be a barrier to the valid outcome of your research. You now need to turn your area of interest into a research question; you need be clear about the reasons for the research, set out your aim and form a **hypothesis** to be tested.

Key term

Hypothesis – a theory or an assumption to be proved or disproved

Developing the proposal

At this stage of the process you will begin to consider who might be invited to take part in your research. This will depend upon the nature of the investigation, but if you can focus on your intended audience now, you are more likely to be successful.

Sampling

The next area to consider is the method you will use to select your sample. Do you want the views of just the senior managers within your identified organisation or do you think the results would be more meaningful if you collected responses from the rank and file within the public service you have selected?

User involvement

At the outset you will need to decide who will be involved in your research project. To ensure that your outcome meets the needs of those it affects, you should consider involving these people at all stages of your research. In the earlier example of investigating a public service pension scheme, you might wish to consider involving serving officers in that service, as they are the ones who will be affected by the issue.

Similarly, if you wish to explore the background to comment on situations, you will need to rely on evidence provided by former personnel in the service of your choice.

These individuals will provide a perspective on your research that would not be possible by relying only on 'outsiders'.

You might consider involving users early on in the research project, to find out what is important to them and not just of academic interest to you. You will need to consider the effect of your research on the user and whether it might pose practical or ethical problems for them. If you decide to involve users in your project, early involvement (during the design stage) should ensure a more successful outcome than consultation at a later time. This could be in the form of a small focus group or by using a questionnaire.

If you continue to involve these users as your project progresses, you should be able to identify any problems as they occur and make improvements to overcome them, thereby ensuring the project runs smoothly, achieves a successful outcome and is completed on time.

Activity

You might wish to practise carrying out focus group interviewing. Working in groups of three or four you can try out your interview questions and techniques as a pilot. It will also give you the opportunity to become familiar with the tape recorder or other equipment you intend to use later on.

For about 10 minutes each member of the group uses their interview guide questions with their classmates and records the results. After the 10 minutes is up the next student can ask their questions about the topic, and so on. When everyone has discussed their topic it is a good idea to give feedback to each other about how well (or otherwise) you feel the interviews went.

Research methods

When you have decided on your research hypothesis and completed your literature review, you will need to consider the method by which you will conduct your research. The following paragraphs describe the main methods of research and suggest reasons why one method might be more suitable than another. Your choice of research method should reflect what is needed to test the hypothesis you have put forward.

Primary research

Primary research is the term used to describe the gathering of information by the person who is carrying out the research. It will provide the latest relevant information on the subject being researched. When you are watching a video or asking questions of a visiting speaker, you are carrying out primary research. Your notes or results might be different from other class members, but that does not mean either of you is incorrect.

Key terms

Primary research – original research; information is collected personally by the person undertaking research

Secondary research – information collected by others

Secondary research

Secondary research describes the way you use information that has been collected by other people. You will use this method to complete a large proportion of your coursework. You will read, watch and listen to information from a wide range of sources and then use the knowledge you have gained to present your own work.

Sources of secondary research

- Books
- Newspapers
- Magazines
- Journals
- Official websites
- Case studies

Before you can carry out your own research you need to be aware of what has already been published on the topic. This will be covered in more detail in the literature review section.

Research by survey

Survey research is one of the most important areas of research. It includes asking questions of respondents. A 'survey' can be anything from a short paper-and-pencil feedback form to an intensive one-on-one, in-depth interview. Surveys fall into two general categories: questionnaires and interviews.

Questionnaires

Many people will think of a mail survey in relation to questionnaires. This is one way to target many people at relatively little cost to the company managing the research. There are other advantages also: you can be certain that every respondent is being provided with the same set of questions, and they can complete them in their own time. However, there are some down sides to using questionnaires that you will need to consider: traditionally the return rate of questionnaires is low, and there is no opportunity for either the researcher or respondent to explore questions or responses in depth.

In some situations, questionnaires are given to a group of respondents at the same time, for example within a business. The respondents are brought together to complete the questionnaire, which is collected after the event, resulting in a high response rate. Additionally, if any respondent was unsure of what a question meant, they could ask their colleagues for clarification. One disadvantage of this type of questionnaire is that some respondents might give the same answer as a colleague, without considering their own response.

Another variation on the questionnaire survey is when the researcher hands the survey to the respondent at their own premises. This is then left to be completed and is collected by the researcher at an arranged time. In some ways this approach could benefit both the researcher and respondent: the survey is completed in private at a convenient time (as with the mailed version), but they also have personal contact with the researcher in the same way as the group survey. There is the added advantage that the respondent can ask questions on any aspect they do not understand or wish to explore in greater depth.

If a survey is your chosen method of gathering data for your research project, you will need to consider which type is best for your purpose. This will depend on the intended participants and their attributes. If you are to use questionnaires, it is assumed that the respondents are able to read. You will need to consider the language used in the survey. Do all your respondents speak the same language as you do or will you need to produce the survey in different languages?

How will you access the intended participants? You will need to consider the geographical area over which they are spread and then consider whether to conduct a mail survey, personal interview or a combination of the two.

You will need to consider *and justify* the reasons why you wish to use a questionnaire. Remember that this method of gathering information is only part of the response you will need to answer your research questions. Questionnaires will need to be used alongside other methods, for example interviews and observations. Using a variety of methods ensures that your research will be more valid and reliable than using one method in isolation.

Interviews

Conducting research by the interview method is a more personal approach than

Activity

When planning your questionnaire consider the following points:

- **what are your questions?**

- **what type of (and how much) information do you need to answer the questions?**

- **can you really justify using a questionnaire?**

- **what other types of methods will you use (and why)?**

using a questionnaire. The interviewer speaks directly with the respondent and is able to explore the answers given. This could be by probing more deeply to gain understanding or even by asking follow-up questions. The respondent is also able to provide their own opinion or explanations. By their nature, interviews can take a long time to complete. If the interviewer is to rely on notes, they will also need to be able to write very quickly. Another alternative is to use a voice recorder (with the knowledge and permission of the respondent).

Telephone interviews allow the interviewer to gather a large amount of information in a relatively short period, compared with the face-to-face method. Many of the large-scale opinion polls that appear in national newspapers and other forms of media are based on telephone interviews. This method also allows the interviewer to ask follow-up questions, if clarification is needed. Negative aspects of this type of interview include some people not having their number listed in directories, while others resent the disturbance that such a call can make to their home life. Telephone interviews also need to be kept relatively short, so that the respondent will complete the process.

Figure 23.1 A population from which the sample will be derived

Think about it!

What other methods of interviewing can you think of?

What are the good and bad points about each type you have identified?

Figure 23.2a Face-to-face interview

Figure 23.2b Telephone interview

Interviewing is undoubtedly among the most testing of research methods. When they are conducted properly the results can be very precise, but there are many pitfalls to be negotiated along the way. The interviewer needs to keep focused on the task and not be distracted away from the purpose of the questions. He or she also needs to be available at a time best suited to the needs of the respondent.

There are many skills involved in conducting a good interview, including motivating the respondent throughout the session. The interviewer also needs to be flexible in approach. If the respondent is unsure of the meaning of a particular question, he or she must be able to clarify and also complete the entire interview.

Creating the survey

Once you have decided on the method you will use to carry out your research project, you will consider what to include. You must consider the content, the use of words and the ways in which the questions are set out. Attention to detail at this early stage could reap benefits later on. There are three main areas to be addressed when writing a question:

1. The content – it is essential that *you* understand the purpose of the question.

2. Selecting an appropriate system to collect responses.

3. Determining the wording of the question to achieve the result.

Once you have written your questions you will need to consider where they will be placed in the survey. For example, will you ask a number of questions that lead up to the one you really want answered or will you get straight to the point? Once again it is important to spend time on the preparation stage so that things move smoothly once the project is launched.

Literature review

Now you have identified exactly what it is you will be investigating, you need to research what information already exists on the subject. There is nothing to be gained from spending a lot of time (and huge effort) duplicating what someone else has done previously. In fact, you could find yourself accused of copying someone else's work and claiming it as your own. No doubt you have already been warned of the possible consequences of plagiarism!

A literature review is a well thought-out and organised search for all the literature published on a topic. A well structured literature search is the most effective and efficient way to locate sound evidence on the research subject. Evidence may be found in books, journals, government documents, newspapers and television or radio programmes. You will need to be aware of where the most likely sources of your information will be. Internet search engines may be useful in providing some information – *but beware* – some information given on internet sites may be just opinion and not very reliable.

If you limit your search to professional websites you should be able to access reliable information. One advantage of the internet over other published materials is that the information is available almost immediately.

Methodology

You will need to decide how you are going to present the information (data) your research produces; this will be either in quantitative or qualitative format. Qualitative data is descriptive, and is produced in written format, while the basis for quantitative data is numerical. Qualitative data might include text taken directly from respondents' answers or it can be a summary of what has been said, perhaps from notes taken at the time.

Data needs to be presented in a way that makes it straightforward to read; this will result in the reader being better able to understand the argument and conclusions. It is possible to combine both types of data within the same work, for example, pages of text with tables, graphs or other numerical information added, where appropriate. Although it is possible to combine more than one method of undertaking research, it is more usual to select *either* a quantitative *or* a qualitative approach to data collection.

Quantitative research takes the form of processes and methods that allow for statistical analysis of data. This method can be used to compare research in sub-groups; the results are usually in number format, e.g. a tally chart.

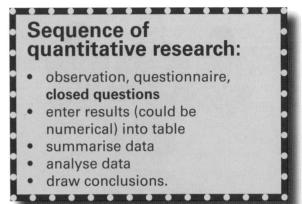

Sequence of quantitative research:

- observation, questionnaire, **closed questions**
- enter results (could be numerical) into table
- summarise data
- analyse data
- draw conclusions.

Where it is considered necessary to explore participants' understanding of questions, it is more appropriate to adopt a qualitative research. Rather than using a questionnaire or telephone call as a 'one-off' method of data collection, this method aims to study the subject in their natural surroundings and collect naturally occurring non-biased data. This method uses words rather than numbers to describe the views of the participants. Qualitative research methods might include individual and group interviews or focus groups. With this method it is possible to identify key themes or patterns as they emerge; these can then be used to manage the data and test the hypothesis.

There are many different types of questions that can be used for research. Amongst the most commonly used are:

- making a list
- questions that require a yes or no answer
- choosing from a list of options
- ranking answers in order
- open-ended questions
- agreeing or disagreeing with a statement.

When writing your questions it is a good idea to use a variety of question types to keep the respondent interested in the research. It will also generate different types of evidence that you can manipulate in your findings.

Key terms

Closed question – a question that is often accompanied by a set of answers from which the interviewee must select one

Objective – looking at the facts, remaining free from bias

Open question – a question that allows varied responses rather than simply answering 'yes' or 'no'

Subjective – looking at things from your own point of view; not being impartial

Reliability – the method used to obtain information is consistent and can be repeated

Validity – the method used and information gathered are relevant to the study

The quantitative method of research allows responses to be **objective**, while the qualitative method provides data that can be **subjective**.

Sequence of qualitative research:

- Ask **open questions**
- Record results (can be very labour intensive)
- Interpret results
- Ask more questions if necessary
- Theorise
- Draw conclusions.

Other considerations

Now you are almost ready to get down to the practicalities of undertaking your research project – there are just a few more things you need to understand before this can occur. In addition to the research method you select, you will need to ensure that the results of your research will be valid and reliable. **Validity** means being able to describe whether the results you have obtained tell you what you want to find out. **Reliability** is concerned with being able to reproduce the method and get the same results. Sometimes it is possible to produce results that are valid but not reliable; the level to which your research meets the criteria of being valid *and* reliable will depend on how you have planned the project and carried out the methodology of data collection.

Table 23.1 Comparison of research methods

Qualitative research methods	Quantitative research methods
Holistic (explores in depth)	Particularistic (direct response to question)
Subjective	Objective
Process centred	Outcome centred
Possible lack of control (open questions)	Relative level of control (closed questions)
Discovery focused	Verification focused
Explanatory	Confirmatory

Source: Adapted from Cook and Reichardt (1979)

Now you have a good idea of what research involves, and have selected your topic, you will decide the best way to gather the evidence you need. You will need to identify those individuals who will be involved, make arrangements for a convenient time to interview them, or send a questionnaire. If you are relying on questionnaires being returned by post, remember to make allowances for a potentially low response rate.

If you are sending a questionnaire through the post it is a good idea to telephone the recipient beforehand, and enclose a letter with the questionnaire to remind them of who you are and why you are asking for their help (see below for an example). You might consider using a letter similar to the following template:

It is also important to remember that you will be doing this alongside the other units on your course, and you must allow sufficient time to do the best you can. It would be very embarrassing if you have carried out a very good research project and this is then spoiled because you have not allowed enough time to complete it.

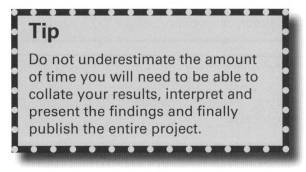

Tip

Do not underestimate the amount of time you will need to be able to collate your results, interpret and present the findings and finally publish the entire project.

The Great Town College
Great Town Road
Great Town

e-mail: **nora@greattowncol.com**

mobile: 07834 788312

10 October 2010

Dear Sir/Madam *(or name, if you have spoken with them)*

Further to our previous telephone conversation concerning my research project on Police Pensions, I am enclosing the questionnaire. Please see the accompanying letter from my tutor which confirms my identity as a student on the BTEC National Diploma in Public Services.

I would very much like you to take part in this research. I must stress that you will remain anonymous and that you may withdraw from the project at any time.

My timescale for completion of this project is restricted, so I would be grateful if you could complete the questionnaire and return it in the enclosed stamped addressed envelope by the 31st October.

Thank you very much for taking the time to read this letter. After I have completed the study I will be pleased to send you a copy of my findings.

If you have any comments or questions, please do not hesitate to contact me by email.

Yours sincerely

Nora Davies

Grading Tip!

To achieve P1 you will need to produce a well-founded research proposal; it is likely that you will require some support from your tutor in determining this.

For P2 you need to plan and describe the design of your research project. While you are doing this you will probably uncover many questions that you will need to address when you begin to put you proposal into action.

M1 will be awarded if you are able to demonstrate a high degree of autonomy in producing your proposal.

For M2 you will need to provide an *explanation* of the design for your research project.

To achieve D1 you will have worked independently to produce your research proposal.

A *justification* of the adopted project design is needed to achieve D2.

23.2 Reviewing the results and presenting the research project

So the planning went well, you finally nailed down the purpose of the research and have gathered lots of information. Well done! Now what are you going to do with it? As identified at the end of the previous section, at this stage your work is far from being complete. Developing an effective and concise report to present the findings of your research project could take a considerable amount of time.

This is probably a good time to book another session with your tutor, so that you can talk through what you propose and be reassured that it is the way to proceed. If any potential problems are identified at this stage you will have the opportunity to make appropriate changes to your plans.

There are a number of considerations to keep in mind when you decide on the format of your work. The first of these is the audience – who is going to read the report? Is it your peers, tutor, the participants, their bosses (or anyone else you can identify)? Are they going to want to know every step of the research or just the outcome? Of course, you will be assessed against the grading criteria for the unit, so you will want to make sure you have covered every step in sufficient detail.

The way in which you have conducted the project is also important. If you ask your participants for feedback on how they found the experience, you will be able to overcome problems as they arise and possibly make improvements to your original proposal. Remember too that your classmates are involved in a research project at the same time as you – by regularly discussing progress with them you will be able to assist each other in overcoming any common issues that might occur.

Writing up the report

It might help to think of your report as telling a story: you will need to have a beginning, middle and end. When you write your report, assume that the reader has no previous knowledge of the subject, so you will need to 'spell it out'. Most research projects will have one story line – sometimes this will centre on a particular research finding, other times the focus will be a problem or challenge that resulted from the methodology. You will need to be concise and at the same time provide sufficient detail for the reader to understand the story. One of the most difficult parts of telling a story is to keep the attention of the audience. Think about the type of book or film you enjoy – what is it that makes you want to read or watch to the end?

It probably seems a long time ago since you started thinking about your research subject; you have presented the hypothesis and read countless articles on other people's take on this. You decided on what type of research you would use, have carried out interviews or sent and received questionnaires and gathered the necessary data. To be able to discover the basis for your story you now need to take a step back from the detail and see the big picture – try to observe the work from the viewpoint of your audience. It might be that some of the detail you believed was essential to the meaning of the project is in fact not now necessary – if it does not add anything to the outcome, it could (and should) be left out.

Deciding what is important comes down to personal preference – at this stage you are the only one who owns the information. However, different people see the same thing in different ways – they have different perceptions of it. It is only natural that as you have devoted so much time and energy to the project, you want everything to be included; you could be said to have a biased view because of this. You need to try to adopt an impartial view and make decisions based on logic only.

The figure represented opposite provides the viewer with an ambiguous image. It can be perceived as two black faces looking at each other in front of a white background. Take another look at the image and you might be able to see it as a white vase on a black background.

Once you have been made aware of the available options, it is possible to consider both; however, most find it difficult to perceive both images *at the same time.*

To prevent your own perception from interfering with the outcome of your report, you will need to consider other people's views and adopt an objective, impartial approach.

Disseminating the report

You now need to think about how you will disseminate the result of your research; this includes the format of the report. In many organisations there will be a particular 'house style' that is followed and methodology that is employed. Articles that are presented for publication (e.g. in a journal or book) will need to follow specific guidelines on formatting, and each publisher will have their own rules to follow. Universities will also have guidelines laid down for their students to follow, which typically include labelling of figures and margin width. Although your tutor is unlikely to impose unattainable rules, you will need to ensure you understand how the work should be presented. Whatever regulations are imposed upon the format of your report, it is likely to include the elements described here

Figure 23.3 The Rubin vase

Format of the report

Abstract

This is usually no more than 100 words in length and identifies the topic under consideration.

Look at the beginning of each unit in your course. They all begin with an abstract that 'sets the scene' for what follows.

Introduction

In this first section you will convince the reader why your subject is worth researching. Remember, you have already had the approval of your tutor, so it should not be too difficult to persuade others too. This is where you will state your hypothesis; you need to be specific about your predictions.

You should be prepared to go into some depth to explain the extent of your topic. This will clarify things and provide reasons why you have undertaken a review of particular literature.

You will need to explain the factors that led to you selecting the literature. There should also be evidence of a comparison and analysis of literature sources. This is where you will bring things together, by identifying any trends or theories that emerge, or indeed any conflict or apparent gaps, which your research will identify. Remember, this is only an introduction to the literature review – its outcome will be in another section.

The literature review

This is where you will show that you have a good understanding of the current state of information that is available in your chosen topic. If you have read many types of literature, you will probably find it more manageable to group these into categories. These sub-groups could include, for example, those that come to similar conclusions or those that have used qualitative or quantitative methodology. You will

> ## Checklist
>
> Include in this section:
> - why the subject is worth researching
> - a *brief* overview
> - a summary of the questions you will try to answer
> - how your research links with current thinking
> - proof that you have considered others' views at the outset.

need to provide a brief summary of each piece of literature and ensure you provide a critical analysis of the content – remember that you are not just describing the work. As well as providing information on what has already been written on your topic, the literature review will assist in your understanding of the issue and could open up new avenues for you to explore. You might also have discovered contradictions in the work carried out by others; this will allow you to consider both sides of the argument and provide a valid outcome to the issue under discussion.

You will summarise how the literature has added validity to your topic and you also need to discuss the significance of this to the issues identified in your introduction.

The main section

You have asked your questions and got lots of information; now you need to present this data in a way that is suitable for the purpose of your project and will keep the attention of the audience. Your hope is that the data will support your hypothesis, but do not be unduly concerned if the opposite is true – it is perfectly valid if the hypothesis you set out is disproved. The important thing is to show that the methods you utilised in carrying out your research were valid and that they were carried out in an appropriate manner. Remember, if you are tempted to stage-manage the outcome, you are allowing your own perceptions and bias to come to the fore.

The data you have collected now needs to be analysed and conclusions drawn from this. The type of data you have collected will have an effect on the way you present your findings. You should attempt to present your data findings in more than one way (remember, you want to keep the audience interested, and they might get a bit fed up of reading pages of figures or percentages).

Some different types of data are outlined in the following paragraphs and demonstrate some of the limitations associated with their use.

The simplest type of data is known as 'nominal'. Typically responses will be a single word. This data will allow you to achieve a total number of respondents who gave the one-word answer. This type of data will not allow you to carry out comparisons or evaluate the level of response. Examples of this are provided in the boxes below.

In these examples you could only count the number of people who smoke or identify the group to which they belong.

The second type of data collected is 'ordinal'. As its name suggests, this allows you to arrange the data according to importance or frequency. An example of ordinal data is provided below.

The numbers underneath the response statements allow the researcher to interpret them in numerical format, so permitting statistical data to be provided. When you have ordinal data the results can be represented in a number of ways, including pie charts, tally charts and bar charts. They can also be used to describe the results.

You need to be able to demonstrate how, and to what extent, your data answers your original research question. By analysing the data you might be able to identify themes emerging. If this is the case these themes will need to be explored further and analysed; this will involve linking them back to any relevant information in your literature review. On occasions a single data source will contribute to more than one theme; in these situations their relevance to each theme should be explained.

Evaluating your data

You began your research project by planning what you would explore; this led to your hypothesis and implementation of your chosen method to test it. Now you have

Type of question providing nominal data

Q: Do you smoke?   **A:** YES / NO
Q: What is your nationality?
A: Select from the following ...

Example of question providing ordinal data

Q: All police officers in the UK should carry firearms.

Strongly agree	Agree	Neither agree nor disagree	Disagree	Strongly disagree
1	2	3	4	5

gathered all your data and organised it into various formats. The evaluation phase of the project is closely linked to the initial planning stage in what is often referred to as the planning–evaluation cycle. In the planning stage you identified a set of actions you were going to take and the means by which these would be executed. The hypothesis was refined and any potential problems recognised were dealt with. These steps allowed you to focus on the matter to be addressed.

The evaluation stage also involves a succession of actions that will include formulating the objectives and goals, selecting and organising relevant data, an analysis of that data and the intended use of the evaluation results.

Data analysis

Data analysis is a process of examining, cleaning, transforming and modeling the data you have collected so that you may highlight useful information. This will allow you to make conclusions and will add weight to support the decisions you make. There are many different varieties of data analysis, each used for a specific purpose. All varieties of data analysis follow the same phases.

Process of data analysis

- data cleaning
- initial data analysis (assessment of data quality)
- final data analysis (answer the original research question)
- final data analysis (necessary analyses and report)

Data cleaning

Data cleaning is a vital procedure during which the researcher inspects the data and, if any is found to be incorrect, it may be put

right. Similarly, it is at this stage that any data that is found to be unnecessary should be removed. As mentioned previously, it is essential that any decisions made about the validity of data are not subjective. If any data is removed it should be kept in a retrievable format, so that it could be used later, if needed.

Initial data analysis

During the initial data analysis phase you should steer clear of any analysis that is aimed at answering the original research question as this will occur during the next phase. The initial data analysis phase considers the quality of the data that has been gathered.

The quality of data should be checked as early as possible. This can be undertaken using different techniques including frequency counts, descriptive statistics (mean, median, standard deviation), normality or associations. Other methods will check whether the decisions made at the cleaning phase have had any effect on the distribution of the variables. Similarly, if there are any missing observations or values it should be possible to determine whether they are missing due to the cleaning or whether it is a random phenomenon. The choice of analyses to assess the quality of data during the initial data analysis phrase depends on the analyses that will be employed in the main analysis phase.

The findings of the initial data analysis are documented and any necessary or possible corrective actions are taken. At this stage the original plan for the main data analysis can, and should, be specified in more detail, or even re-written.

Main data analysis

In the main data analysis phase, you will consider the data in relation to answering the original research question.

Final data analysis

The final data analysis concludes the process, by using the evidence gathered to support your conclusions in relation to the research question.

Conclusion

You are nearly there now, but it is not quite time to take your foot off the accelerator. Many otherwise good pieces of research have failed to keep the attention of the reader because the author has failed to accurately 'bring it all together' at this stage. Here you will remind the reader why you have included particular points and justify their relevance to the project as a whole. You must ensure that your arguments are clear and easy to follow, and that any common threads which have emerged are properly connected. The entire report must be written in a logical sequence and must contain sufficient detail to allow the reader to understand it.

Choosing your methodology

The choice of analysis method employed during the initial phase depends on the way in which the data was collected. You will need to choose a methodology that is suitable for the chosen problem. Even if you use the same method to look at two problems, the methodology you employ

may be different. Qualitative research uses qualitative data analysis to analyse data that includes text, transcripts of interviews, photographs and observation notes.

When quantitative research has resulted in a large number of responses it is usual to employ a quantitative data analysis. For example, you will need to know not only how to calculate the mean, variance and distribution for a set of date, but you should also understand which one is an appropriate method to present the information. Considering these aspects will assist you in selecting the methodology best suited to your research.

You need to be able to state with confidence the conclusions you draw from the research project; these need to be based on facts that are clearly evident within the findings of your project. Also you will consider how the data you have gathered add weight to existing literature that you examined earlier on.

The ability to identify what went to plan and what would need to be adapted in a future project is a skill that will identify you as a researcher with true ability. So, how could you improve a future study? Maybe you would ask further questions, so you could glean additional data; or perhaps you would adjust the methods you employed. These are examples of the reflection that all researchers should carry out and you need

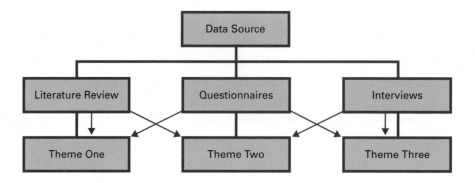

Figure 23.4 Different pieces of data may contribute to more that one theme

to write this clearly in your conclusion. It is important for you to admit that you have not provided all the answers to your hypothesis, and you might consider suggesting avenues for further investigation in this field.

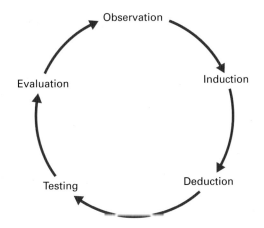

Figure 23.5 The steps involved in research

Grading Tip!

Having successfully completed your research proposal and design, you will put your plan into action; this will include collecting and interpreting data (P3).

To achieve M3 you will need to implement your project *and explain* the techniques you use for collection of data.

For P4 you will demonstrate sound data collection techniques *and* interpret data *through application of statistical analysis*.

M4 is an extension of P4 – you will need to present and interpret data, and explain the results of your research.

To achieve D3 you must present and interpret the data you have collected, and also provide an analysis of your research results.

To achieve P5 you must review the outcome of your project and fully explain how you might do things differently on a future occasion, providing valid reasons for this.

M5 will be awarded if you provide a *critical analysis* of your research results. You must also justify the areas for future consideration that you identified in P5.

The final pass criterion (P6) will be achieved if your final report meets the required standard and is set out in the accepted format provided by your tutor.

Key terms

Action research – the purpose of action research (or practitioner research) is to bring about changes for the better within an organisation

Case study – a useful way of finding out what 'makes people tick' and the ways that different aspects work together towards an outcome

Documentation – this refers to all materials gathered during the course of your research; it might include photographs, reports, newspaper articles, audio or video recordings and many more examples

Ethics – ethical research requires respect and being aware of the rights and feelings of everyone involved in the research. It is essential that no unintentional harm or distress are caused to any person

Focus group – this is a particular type of interview technique where the participants are gathered together. People might feel more comfortable in this set-up

Informed consent – the ethical principle of participants voluntarily agreeing to be involved in research

Interview – a structured format for collecting evidence, by asking questions or by discussion

Methodology – the principles and values that underpin the research process

Methods – the actual techniques employed by the researcher to gather data

Objectivity – a neutral approach to research

Probing – an interview technique aimed at bringing out information from the respondent

Qualitative method – non-numerical data

Quantitative method – numerical data

Reliability – the method used to obtain information is consistent and can be repeated

Subjectivity – biases that might affect the outcome of research

Survey – an attempt to produce a large volume of data by using a large sample

Validity – the method used and information gathered are relevant to the study

End-of-unit knowledge check

1. Suggest three reasons why public service research might be undertaken.
2. Explain the importance of undertaking a literature review.
3. Describe at least two methods of collecting data.
4. Outline the main reasons for selecting quantitative methods of research.
5. Identify ways of presenting research findings.

Grading criteria

In order to pass this unit, the evidence you present for assessment needs to demonstrate that you can meet all the learning outcomes for the unit. The criteria for a pass grade describe the level of achievement required to pass this unit.

To achieve a pass grade the evidence must show that you are able to:	To achieve a merit grade the evidence must show that, in addition to the pass criteria, you are able to:	To achieve a distinction grade the evidence must show that, in addition to the pass and merit criteria, you are able to:
P1 Produce a valid research proposal for a public service based research project, with teacher support	**M1** Produce a valid research proposal for a public service based research project, with limited teacher support	**D1** Independently produce a valid research proposal for a public service based research project
P2 Describe the research design for a public service based research project	**M2** Explain the research design for a public service based research project	**D2** Justify the research design for a public service based research project
P3 Implement the research project, describing data collection techniques	**M3** Implement the research project, explaining data collection techniques	
P4 Present and interpret collected data, applying statistical techniques to describe the research results	**M4** Present and interpret collected data, explaining the research results	**D3** Present and interpret collected data, analysing the research results
P5 Review the project results, explaining areas for future consideration	**M3** Analyse the project results, justifying areas for future consideration	

Unit 30
Practical team sports

Introduction

Many centres that provide public services courses also deliver a sports curriculum alongside, which will make delivery of this unit much easier. Many learners will participate in the variety of **team sports** offered by the centre as well as those offered in the wider community, and you are expected to provide evidence for this unit by selecting sports in which you either excel or have a particular interest. The aim of the unit is to allow you to explore the **skills**, **techniques**, **tactics**, rules and regulations of two team sports, through practical participation, in order to develop your knowledge and understanding of team sports in general.

The unit focuses upon your practical sports performance in team sports, especially on the application of skills, techniques and tactics which is achieved through participation in practical activities, and reflecting on your own performance and that of other team members. You will reinforce the knowledge and understanding required to study aspects of coaching and leadership, fitness and training, physiology and health and safety. All the public services, uniformed and non-uniformed, encourage their personnel to participate in team sports as it helps with aspects of teamwork, cohesion and communication, and also bonds them into a social network on which all businesses thrive.

Key terms

Team sports – skilful, physical activity in which individuals come together to take part in meeting a particular challenge

Skills – an action or set of actions in sport; the learned ability to perform the right techniques at the right time, effectively, efficiently and consistently

Techniques – basic movements in sport; combination of a number of techniques into a pattern of movement called skill

Tactics – methods used to put strategies into practice in a sport; plan or procedure designed to gain advantage or success

You will also have the opportunity to investigate the rules and regulations of team sports, as well as tactics and formations, before reviewing your own performance by different assessment methods and making suggestions relating to the development of a team. The public services encourage employees to participate in team sports as it helps to build teamwork and cooperation, ensures that the workforce keeps fit and helps with leadership skills.

Learning outcomes:

By the end of this unit, you should:

1. Know the skills, techniques and tactics required in selected team sports.

2. Know the rules and regulations of selected team sports.

3. Be able to assess your own performance in selected team sports.

4. Be able to assess the performance of teams in selected team sports.

30.1 Know the skills, techniques and tactics required in selected team sports

Skills, techniques and tactics required in two team sports

There are a variety of team sports available to you, but only two that you have to participate in for this unit. The more contrasting the team sports are, the better chance you have of assessing your own performance and that of the team, and the more likely you will be able to achieve a Merit or a Distinction. First you need to know, understand and explain the skills, techniques and tactics for two team sports.

Skill is present in all team sports and can be seen as a pattern of movement. Techniques are put together as a part of that skill and, along with natural ability, you are able to develop these techniques and skills to improve individual and team performance. In most cases, skill is a combination of physical and mental qualities, so by learning techniques and participating in the correct training, you will find that decision-making becomes easier and you will become more skilful. The learning of skills and techniques is affected by the training and practice that you take part in, the coaching given and the feedback you get.

All team sports require tactics in order to achieve success. You need to plan the tactics prior to every match, as they may change from game to game and may depend upon many factors, including the weather, the opponents, the facility, and any injuries and suspensions of your team players. As a team you will practise tactics both in attack and defence, with drills for all the different situations the team will find itself in. It is imperative that all the players understand each tactic and when to employ it, otherwise it will lead to confusion and disrupt the team's performance.

Hockey

The general aim of hockey is for the players to get the ball into the opponent's attacking circle and attempt to hit, push or flick it into the goal. The team that scores the most goals in a game wins. The way that you do this is to practise your skills and techniques individually, in accordance to the position in which you are play, and work out tactics as a team to score goals and prevent the opposition from scoring.

In hockey there are two teams, each with 11 players on the pitch, and you play two halves of 35 minutes each. At the beginning of the game and after every goal, the game starts from the centre of the field, with each team on its own half, and the ball is played in any direction across the pitch throughout the game. The playing field is rectangular – 91.4 m × 55 m – with a goal at either end set within a semi circle 16 m from the goal. A centre circle sits on the centre line and there are two 22.9 m lines at both ends of the field, with 'D' markings around each goal.

Hockey is a very fast game that requires highly skilled players who can manoeuvre the ball with great precision and speed, keeping possession as much as possible before hitting the ball hard, with accuracy, to score a goal.

Skills and techniques

Skills and techniques used in hockey include the following.

- Dribble – when you control the ball with your stick as you run, moving it along the floor in front of you and away from

Figure 30.1 Hockey is one of many team sports played in the public services

your feet. Keep the stick in contact with the ball as much as possible to make it easier to pass and harder for an opponent to tackle without giving away a free hit.

- Hit – when the stick is moved back from the ball and then brought forward quickly to contact the ball with force in order to get the ball running smoothly along the ground to reach the target.

- Push – the best way to pass the ball over a distance, using the wrist to force the ball forward to another player and following through after contact. It is an easy move to disguise as your hands are further apart on the stick than for a hit. Keeping down low will give you more power and pace.

- Clip hit – also called a 'scoop', the ball is lifted off the ground to pass, shoot at goal or to lift the ball over an opponent's stick. The stick is placed at an angle in order to lift the ball slightly, but not so high as to be called dangerous by the umpire.

- Trap – when you receive a ball and stop it in a controlled manner. You have to remain low, bending the knees and waist, with the stick low to the ground also. Keep your hands 'soft' and relaxed while angling the stick to control the ball.

- Drive – similar to a hit, but the stick goes further back and is brought forward in a swinging motion to strike the ball, forcing it to travel further.

- Long-handled slap – a quick, hard shot on goal when close in. It is stronger than a push so is useful when you are being closed down by an opponent. The backswing is short and flat with the stick parallel to the ground.

- Tackle – one of the ways to stop your opponent by placing your stick in the path of the ball, keeping your stick close to the ground and waiting until the right moment. Your stick should not touch the opponent's stick before or after the tackle and you cannot use your body to force them out of the way.

- Reverse stick backhand – a reverse hit, but not with the rounded back of the stick, that is used for passing, shooting and as an element of surprise. The backswing is short and, using your wrists to turn it, use the inside edge of the stick, keeping it in contact with the ground, and follow through.

- Aerial – the ball is raised off the ground to above head height, falling into space, but the opponent must be at least 5m away. It is used to relieve pressure from the defence, present a counter attack or eliminate players.
- Drag flick – this can only be used at a penalty corner and is a relatively new technique.
- Sweep – similar to a long-handled slap, but you are in a full lunge position when playing the ball. This generally allows more accuracy and similar amounts of speed and power.
- Jab – a quick movement made while running alongside your opponent, to move the ball out of play or break down a run. It is mainly used when a player has been channelled or pressured when in possession of the ball.

Tactics

Tactics used in hockey include the following.

- Full pitch – the opposition team press every situation on the pitch.
- Half pitch – you only put pressure on the opponents playing inside your own half; all of the players are behind the ball and the opposition's half is free.
- Three-quarter press – this leaves the defensive quarter free for play without pressing the opposition.
- Zonal marking – the entire defensive team aligns itself according to where the ball is in relation to the most dangerous play available to the opposition.
- Man marking – you follow your opponent wherever they move on the pitch.
- Switch play – eliminates players to create space and allow a better chance of scoring or when no other options are available when attacking, so you move over to the opposite side of the pitch.
- Turn over – this is classified as a breakdown of play which the opposition use as an advantage.

Rugby Union

Rugby Union is very popular in the uniformed public services, particularly the Armed Forces, which organise a tri-service tournament annually. It is a competition between two teams in a match lasting for 80 minutes plus added time for injuries and stoppages in the game. It is controlled by a referee, two touch judges and sometimes a video referee who can replay incidents using television replays. The object is to score more points than the other team by scoring tries, conversions, drop goals and penalties in your opponent's goal area. If both teams score the same number of points, it is classed as a draw.

A team consists of 15 players, 8 forwards and 7 backs, with up to 7 replacements allowed during the game. The forwards gain and retain possession of the ball by driving the ball forwards into the opposing forwards, and take part in the scrums and line-outs. The backs move the game forward by running or kicking the ball, and try to cause the opposition defence to commit too many players at strategic points to create space for the backs to run in and score a try.

Some of the skills and techniques used in Rugby Union are shown below.

Kicking

- Place kick awarded for penalties and conversions. Using a kicking tee, a pile of sand or a divot in the ground, place the ball tilted towards its intended direction of travel. Measure out a run up, relax and look between the posts, then run at the ball at a 45-degree angle, keep your body weight forward and kick the ball with a follow-through in the direction of the ball.
- Punt kick into touch if the opposition have given away a penalty. Hold the ball at 35 degrees, with one hand towards the front of the ball and the other towards the rear. Step forward and drop

the ball onto your kicking-foot laces and follow through.

- Drop kicks are used to restart the game or kick for a field goal. Hold the ball in both hands, pointing down. Keep your eyes on the ball, then step forwards and raise the ball to waist level. Drop the ball and, as it falls, strike it with the lower part of your instep and follow through.

Tackling

The side tackle is very effective in bringing your opponent down. Timing is all important as you will both be running and you do not want to injure yourself. Your shoulders should be at your opponent's hip height. Grab the thigh, crouching down and driving the legs for impact. Keep your head behind the opponent's body, wrap your arms round, grip tightly and hold on. Quickly get to your feet and try to get the ball.

Tackling from behind needs good timing and determination to stop your opponent gaining ground on you. Get as close as possible to them and aim for their thighs with your shoulder, placing your head to the side of their leg and wrapping your arms round their legs. Land on top of your opponent and get to your feet quickly.

Catching

Catching a high kick and calling a 'Mark' inside your own 22 m line is a difficult technique. Call for the ball and get into line with the path of the ball, keeping your eyes on it at all times. Extend your arms towards the ball with elbows bent and side-on to the opposition. Catch the ball at eye level and bring it into your hands, then your body and, if in the air, land on your feet and prepare for contact.

The line out is crucial, especially near to the opposition's goal line. The jumper has to catch the ball from the hooker and pass the ball to the scrum half after listening for a call

from either of them. As the ball is released, coil your legs and jump, raising your arms above your head and keeping your eyes on the ball – you may be allowed support from your team. Catch the ball and land with your back to the opposition, and then pass the ball.

Figure 30.2 Rugby Union is a popular team sport in the Armed Forces

Evasion – running with the ball

The dummy fools your opponent into thinking that you are about to make a pass. Run towards the defender with the ball in both hands and make the passing motion to a team mate, then drop your shoulder, stop and do not pass. The opponent will be drawn to your team mate and you set off running again, looking for players in support.

A sidestep is a way of evading your opponent and shaking off a tackle. As you approach the tackler, shorten your stride and step wide as if you were going to go that way, but then shift your body weight in the opposite direction and accelerate past them.

The swerve is similar to the sidestep, but not as extreme, and is used mainly by the backs. Run straight towards the defender, holding the ball in both hands, then change your line of running and lean away from the tackler using your hips. Sprint away from the off-balance defender.

Passing

For a basic pass, be relaxed and pass for the player, not at them. Hold the ball in two hands, fingers spread, and sweep the ball off your hips in an arc. Release the ball, flicking your wrist and fingers with a follow-through.

Rugby Union tactics

Tactics in Rugby Union are similar to those of other team games in that you are trying to stop the opposition from scoring while trying to score as many points or goals as possible yourselves. So, teams may decide on defensive tactics for part of the game, or width in attack could be the main tactic decided before the game. However, it is the set pieces or stoppages in play that allow rugby teams to use different tactics. Depending upon the area of the pitch where the re-start takes place, or the time left, different tactics will come from the ball out of play. They include:

- Line out – it may be a short or long throw to the line out; there may be a dummy run or players could turn it into a maul and move forwards.
- Drop goal – when the end of the game is close and any score will win the game, some teams will position themselves for a drop goal attempt.
- Scrum – a heavy pack near to an opposition line may try to push the scrum over the line to score a try.
- Maul – if there are enough players to drive and roll the maul, it may be a tactic to either score or to encourage the opposition to bring more players into the maul, leaving gaps across the field.

Other tactics could involve changing formations at different phases of play, spreading the backs further across the field or breaking from a ruck quickly to catch the opposition off guard. Some tactics can be planned before the game, but many will be from practices and drills during training which come into play during the game.

30.2 Know the rules and regulations required in selected team sports

P2   M2

Rules and regulations in two different team sports

The rules and regulations in sport are continuously changing and evolving to improve the safety or the experience of the players and spectators. Officials are essential in applying the rules of the game and ensuring the health and safety of the individuals, and they will punish players if they break the rules or regulations. Rules encourage good sporting behaviour, help games to flow and protect players from injury, so it is important that you, and your team players, know and understand all the rules and regulations of the sport. National Governing Bodies of sport update their rules and regulations each year and issue a handbook with any changes, so you need to ensure that you keep up to date with the latest edition.

Hockey

There are two umpires used to officiate each match, with each one controlling one half of the field divided diagonally. A time keeper and record keeper assist in the decisions of the umpires.

A green card is issued as a warning; a yellow card is a temporary suspension of a player for a minimum of five minutes without substitution; and a red card indicates that the player is permanently excluded from the game with no substitute allowed.

- Each team is allowed 5 substitutes and 11 players on the field, and there is no limit to the number of substitutions during a game, though they cannot occur during a penalty corner.

- The goalkeeper may wear protective clothing, including a full-face helmet, body padding, leg guards, gloves and kickers, and can use any part of their body to deflect or propel the ball within the defensive circle.
- There is no offside rule.
- Set plays include: penalty corner; penalty stroke; penalty goal; free hits; long corner; 15m hit; sideline hit.
- If you raise the ball off the ground and the umpire decides that it is dangerous, then the opponents get a free hit from the place where the offence occurred. Dangerous play is also called when you try to play the ball above the height of the shoulders or hit the ball while it is in the air.
- Types of foul include: obstruction; advancing; back sticks; sticks; stick interference; and third-party obstruction.

If the teams are tied at the end of the game, the game proceeds to a 'tie breaker'. This usually consists of two halves totalling 15 minutes, with a sudden death, where the first team to score a goal wins. If no goal is scored, a penalty shootout will commence to determine the winner.

'England Hockey's Code of Ethics and Behaviour encapsulates all the sporting, moral and ethical principles that hockey represents. The Code is intended for all participants and disciplines within the sport. Everyone involved in the sport should promote equality of access and opportunity, fairness and respect.'

Source: www.englandhockey.co.uk
With kind permission from England Hockey

Rugby Union

There are twenty laws that govern Rugby Union, including:

- The pitch should not exceed 100m in length and 70m in width.

- There are 5m, 10m, 22m and centre lines.
- The goal is 5.6m wide and the posts 3m to the top of the bar, with a minimum height of 3.4m.
- A match is started by a kick-off, when any player may throw or kick the ball.
- Any player can tackle, hold or push an opponent holding the ball.
- Any player can take part in a scrum, ruck, maul or lineout.
- The advantage law takes precedent over most other laws as it makes play continuous.
- At the start of play, all players are onside, but during the game may find themselves offside. If a player is offside they are temporarily out of the game

There are then laws on the set plays of rucks, mauls, lineouts and scrums, a knock-on or throw forward and the kick-off and re-start kicks.

Think about it!

Apply the rules and regulations in two team sports of your choice to three different situations that may arise during a game. Particularly think about when the game is stopped by the officials and the reasons given. Also determine the role of the officials in your team sports.

Grading Tip!

In order to achieve the higher grades for the skill, techniques and tactics criteria, and the rules and regulations of two different team sports, you must explain your choices in much more detail than you did for the Pass. Give reasons why you chose your two particular team sports and ensure that you cover all the necessary criteria for each of them.

30.3 Be able to assess own performance in selected team sports

Participating in two team sports

You are required to take part in two different team sports for this outcome, and to demonstrate all the skills and techniques that you have mastered. You are expected to play a part in the tactics decided before the game. Immediately after the game you will need to write down your thoughts about your performance, assess how well you executed your skills and techniques, and identify your strengths and areas for improvement. At a later time, self-evaluate your performance again, once you have had time to think about your contribution to the team, in order to have some information to hand for a self-analysis. Ensure you do this for both team sports in which you participate.

Self-analysis – identifying strengths and areas for improvement in two team sports

Using the information gained from your participation in the two team sports, carry out a self-analysis using two different assessment methods. Consider the physiological, psychological, technical and tactical factors, highlighting how you feel you can address each of these in the future. By analysing your performance you can address the issues that may be affecting you, and make some changes to your strengths and areas where you need to improve. Analysis is even more important when you have not performed well, in order to put the correct things in place for the next game.

There are a number of assessment methods you could use in order to look at your own performance both objectively and subjectively through technology, testing, observations, interviewing, analysis and performance profiling.

Physical assessment

You need a high level of fitness to perform at your peak each week when participating in team sports. Fitness tests can be carried out to measure your health-related components of fitness – cardiovascular endurance, strength, muscular endurance, flexibility and body composition – and repeated at regular intervals to show your improvement and development.

Psychological assessment

Having the ability to concentrate, be aroused, feel confident and be motivated when performing are some of the psychological factors required to achieve success. Your motivation could be intrinsic, coming from within yourself, or extrinsic, coming from somewhere else, depending upon your direction and intensity of effort. Self-confidence will grow when you can achieve your aims and objectives which will, in turn, help you to achieve success as your performance improves.

Technical assessment

As you learn and practise your skills and techniques, they will become easier to do and more natural to you. Therefore you will need feedback from others regarding how you carry out more complex skills, by breaking down the techniques. This can be carried out by observation or video analysis. The study of biomechanics examines the forces acting on your body and analyses specific movements in order for improvements to be made.

Tactical assessment

Tactics in team sport are vital to achieve success. You, and your team members, will need to understand and carry out the tactics set out by the coach in order to perform effectively and will include team formations, set plays, phases of play and attack and defence, among others.

One form of assessment used by many public services is a SWOT analysis, which is a subjective analysis of a performance. It helps you to analyse your current strengths and weaknesses in relation to your, and your team's, performance as well as the opportunities available and the threats to your performance. The strengths and weaknesses are internal to you and your team, while the opportunities and threats relate to outside influences and barriers to the opportunities.

SWOT:

- **S**trengths – What parts of your performance went well and what skills and techniques did you perform to a high standard? Did any of the tactics work and could you use them again?
- **W**eaknesses – The parts of your performance that did not go so well or the skills and techniques that did not work. Did any of the tactics break down and therefore hand the initiative to the opposition?
- **O**pportunities – What needs to be done to make improvements for the next game? What tactics need to be practised and how can you improve your skills and techniques? What resources do you have, or need, to help in making those improvements?
- **T**hreats – The barriers that may not allow you to carry out your improvements whether it be money, time, coaching or other such problems. How could they be overcome?

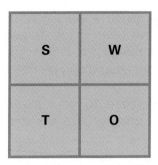

Figure 30.3 SWOT analysis can be used to assess performance

Explain and analyse the strengths and areas for improvement in two team sports

All the strengths and areas for improvement assessed must be analysed with a mind to improving future performances. You need to ensure that you include knowledge of the rules, regulations and officiating alongside the skills, techniques and tactics when referring to your strengths and areas for improvement.

Performance profiling is a way to analyse your own strengths and areas for improvement as it considers what you feel is important and will help to motivate and monitor your improvements in performance. You need to think of up to ten psychological or technical factors which are vital to your performance and rate them on a scale of 1 to 10, with 1 being the lowest and 10 being perfect. First, rate your current level of performance against each of the factors and then a level to where you would like to progress to in the next few months. Plot the results onto a chart or graph and review them at regular intervals.

Analysis of strengths and areas for improvement will lead to an evaluation of the things that are going well and things that are going wrong. From this you will need to set targets which you can formulate into a plan, then carry out the targets in training or the next match, before analysing your performance again to see if any improvements have been made. Target setting is a useful strategy for increasing motivation and confidence and can be used for short-, medium- or long-term objectives. Performance targets relate to your skills, techniques and performance in the sport, and outcome targets are concerned with the end result – if you win or not.

> ## (g) Grading Tip!
>
> To move from a Merit to Distinction in this outcome you must distinguish between a description of the reasons and a comparison and contrast of the strengths and areas for improvement in two different team sports. You also need to give a conclusion to your analysis for the top grade

Activity

Design your own performance profile for the team sport you currently play. This will enable you to assess your strengths and weaknesses and show what you feel is important in your sport. It could also improve your fitness levels and your performance in the skills and techniques required by the sport.

30.4 Be able to assess the performance of teams in selected sports

Performance analysis using different methods of assessment identifying strengths

Performance analysis must be specific to the actual sport being played and should take into account the application of the skills, the techniques performed and the different tactics used. The assessment will identify the strengths that need to be at least maintained and the weaknesses, or areas for improvement, that need to be practised and perfected by setting targets, goals aims and objectives. It may be possible to observe your team in action and provide them with evidence of their performance in a report, a witness statement or even with video analysis.

You could use objective performance data or subjective observations as two different types of assessment. Objective performance data look at your results or outcomes, such as goals scored or distance run, time in opposition half, percentage of possession and other facts from the game

Figure 30.4 Video analysis is an excellent way to assess a team performance

– often seen on your television screen during live matches – that you can analyse and make comments on. The subjective analysis requires someone to watch a performance and make notes, then give verbal and written feedback on what they saw, similar to a half-time talk or a substitution taking place.

There are also now many more fun ways of performance analysis using advanced technology and a variety of different equipment to give readings and measurements. Heart rate monitors, pedometers, video cameras and mobile devices for recording action can be coupled with software such as Kandle's 'Deja Vu' computer program, which delivers instant action replays and analysis of performances, or DartTrainer's 'Dartfish', where an overlay of a learner's performance can be directly compared with that of a world-class athlete in a split-screen mode. These really help you to review, evaluate and improve skills, techniques and tactical performances in a virtual world.

Explain and analyse strengths and areas for improvement in the development of a team

Suggestions should be made relating to the development of the team, with a justification of the suggestions in a detailed report which gives an account of the strengths and areas for improvement, and the methods the team could use to improve performance. In order for you to set aims, objectives and goals and to improve the areas for improvement, it is necessary to use SMARTER targets:

- **S**pecific – goals will be attained if they are clear and unambiguous.
- **M**easurable – this makes you accountable and allows progress to be monitored.
- **A**chievable – set goals that can be reached, to help with motivation.
- **R**ealistic – the goals need to be within your limits and without barriers.
- **T**ime constrained – using short-, medium- and long-term goals will make setting targets easier.
- **E**njoyable – if the targets are boring and do not involve a range of activities, your motivation will decrease and targets will not be achieved.
- **R**ecorded – you must monitor your progress and have the facts and figures to hand when next evaluating your performance and setting new SMARTER targets.

Grading Tip!

To gain the Distinction grade for this outcome you are required to break down each of the strengths and areas for improvement in the development of a team and analyse them in much more detail, giving reasons why you chose each of them, and finishing with a personal conclusion.

End-of-unit knowledge check

1. Define the terms 'skill' and 'technique'.
2. Why is it necessary to have rules and regulations in team sports?
3. Describe the roles and responsibilities of officials in team sports.
4. What is a SWOT analysis used for?
5. When would you use a 'performance profile'?

Grading criteria

In order to pass this unit, the evidence you present for assessment needs to demonstrate that you can meet all the learning outcomes for the unit. The criteria for a pass grade describe the level of achievement required to pass this unit.

To achieve a pass grade the evidence must show that you are able to:	To achieve a merit grade the evidence must show that, in addition to the pass criteria, you are able to:	To achieve a distinction grade the evidence must show that, in addition to the pass and merit criteria, you are able to:
P1 Describe skills, techniques and tactics required in two different team sports	**M1** Explain skills, techniques and tactics required in two different team sports	
P2 Describe the rules and regulations of two different team sports, and apply them to three different situations for each sport	**M2** Explain the application of the rules and regulations of two different team sports, in three different situations for each sport	
P3 Demonstrate appropriate skills, techniques and tactics in two different team sports		
P4 Carry out a self-analysis using two different methods of assessment identifying strengths and areas for improvement in two different team sports [RL1, RL2, RL3, RL5, CT2, IE3, IE4, EP4]	**M3** Explain identified strengths and areas for improvement in two different team sports, and make suggestions relating to personal development	**D1** Analyse identified strengths and areas for improvement in two different team sports, and justify suggestions made

To achieve a pass grade the evidence must show that you are able to:	To achieve a merit grade the evidence must show that, in addition to the pass criteria, you are able to:	To achieve a distinction grade the evidence must show that, in addition to the pass and merit criteria, you are able to:
P5 Carry out a performance analysis using two different methods of assessment, identifying strengths and areas for improvement in the development of a team in a team sport [RL1, RL5, IE3, IE4, IE6, CT4, TW2, TW4, TW6]	**M4** Explain identified strengths and areas for improvement in the development of a team in a team sport, and make suggestions relating to development of a team	**D2** Analyse identified strengths and areas for improvement in the development of a team in a team sport, and justify suggestions made

Unit 32
Instructing physical activity and exercise

Introduction

More people than ever are attending gyms, taking part in exercise sessions or entering physical activity events in an effort to stay fit, lose weight or improve their health. As everyone has individual needs, it is the job of the instructor to meet their clients' needs by providing them with safe and effective exercise sessions. The aim of this unit is for you to be able to design, plan, lead and review exercise sessions which meet the needs of different client groups. The Armed Forces have their own Physical Training Instructors (PTIs) who regularly put new recruits and serving personnel through their paces in order to keep fitness levels high. Other public services, such as the police, also have dedicated physical training instructors to run the entrance tests for new recruits, while others have their own gyms for staff to use on a regular basis.

As an instructor you will need to understand the principles of safe and effective exercise sessions and how the body adapts to training when taking part in a fitness programme. You will also require a good understanding of health screening methods and health and safety factors, which include warming up and cooling down, as well as carrying out risk assessments.

From all the knowledge gained you will be able to design an exercise programme for individual clients and then plan and lead an individual exercise session following the correct procedures. You will then be required to review the individual session and the fitness programme, obtaining feedback on your performance, enabling you to identify your strengths and areas for improvement. The unit uses a combination of theory and practical aspects to help you gain an improved understanding of working as an instructor in the fitness industry or for the uniformed public services.

Learning outcomes:

By the end of this unit, you should:

1. Know the principles of safe and effective exercise sessions.

2. Be able to design an exercise programme.

3. Be able to plan and lead an exercise session.

4. Be able to review the design of an exercise programme and leading of an exercise session.

32.1 Know the principles of safe and effective exercise sessions

`P1` `P2` `M1` `P3`

Principles and components of fitness training

In order for you to meet the needs of a client you will require a good understanding of the health-related components of fitness, and how the body adapts to training within different client groups. As an instructor you will also need to have knowledge of health screening methods and risk assessments to ensure the safe and effective delivery of the exercise sessions.

Health-related fitness is the minimum level of physical fitness that you need to keep in good health. If you have good health it is possible to lead a full and active life where the physical, cultural, mental and social aspects work well together. For this you need a balanced diet, regular exercise, plenty of rest, limited alcohol intake, to avoid social drugs and control your stress levels; in other words, live a sensible lifestyle.

The following components of fitness link to health-related fitness and are important if the human body is to work efficiently.

Aerobic endurance

Sometimes referred to as 'cardiovascular endurance' or 'stamina', this is the ability of the heart, blood and respiratory systems to supply fuel and oxygen to the muscles so that the body can work for relatively long periods of time at a steady, constant level without becoming tired.

Strength

Sometimes referred to as 'muscular strength', this is the ability to exert an external force to lift a heavy weight, or use various muscles to apply maximum force to an immovable object.

Muscular endurance

This is the ability to repeatedly exert your muscles very hard over a period of time. Without this you would suffer fatigue very quickly and your arms and legs would feel tired and heavy. It is also important for body posture, as our muscles keep us upright when we sit or stand.

Figure 32.1 Health-related components of fitness

Flexibility

This is the ability to move your joints through their full range of movement, sometimes referred to as suppleness. This is important in helping you to reduce the risk of injury and is linked to the muscular and skeletal systems.

Figure 32.2 Flexibility is often overlooked when training

Body composition

This refers to the body's physical make-up in terms of fat, muscle and body tissues measured as a percentage. An adult male should have 12–18% fat and an adult female 14–20% fat. You can change the amount of fat and increase muscle by exercise and the correct diet.

The FITT principles of planning training programmes

For your clients to improve their fitness they will need to plan an exercise programme that follows the **FITT** principles. In order to gain full benefit from the exercises you need to train in a specific way, to your needs, to improve the level of fitness. The only way to make this improvement is to overload the body systems so that they will gradually adapt to a higher level of work, but beware of doing too much too soon – the secret is little and often.

The FITT principles are:

Frequency
Intensity
Time
Type.

> ## Key terms
>
> FITT – an acronym for four of the principles of training: frequency, intensity, time and type
> Training methods – continuous, interval, circuit, Fartlek, plyometric, weight or resistance and flexibility training

Frequency – how often your clients should train

This relates to the number of times you recommend your clients train each week. Current practice points to a minimum of three times a week, giving the body time to rest after each session and spreading the sessions out over the week.

Intensity – how hard your clients will train

You will have to work the clients' body systems hard enough for them to adapt, looking at their current fitness, starting at the correct intensity and not exercising above the training thresholds.

Time – how long your clients will train for

Gradually increasing the duration of the exercise will start to overload the body, and the working heart rate level should rise. A session should start at a minimum of 20 minutes in order for the body to see any real benefit.

Type – what kind of training your clients will take part in

You should have specific exercises and activities for your clients to perform so that they can develop their skills and fitness. Variation in **training methods** will overcome boredom and lack of motivation.

If your clients follow their training programme correctly they should find that they are able to carry out the exercise much more easily as the weeks progress. This is because their bodies are adapting to the exercise and improving their performance. The long-term adaptations will strengthen the heart, making it capable of pumping more blood around the body, and will allow the lungs to get more oxygen to the muscles and increase the size and strength of the muscles (muscle hypertrophy).

> ## Activity
>
> Relate the FITT principles to an activity or sport that you participate in currently. How could you progressively overload the training that you undertake to make you fitter and more competitive?

Health and safety considerations associated with exercise programmes

Before your clients can begin to start exercising and training, it is imperative to find out if they are fit enough to participate, and whether they have any medical conditions that could affect them if they do start taking part in physical exercise. The first step is to ask them to complete a Physical Activity Readiness Questionnaire (PAR-Q) and to determine their current physical activity level.

The PAR-Q will identify those who should seek medical advice concerning the type of exercise or activity most suitable for them, and those for whom physical activity might be inappropriate.

Physical Activity Readiness Questionnaire (PAR-Q)

Many health benefits are associated with regular exercise, and the completion of the PAR-Q is a sensible first step to take if you are planning to increase the amount of physical exercise in your life.

For most people, physical activity should not pose any problem or hazard. The PAR-Q is designed to identify the small number of adults for whom physical activity might be inappropriate or those who should seek medical advice concerning the type of activity most suitable for them.

1. Do you have a bone or joint problem such as arthritis, which has been aggravated by exercise or might be made worse with exercise?	YES	NO
2. To your knowledge, do you have high blood pressure?	YES	NO
3. To your knowledge, do you have low blood pressure?	YES	NO
4 Do you have Diabetes mellitus or any other metabolic disorder?	YES	NO
5. Has your doctor ever said that you have raised cholesterol (serum level above 6.2mmol/L)?	YES	NO
6. Do you have or ever suffered a heart condition?	YES	NO
7 Have you ever felt pain in your chest when you do physical exercise?	YES	NO
8. Is your doctor currently prescribing you drugs or medication?	YES	NO
9. Have you ever suffered from shortness of breath at rest or with mild exercise?	YES	NO
10. Is there any history of Coronary Heart Disease within your family?	YES	NO
11. Do you ever feel feint, have spells of dizziness or have ever lost conciousness?	YES	NO
12. Do you currently drink more than the average amount of alcohol per week (21units for men and 14 units for women (1 unit = ½ pint of beer/cider/larger or 1small glass of wine))	YES	NO
13. Do you currently smoke?	YES	NO
14. Do you NOT currently exercise regularly (at least 3 times per week) and/or work in a job that is physically demanding.	YES	NO
15. Are you, or is there any possibility that you might be pregnant?	YES	NO
16. Do you know of any other reason why you should not participate in a programme of physical activity?	YES	NO

If you have answered YES to any of the above please give details: _____

_____

If you answered YES to one or more questions:

If you have not already done so, consult with your doctor by telephone or in person before increasing your physical activity and/ or taking a fitness appraisal. Inform your doctor of the questions that you answered 'yes' to on the PAR-Q or present your PAR-Q copy. After medical evaluation, seek advice from your doctor as to your suitability for:

1. Unrestricted physical activity starting off easily and progressing gradually, and ...

2. Restricted or supervised activity to meet your specific needs, at least on an initial basis.

If you answered NO to all questions:

If you answered the PAR-Q honestly and accurately, you have reasonable assurance of your present suitability for:

1. A graduated exercise programme

2. A fitness appraisal.

Assumption of Risk

I hereby state that I have read, understood and answered honestly the questions above. I also state that I wish to participate in activities, which may include aerobic exercise, resistance exercise and stretching. I realise that my participation in these activities involve the risk of injury and even the possibility of death. I hereby confirm that I am voluntarily engaging in an acceptable level of exercise, which has been recommended to me.

Client's Name (Print):	Trainer's Name:
Client's Signature:	Trainer's Signature:
Date:	Date:

Figure 32.3 A typical PAR-Q to be completed by all clients

In addition to the questionnaire, you will need to be aware of any of the clients' contraindications, such as asthma, injury, diabetes or other conditions that are likely to affect their ability to exercise, by conducting an interview or a short questionnaire. Then a risk assessment of the equipment and the facility that is being used for the training must to be carried out before each session to identify any hazards or risks to the clients or yourself.

To ensure the safety of your clients you will need to make them aware of the importance of wearing the correct clothing and footwear in order that they can perform to the best of their ability. Clothing should allow unrestricted movement but not be too loose, and footwear should provide grip and support as well as being tied or secured correctly. Jewellery should always be removed and long hair tied back. If there are any rules and regulations to follow then they should be obeyed at all times. Get to know the emergency procedures and health and safety procedures of the facility and equipment that you will be using. Make safety your first priority.

Grading Tip!

To upgrade from a Pass to a Merit for this outcome, you need to give more detail of the descriptions you have already carried out for P2. Give reasons why you have to carry out certain health and safety questionnaires or interviews, and why risk assessments are so important to you and your clients. You could even design your own questionnaires or risk assessments. Cover as many of the health and safety issues as you know about and ask others if they know of any more.

The importance of warm-ups and cool-downs in exercise programmes

A warm-up is carried out before taking part in exercise or training to avoid the risk of injury, prepare the body systems and activate the energy systems required for the particular activity. It generally consists of a gradual increase of intensity and could be specific to the activity that will follow, or more general if your clients are using low repetitions on resistance machines.

The functions of the warm-up are to:

- slowly increase the heart rate
- raise the breathing rate to exercise levels
- raise the body temperature
- prepare all the joints ready for exercise
- prepare the muscles
- focus the mind on the exercises to come.

There are usually three phases for a warm-up. The first one consists of pulse-raising activities, which is gentle movement and cardiovascular exercise to raise their heart rate, and includes walking, jogging or sidestepping. This is followed by mobility or flexibility activities such as rolling your shoulders, swinging your arms, bending to each side, circling hips and bending the knees. To conclude, the clients must stretch all the muscles in a slow and balanced way to improve joint mobility.

Safe stretching exercises

There are four main types of stretching used to improve flexibility:

- Static stretching, where you use your own strength to extend the limbs beyond their normal range. Hold the stretch for 10 seconds and release slowly. Rest and repeat the stretch.
- Passive stretching is done using a partner to apply an external force to

move the limb to its limit and holding it for a few seconds. Only stretch the muscle to the point when it becomes uncomfortable.

- Active stretching allows you to move rhythmically and under control to extend the stretch over 20 seconds. This should be carried out very slowly and carefully in order not to bounce in the stretch.
- PNF (proprioceptive neuromuscular facilitation) stretches are used when the muscles are relaxed, then you contract the muscle as hard as possible before stretching fully for a few seconds.

Muscles must be warm before your clients begin to stretch. You can stand, sit or lie down to carry out your stretching, and concentrate on the specific muscle groups being worked. Always repeat the stretches a number of times and follow the same pattern of starting at the neck and working down, or at the ankle and working up, so that you do not miss out any muscles.

Ask Yourself!

What kind of pulse raisers could you use in a small space?

Why do you need to stretch all the muscles before exercise?

How long should the warm-up last?

The cool-down is used to return the body to its normal state as quickly as possible, and involves exercising the whole body followed by gentle stretching. This will keep the blood flow high and remove lactic acid waste from the muscles created by the exercise. The functions of the cool-down are to return the heart rate and breathing back to normal, remove any waste products and return the muscles to their normal temperature slowly.

To begin the cool-down, let the clients go through the full stretch routine of the warm-up, but hold the stretches for a few seconds longer. Follow this with some gentle rhythmic and mobility exercises, similar to the warm-up but at a slower rate, and finally shake out the limbs and the relaxed muscles to help the blood return to the organs and help you feel relaxed.

32.2 Be able to design an exercise programme

A six-week exercise programme of activities for two contrasting clients

In order to design an exercise programme you must gather as much information about your clients as possible. After they have completed a PAR-Q, discussed their lifestyle factors, stated the specific reason for wanting to exercise and you have established their physical activity level, it is possible to plan their six-week exercise programmes of activities. Use two very contrasting clients either of different age, gender or body build to design your programmes, or they will be very similar and difficult to compare and contrast.

Each of the sessions within your exercise programme must be structured correctly and should follow the same procedures, taking into account the body's adaptations to the training as the weeks progress. Remember to take into account the specific needs of the varied client groups which you may be training, such as the elderly, the obese, or those of very differing abilities. Also, be aware of any specific barriers the client might face in adhering to, or understanding, the sessions within the programme.

Always introduce yourself and chat briefly in order to relax the client and make them feel welcome. Explain the aim and objectives of each session before starting the warm up and moving into the main content of the session. The FITT principles will apply to each session as the clients body adapts to the training programme so be aware of increasing the frequency, intensity or length of time of the exercises for each session. As a qualified instructor you should be aware of the code of ethical practice laid down by your Governing Body when dealing with clients, which will include their rights and your responsibilities in addition to following the professional standards required by your qualification.

There are many training methods that can be incorporated into the programmes.

Continuous training

Aerobic endurance training consists of either long, slow, steady distance or high-intensity continuous training. Distance training includes running, swimming, cycling, rowing and aerobics at a steady pace for a minimum of 30 minutes, while high-intensity training works for a shorter time but at up to 90% of your maximum heart rate.

Interval training

Any kind of training which uses alternate periods of very hard exercise and rest is classed as interval training. The low activity or rest periods between the repetitions of work at high speed are essential for recovery and enable the client to train for a longer period of time. The training can be any form of cardiovascular activity at a high percentage of maximum heart rate.

Circuit training

Your clients will perform a series of exercises or activities in a set order, working different muscle groups at each of the stations for a short period of time. The circuit can

be altered by increasing the time at each station, the number of repetitions carried out or the number of activities/exercises.

Fartlek training

This is a form of interval training which includes changes of speed and different terrains. It is a Swedish term meaning 'speed play' and incorporates aerobic and anaerobic fitness by walking, running or cycling for a minimum of 40 minutes. It is a favoured training method for team games as it replicates the performer over the period of participating in a game.

Plyometric training

The client performs a series of explosive movements such as leaping, bounding, skipping and jumping which puts stress on the muscles and joints to improve their muscular power. The muscles stretch and contract to produce power in order to jump higher or further.

Figure 32.4 Plyometrics is being used more frequently during training sessions

Weight training

The resistance method of training improves muscular strength and muscular endurance, depending upon the number of sets and repetitions carried out or the amount of weight used. A repetition is one movement of the weights, and a set is a number of repetitions performed one after the other, before resting and then performing another set.

Flexibility training

The client will stretch and move joints through a full range of movement to a point of resistance. There is a range of stretching exercises, including static, active, passive and proprioceptive neuromuscular facilitation (PNF) stretches to improve flexibility and reduce joint injury.

To avoid injury and to get the maximum effect from each of the training sessions within the programme, you need to ensure you carry out a warm-up before the session and a cool-down afterwards. Ensure the session is of appropriate intensity by working out your client's resting and maximum heart rates. The resting heart rate is taken when the client is calm and relaxed, preferably using a heart rate monitor for precision, and for the maximum heart rate you subtract the client's age from 220. This will allow you to calculate the training zone of your client and ensure your programme is at the correct intensity for the percentage of maximum heart rate which they will exercise at.

As a professional instructor you will be expected to be properly qualified, to treat your clients as individuals, regardless of their race, gender, age, disability, religion, ethnicity or sexual orientation, and to keep all information confidential under current legislation. You will be expected to be aware of your clients' needs and treat them with courtesy, trust, dignity and professionalism.

> ### (g) Grading Tip!
>
> Once you have designed the six-week exercise programmes for the two contrasting clients – try to use very different clients in order to be able to contrast the programmes – for the Merit grade you will need to give reasons why you chose the particular exercises for each of the clients.
>
> For the top grade it is necessary for you to suggest alternative activities or exercises from those chosen, give the strengths and weaknesses of all the activities and exercises, and contrast the two clients' programmes, giving a conclusion.

32.3 Be able to review the design of an exercise programme and leading of an exercise session

P5 M3 D2 P6 M4

Planning a safe and effective exercise session

Using your six-week exercise programme, take out one of the sessions planned and be prepared to deliver it to a client in a safe and effective manner. Determine a date, time and venue with your client for the session, then carry out risk assessments of the equipment and the facility in advance, as well as on the day of the session. You should have all the information from previous health screening procedures, such as the PAR-Q and lifestyle questionnaire, in preparation for setting an aim and objectives for the session. The target of the exercises is to make them achievable but to stretch the client and complete the objectives set. These could include flexibility, weight loss, muscle tone or cardiovascular fitness.

When considering the exercises for your client, think about those they enjoy taking part in, ensure that there are no cultural limitations and that the correct equipment is available. Your session plan should be complete, with the three main parts of warm-up, main activity and cool-down. The usual duration of a session is one hour, and the timings will vary depending upon the requirements of the client.

Make sure you work muscles in pairs, and train the large muscle groups first by carrying out the difficult exercises first and end the session working the abdominals and lower back muscles. Be early for your appointment, correctly dressed and ready to meet the client.

> ### Activity
>
> **Plan a 30-minute specific exercise session for a client without the warm-up and cool-down included. Design and complete your session to include the aim and objectives, the correct exercises and equipment required, and all the health and safety considerations. Be prepared to deliver the session at a later date as part of a complete one-hour session.**

Before the session starts you need to make last-minute checks of the equipment and the venue. Ensure that the equipment is working correctly and set up in advance, the floor is clear and clean and the temperature and ventilation are set correctly – not too hot. Also take into consideration that not all sessions will take place in a nice, warm gym. A great many training sessions take place outdoors or in a swimming pool, especially the cardiovascular fitness training, so you must be aware of all the barriers that may exist if this is the case, for instance the weather or incorrect clothing and footwear.

Explain and justify choice of activities for the planned exercise session

You will have gathered all the necessary information about your client and used this to plan the session. Were there any contraindications mentioned on the PAR-Q that would prevent your client from exercising? These include high blood pressure, diabetes, high resting heart rate, a history of heart disease, angina and any joint conditions. Have you considered all the components of fitness and principles of training and taken health and safety factors into consideration?

> ### Think about it!
>
> Why did you choose the specific exercises and activities for your client in the planned session? What activities did you use for the warm-up and cool-down and why? Give reasons why you chose each individual activity and which of the components of fitness you are hoping to exercise. Ensure that your aim and objectives will be met, otherwise the session is pointless.

Deliver a safe and effective exercise session with support or independently

Using the session plan completed in the previous activity, you are now required to extend it to a full hour and include the warm-up and cool-down so that you may lead a client through the safe and effective exercises designed in the programme. Ensure that you go through all the checks mentioned in the planning stage and be prepared to meet your client. Here is a checklist of points you will need to consider.

- Be early for the session.
- Ensure that you are dressed correctly.
- Meet your client and introduce yourself.
- Talk through health and safety procedures – for example, fire and first aid.
- Ask if the client has any injuries or illness before they take part.
- Check that they are dressed appropriately.
- Ask if they have eaten recently.
- Explain about drinking water or a sports drink throughout the session.
- Show the client your session plan and what you expect from them.
- Mention the main aim and objectives of the session.
- The session can now start with the warm-up.

Throughout the session you need to communicate with the client, either verbally or through signs and body language, and give instructions if required. You may be required to carry out a demonstration if the client does not understand what you are asking them to do. Observe and correct any poor techniques while constantly motivating the client through all the exercises of the session. Don't forget that if any injury occurs at any time, or the client shows signs of fatigue, you must stop the session immediately. If any exercise seems too difficult or too easy, you may need to modify it accordingly.

At the end of the session, once the client has cooled down, you need to ask questions about the session in order that you can review and make necessary changes to

Figure 32.5 Delivering a safe session for a client

the next session and even to the overall programme. When the client has given their details on what they enjoyed the most about the session, whether it was the correct intensity and if they felt the aim and objectives were achieved, you can write down your self-evaluation. Check that you leave the equipment in working order and the venue as you found it.

32.4 Be able to plan and lead an exercise session

Review of own performance in the designing, planning and delivering of the exercise session

Physical activity and exercise is linked to beneficial effects on arthritis, heart disease, lung disease, cancer, diabetes, obesity and falls and fractures in older people. All these conditions threaten an adult's ability to function by themselves, and now exercise is shown to be associated with a reduced risk, or slower progression, of several age-related conditions, as well as improvements in overall health in older age. Therefore, your clients will not only be young people trying to get fit, but also those of a more mature age who wish to remain active until much later in life. Designing, planning and delivering exercise sessions will need to be reviewed for all members of society, regardless of their age.

There are various methods of gaining evaluative feedback at the end of your exercise session and from the design and plan of the exercise programme itself. One of the most important sources of feedback is your client, immediately after each session and at the end of the programme, who can give you valuable information. This can then be followed up at a later date by interviewing your client and assessing the programme and the individual sessions in order to design and plan the next programme.

You need to ask them a number of questions, including:

- Did the programme meet their aims and objectives?
- Which exercises did they enjoy and which did they not enjoy?
- How did they feel immediately afterwards and the following day?
- Did they notice any improvement of any kind?
- Which exercises did they find the most useful?
- What improvements could be made to the sessions or programme?

Next you must carry out a self-evaluation by answering the same questions as your client, to see if there are any similarities or any glaring contrasts which would need to be addressed immediately. The feedback will help you to improve your performance as well as that of your client. There may also have been an observer, a trainer or someone else watching your session, who may also be able to provide you with valuable verbal or written feedback.

With all the feedback information collected and collated, you can now plan the next set of sessions to be included in the design of the next training programme for your client. Ensure that overload and progression are included, use the FITT principles (mentioned earlier in this unit), and make the necessary changes to keep it fun, interesting and to maintain their motivation. Set the client SMARTER targets so that you can monitor their performance.

Another way to review your performance, your design of an exercise programme and the leading of the session is to carry out a **SWOT analysis**, which will identify your strengths and areas for improvement and improve you as a physical activity trainer and as a professional. SWOT analysis involves you analysing.

Key term

SWOT analysis – an acronym for Strengths, Weaknesses, Opportunities and Threats

- **S**trengths – the parts of your design for the exercise programme, the planning, delivery and performance of the exercise session that went well and you will use again.
- **W**eaknesses (areas for improvement) – any areas which did not go as planned that you will need to change or discard for the next session.
- **O**pportunities – further exercises or ideas you could put into a future session to make it more intense, interesting or rewarding.
- **T**hreats – possible barriers to your next exercise programme or the running of an exercise session.

In order to improve your skills and performance as a physical activity and exercise instructor, you need to continue with your professional development by taking the time out to watch other

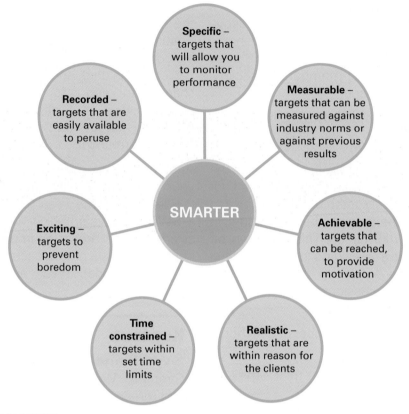

Figure 32.6 SMARTER targets

instructors delivering exercise sessions, register on training courses, take further qualifications and attend conferences. The fitness industry grows daily and there is an ever-increasing need for competent and qualified fitness trainers and instructors either working in local authorities or private providers, as well as personal trainers for individual clients. The uniformed public services will always require personnel with such skills to get new recruits into shape and to keep the present staff at the required fitness levels.

End-of-unit knowledge check

1. FITT is a mnemonic. What does it stand for?
2. Why does a client need to complete a PAR-Q?
3. What are the four types of stretching?
4. What is a contraindication and why will it prevent you from exercising?
5. Why are physical activity and exercise important to the public services?

Grading criteria

In order to pass this unit, the evidence you present for assessment needs to demonstrate that you can meet all the learning outcomes for the unit. The criteria for a pass grade describe the level of achievement required to pass this unit.

To achieve a pass grade the evidence must show that you are able to:	To achieve a merit grade the evidence must show that, in addition to the pass criteria, you are able to:	To achieve a distinction grade the evidence must show that, in addition to the pass and merit criteria, you are able to:
P1 Describe the principles of fitness training		
P2 Describe the health and safety considerations associated with exercise programmes and sessions	**M1** Explain the health and safety considerations associated with exercise programmes and sessions	
P3 Describe the importance of warm-up and cool-down in exercise programmes and sessions		
P4 Design a six-week exercise programme for two selected contrasting clients [IE2, IE3, IE4, CT1, CT3, RL2, SM3]	**M2** Explain choice of activities for exercise programmes for selected clients	**D1** Justify choice of activities for exercise programmes for selected clients, suggesting alternative activities
P5 Plan a safe and effective exercise session [IE2, IE3, IE4, CT1, CT3, RL2, SM3]	**M3** Explain choice of activities for the planned exercise session	**D2** Justify choice of activities for the planned exercise session and suggest alternative activities

To achieve a pass grade the evidence must show that you are able to:	To achieve a merit grade the evidence must show that, in addition to the pass criteria, you are able to:	To achieve a distinction grade the evidence must show that, in addition to the pass and merit criteria, you are able to:
P6 Deliver a safe and effective exercise session, with tutor support [CT5, CT6, RL6, TW3, TW4, TW5, TW6, EP4, EP5]	**M4** Independently deliver a safe and effective exercise session	
P7 Review own performance in the designing of exercise programmes and the planning and delivery of the exercise session, identifying strengths and areas for improvement [CT4, RL1, RL2, RL3, RL4, RL5, RL6, EP4]		

Unit 33
Volunteering in public services

Introduction

Most public services employers, particularly the uniformed services, are placing more and more importance on volunteering. There is now a variety of volunteer roles within the public services, such as Special Constables in the Police Service, and many employers will expect applicants to have carried out some form of volunteering before they apply to the services.

It is therefore most important that anyone considering a career in the public services should have some experience of volunteering. This unit will help you to gain that experience as part of your BTEC Level 3 National Public Services Diploma.

You may not be aware of how many opportunities there are for volunteering. These can range from helping out at Cadets or visiting the elderly, to becoming a magistrate in court! By completing this unit you will learn about the many opportunities available and the different skills you can gain.

Figure 33.1 RNLI Volunteer Lifeguards

Learning outcomes:

By the end of this unit, you should:

1. Understand the importance of volunteering in public services.

2. Know the different types of voluntary work available.

3. Understand the skills required for voluntary work.

4. Be able to undertake voluntary work.

33.1 The importance of volunteering in public services

What is volunteering?

Volunteering usually means doing work without getting paid for it, although you may be paid expenses for any costs you incur. There are many volunteering opportunities available, both at home and abroad. When considering volunteering you should choose something which interests you, or which is related to the area of work that you wish to enter. For example, if you love animals you could volunteer to help out at your local veterinary practice, pet shop, or at a stables or kennels. If you enjoy working with children you can volunteer by helping with Beavers, Brownies, Cubs or Scouts, helping children to read, hospital visiting, fundraising for children's charities and much more. If you are working directly with children then you will probably need to have a Criminal Records Bureau check – voluntary organisations will usually organise this for you, but it can take some time to process so you need to remember to allow plenty of time to arrange this when thinking of applying to do voluntary work.

If you are hoping to join the Police or Fire Service, there are some specific volunteering roles available which may give you the experience and skills that these services are looking for. For instance, the Police Specials are a voluntary police constabulary that work alongside regular police officers and have exactly the same powers and uniform – the only difference is that they do not get paid. Many Fire and Rescue Services have cadet schemes where volunteer helpers are always welcome.

Why volunteer?

There are many reasons why people choose to volunteer:

- To make a difference – many people become volunteers because they want to make a difference in the community or society.
- To help others who are less fortunate than yourself – there are many people in society who need help from others.
- To support an organisation whose cause you think is worthwhile – this could be a charity or group which you have a connection with or which you just feel is a worthy cause to support.
- Many celebrities carry out some voluntary work, such as raising funds, hospital visiting etc. in their spare time because they 'wish to give something back to society'.

Figure 33.2 David Beckham is involved with many charities including 'Help for Heroes'

Case Study

There are few people in the music industry who have the presence of Bono. The Irish frontman of U2 knows no limitations when it comes to fighting poverty and hunger, and is constantly in direct contact with world leaders and policy makers in his quest to make the world a better place.

Bono was inspired to get involved in charity work after seeing The Secret Policeman's Ball in 1979. In 1986 he helped organise Amnesty International's Conspiracy Of Hope tour alongside Sting, who was one of the Secret Policeman's Ball performers seen by Bono, Peter Gabriel, Lou Reed and Bryan Adams. He also got involved in the Band Aid and Live Aid projects which were organised by Bob Geldof – another Secret Policeman's Ball performer, and later helped Geldof organise the 2005 Live 8 project.

Bono has received three nominations for the Nobel Peace Prize, and was knighted in 2007.

Source: www.looktothestars.org/celebrity/26-bono
With kind permission of www.looktothestars.org

So there are many good reasons for volunteering. However, there are many benefits that you, yourself, can gain by carrying out voluntary work. For instance, you may:

- gain important new skills and experience
- develop existing skills
- make connections that can lead to a job or career
- make new friends
- gain self-confidence and self-esteem
- have fun
- work with different people and increase your awareness of **diversity**
- gain work experience
- become more active and fitter
- feel needed and useful
- see more of your community – or even the world!

Voluntary work is also a good way of '**networking**', which means you meet new contacts and people who may be useful to you later when you are starting out in your career.

Volunteering also lets you try out a potential career area to see if this is something you would enjoy doing full time. You can use the experience and skills you gain from volunteering to prove to a future employer that you can work hard and do a job well. This is particularly important if you are applying for a job in the uniformed public services.

Activity

Carry out some research to find examples of celebrities who carry out voluntary work.

Key terms

Diversity – this word is often used in connection with equal opportunities – it means a variety or mixture

Networking – the practice of building up or maintaining informal relationships, especially with people whose friendship could bring business or job opportunities

Case Study

Elibinayi Nzayisenga, BA Events management, University of Greenwich

What activities have you been involved with as a volunteer?
I have volunteered for some events and I also volunteer for a charity shop owned by Greenwich and Bexley Hospice as a shop assistant.

What made you get involved in volunteering?
I wanted to do something good, which is why I volunteer for the hospice, and I also wanted to gain experience in my field of study, hence the events volunteering.

What has been the best thing about your volunteering so far?
The lessons I've learnt and the knowledge that I am doing something to help others. I have also met some great people that I will cherish.

What has been the most challenging aspect of your volunteering?
Time management. Balancing my time to fit everything in.

Figure 33.3 Elibinayi Nzayisenga, BA Events management, University of Greenwich

What do you feel are the benefits of volunteering?
Experience, the reward of knowing that you are doing something good.

In what ways has your volunteering affected the development of your skills?
I have seen first hand how events are organised and got to understand the planning stages in my text book. I have learnt to work under pressure and a lot of customer service skills like patience. I have also learnt to use a till and how a shop is run.

What would you say to other students about volunteering?
Even if you don't want to give your time for helping reasons, volunteering looks good on CVs and it also teaches you a lot of valuable skills.

Source: www.gre.ac.uk/students/get/volunteering/case-studies

Volunteering is good for you

If the above doesn't convince you that volunteering is a good idea, you may be interested to know that a survey carried out by the Carers' Association discovered that:

- Nearly half of all volunteers (47%) say volunteering improves their physical fitness.
- A quarter (25%) who volunteer more than five times a year say it helps them lose weight.
- Half of people (48%) who have volunteered for more than two years say volunteering makes them less depressed.
- Up to 63% of people say volunteering helps them feel less stressed.

Source: www.carersinformation.org.uk

Grading Tip!

To achieve P2 you should talk about the benefits to be gained by the individual by carrying out voluntary work. Mention the benefits that are listed above and explain a little about each of them.

Key term

Mentor – somebody, usually older and more experienced, who advises and guides a younger, less experienced person

Case Study

Sam's Story
18-year-old Sam from Surrey has benefited from the support of a volunteer **mentor**. Two years ago she was involved in a shoplifting racket, and a year later she became pregnant. Sam's mentor was someone who she could talk to and helped her to make important decisions and get her life in order.

Sam says,

'My mentor helped me because she wasn't like a social worker as I knew she was really interested in me. She didn't have to be there, she was just there because she wanted to be.'

Sam, and other young people like her, have benefited from mentors because they are seen as non-judgmental. It means young people can often talk to their mentors about things they can't talk to their family about

Source: www.timebank.org.uk/ mediacentre/press_release_details. php?id=50

Why is volunteering so important in the public service sector?

There are many deserving causes that require additional finance and resources. Governments and other organisations try to meet everyone's needs, but there are lots of demands for public taxpayers' money and it's impossible to do everything that needs to be done.

For this reason many organisations have to rely on volunteers to help them to achieve their aims. Some organisations rely completely on unpaid volunteers and are funded solely by donations from the public. These include organisations such as the Royal National Lifeboat Institution, search and rescue services such as Mountain Rescue, and many other charities.

Other organisations are partly funded by money from the government but then have to rely on public donations for their main source of income. Organisations such as the Citizens' Advice Bureau and the Samaritans fall into this category.

Ask Yourself!

Can you think of any public service organisations where volunteers are used?

Some organisations employ paid employees, but also use unpaid volunteers to work alongside them, often carrying out the same roles. The Police Service is one organisation where this happens. Police 'Specials' are unpaid volunteers who work alongside regular police officers, carrying out many similar duties. The Specials have exactly the same powers as the paid officers.

Volunteers provide a number of things that are valuable to many organisations. Some volunteers act as fundraisers. Others provide their time, skills and expertise at no cost to the organisation. Volunteers can be called upon to respond to emergencies or to provide new ideas, or sometimes just to be an extra pair of hands to help out.

Because volunteering is so important to the public service sector, employers will look for applicants with volunteering experience when they are recruiting paid staff. If an applicant has experience of voluntary work on their CV, potential employers will recognise that this person is someone who is willing to help others, and this is exactly the type of person they are looking for.

Grading Tip!

To achieve P1 you should explain why volunteering is so important in the public services sector. You should explain about lack of public funding, resources and manpower. Provide examples.

To upgrade to M1 you should focus on two or three different public service organisations that use volunteers (e.g. hospitals, schools, police), and you should examine how the organisations benefit from this. Discuss the different roles that are carried out by volunteers in these organisations and describe what could happen if there were no volunteers. Also discuss why it is important that anyone who is hoping to go into a public services career should carry out voluntary work.

To achieve the D1 grade you could carry out research relating to organisations that use volunteers (many charitable organisations will have their own websites and also printed literature that you can send for). You could discuss possible barriers to volunteering, i.e. what would prevent a person from carrying out voluntary work. This may include lack of time, lack of motivation, not knowing how to apply for voluntary work, etc.

Case Study

The photograph shows Uniformed Public Services students taking part in a sponsored 24-hour 'Run, Ride, Rowathon'. Students gave up their time to row, run and cycle for a period of 24 hours non-stop to raise money for charity.

Figure 33.4 University of Derby college students taking part in a 24-hour 'Run, Ride, Rowathon' for the 'Help for Heroes' charity

Volunteers are involved in many different public sector settings, in schools, police stations, hospitals, prisons and in people's own homes.

The courts are another area where volunteers are used regularly. Victim Support is an agency which trains volunteers to assist victims of crime and witnesses to crimes when they have to attend court. Even the magistrates in the courts are usually unpaid volunteers! There are many other important volunteering roles in the public services sector, such as school governors and

Ask Yourself!

Did you know that anyone (except certain people who are disqualified) over the age of 18 can apply to volunteer as a magistrate?

representatives on Youth Offending Panels. All of these voluntary roles are unpaid, but you will usually receive expenses for such things as travel, telephone calls and postage where appropriate.

33.2 Volunteering opportunities

Assignment tip

P3 You should talk about a range of different types of voluntary work.

M2 You should compare a minimum of two different types of voluntary work.

D2 You should appraise a minimum of two different types of voluntary work.

When considering voluntary work you can choose an area of work which really interests you. If you like animals, you could help out at a local stables or kennels. Many kennels depend on volunteers to keep the dogs happy and well exercised. Remember, exercising the dogs will help you to improve your fitness too!

You may have a particular charity that you would like to raise funds or work for. Or, if you like children, there are many suitable volunteering opportunities – helping out in an after-school club, or helping out with groups like 'Brownies', for example. You will usually need to have a CRB (Criminal Records Bureau) check, as mentioned earlier.

The following is a list of some of the things that volunteers and volunteer groups can do to help others. There are many others:

- Provide food for hungry people.
- Help the homeless.
- Find clothes for those who need them.
- Make neighbourhoods safer.
- Protect wildlife and natural areas.
- Help care for pets and other animals.
- Speak up for people who are unable to speak for themselves.
- Visit the elderly.
- Help to find cures for diseases.
- Help people learn to read or do better in school.
- Preserve buildings or monuments.
- Help to raise funds.
- Join the Police Specials.
- Become a magistrate.
- Become a Samaritan.

You can find local volunteering opportunities by visiting your local library or by contacting your local Volunteer Bureau, which is an agency dedicated to providing volunteers in the community.

Case Study

Volunteers have been helping out in the recent earthquake disaster in Haiti. Voluntary organisations, such as the Red Cross, have been sending workers and supplies such as kitchen kits, shelter kits, personal hygiene kits, blankets and containers for storing drinking water.

As well as distributing vital supplies, the Red Cross is providing medical aid and water for survivors.

Source: www.redcross.org.uk

What sort of voluntary work can I do?

There are no qualifications or other requirements to be a voluntary worker; all you need is to be able to provide some of your time and dedication to your chosen cause. Some volunteer positions do require some training, which they will usually provide free of charge. This will also look very good on your CV!

Voluntary work can be in your local youth club, community centre, mother and toddler group, hospital, hospice, charity office... the list is endless. You will probably gain the most benefit if you choose an area of work that interests you. If you find an opportunity that you are interested in, you should find out as much as you can about it. Many voluntary organisations will have a volunteer manager or coordinator and they should be able to give you a good explanation of what your role will be. If you are under 18 years of age, you do need to check that you will be allowed to do the voluntary work of your choice.

Case Study

Dan and Adam visited the Vitalise Skylarks organisation as students on the BTEC Level 3 National Diploma Course in National Public Services, to spend a week helping people with disabilities to have a holiday break.

Adam says, 'We really didn't know what to expect. None of us had had any experience of being with people with disabilities and we were all fairly nervous and apprehensive about the visit. We spent a week each assigned to a guest who uses a wheelchair and it was an amazing experience. I never expected to enjoy it so much as I did.' Dan says, 'Working with these people really opened my eyes – it was an incredible experience – they were all so much fun. We plan to go back to do it again in our own time as we enjoyed it so much.'

What time can you spare?

When considering what volunteering activity to do, you should think about how much time you have to spare. How big a commitment are you willing to make? How much of your day, week, month or year do you want to spend on volunteer activities? Are you looking for a long-term commitment or just a one-off event?

For example:

- If you have a couple of hours each week, you could visit people in hospital or at a home for the elderly.
- If you have several weeks to spend volunteering, you could plan a bigger project, such as helping out at a summer club for children.
- What skills do you have already? Are you a good organiser? If so, you could use your skills to organise a fundraising event for a charity of your choice.

It is advisable to think long and hard about the type of volunteering work that you would like to do.

Where do I start?

If you wish to offer your time to any organisation, the first thing you should do is contact them directly. Most organisations – again, especially those dealing with children – will ask that you provide a CRB check. This is so that it can be demonstrated that you are not a risk to children, the elderly, or any other group which may be categorised as vulnerable.

You should remember to arrange your CRB check early on so that you can commence volunteering as soon as possible. The law says that you must not start work with children until the check has been made.

The following section will give you some ideas about the different volunteering opportunities that may be available to you. Much will depend upon where you live. You should start to make enquiries about the opportunities that are available to you in your area.

Gap Year Volunteering – Volunteer Work Abroad

Choose a volunteer gap year and make a difference! Many of the organisations that gap year students volunteer to work with are charities. The work they do can range from sustainable development projects to conservation to community health initiatives. Because they are charities, the money you pay to go with them will often be in the form of a donation (they usually suggest the minimum they require), and it is up to you to raise the money in any way you fancy. This means that the voluntary work you do for them and the money you raise is all going towards fulfilling the aims of each gap-year organisation.

Deciding to join a voluntary project abroad or in the UK on your gap year will most likely result in you spending time with like-minded people, doing something you believe in, learning new skills, developing your confidence *and* improving that CV!

Source: www.gapwork.com/ volunteering.shtml

Working with animals

If you enjoy working with animals there is a range of volunteering opportunities available to you. You could offer to help out at a local kennels, stables, cattery or animal sanctuary.

Working with children or young people

There are many volunteering opportunities which involve working with young people. Many organisations – especially those providing services for children – will have a need for volunteers who are good with children and can have a positive influence on them. Community groups, youth clubs and other organisations which exist to offer help and support to young people could be at the top of your list when it comes to deciding what type of voluntary work you wish to do.

There are also playgroups and toddler groups, nurseries and crèches. Other groups include music groups, dance and gymnastics clubs, arts and crafts groups, language groups and many others. Some of these are run privately, while others are run by the local authority. Many of them will welcome help from volunteers once the appropriate criminal record checks have been done.

Youth groups such as Brownies, Scouts, Girl Guides and youth clubs are all run mainly by volunteers. Without people who are willing to give up their time for no pay, such groups would cease to exist. Volunteers are always needed to give up some of their time to help out.

Reservists

The British Army, Royal Navy and the Royal Air Force all have reservist schemes where civilians can join and train to be part of the armed forces on a part-time basis. Reservists can be called up to fight on the front line. Although classed as volunteers, reservists do usually get paid a fee, receive a uniform and expenses.

Police Specials

Special Constables are part-time volunteer officers who have all the same powers as regular police officers. Volunteering as a Special gives you the chance to give something back to your community while learning useful life skills. Police Specials provide a vital link between regular police officers and the community.

If you are successful in applying to become a Police Special you will receive full training, will have a similar uniform to that worn by regular police officers, and will have exactly the same powers as regular officers. You will need to give a minimum of four hours of your time each week, but, in return, you will gain the valuable life skills that the uniformed services are looking for when interviewing applicants.

You can apply to become a Special once you are 18 years of age. Every police force in this country has a Special Constabulary and the duties of a Special Constable can vary from area to area.

Figure 33.5 Volunteer Special Constables on duty

Cadet schemes

Most of the uniformed services have their own cadet schemes. Depending where you live there may be Fire Service Cadets, Police Cadets, RAF Cadets, Army Cadets and Navy Cadets. You may already be a serving cadet. Such schemes are usually run by serving officers and volunteer helpers. By offering your time and services to help as a volunteer, you could gain valuable experience and skills before applying to the service of your choice.

Helping the elderly

There are a number of ways in which you can carry out voluntary work to help the elderly. Organisations such as 'Help the Aged' recruit volunteers to visit the housebound elderly in their own home or care home. Volunteers would need to be checked and vetted and you would need to carry some identification to show to the person you are visiting. There are also other agencies such as Volunteer Bureaux where you can register to do this type of work and they will arrange for you to visit someone, usually for an hour each week. Priority is given to those who live alone and/or have no family contact.

Hospital volunteering

There are plenty of hospital volunteering opportunities for volunteers to help out in local hospitals across the country. In addition to supporting patients, you could also help out in hospital shops or cafés.

Some hospital shops and cafés are open on Saturdays and Sundays, so these roles are ideal for anyone who can only volunteer for a couple of hours on a weekend, as little as once a fortnight or once a month. You can also volunteer with a friend.

There are many reasons to volunteer at a hospital. People who are in hospital and dealing with the stress of illness really appreciate the company and assistance volunteers offer them. When you work with children, it can be especially rewarding. You can brighten their day and give their parents a much-needed break at the same time. You could also gain a lot from hospital volunteering, particularly if you are considering a career in the Paramedics Service.

Working with people with special needs

Many volunteers work with people who have disabilities or other special needs. This can involve accompanying people on shopping trips, or helping with care so that permanent carers can take a break. There are also charitable organisations that run centres where people with special needs can take a holiday or respite care. These centres rely on volunteers to assist the paid staff and ensure that the guests enjoy the time that they spend there. The type of skills and experience you would be likely to acquire doing this type of work would be valued by many employers.

St John's Ambulance Service

Volunteers are trained in first aid to treat all sorts of injuries ranging from headaches to heart attacks. They use these skills to provide first aid treatment at a wide variety of public events.

Over half of St John Ambulance's 43,000 volunteers are under the age of 18. Youth leaders play a crucial part in the development of thousands of young people by broadening their horizons and helping them to realise their potential.

Rescue services

Figure 33.6 Mountain Rescue volunteers in action

There are many different rescue services in this country but they all (apart from the statutory Fire and Rescue Services) have one thing in common. They all rely on volunteers and voluntary donations to ensure provision of the service. Services include the Mountain Rescue, Cave Rescue and the Royal National Lifeboat Institution.

Conservation projects

Are you interested in the outdoors and preserving the countryside? Many conservation projects are run and funded solely by volunteers. Voluntary work may include spending a day picking up litter from trails or clearing out a pond or canal area. Other tasks could include repairing walls and fences.

Charity shop volunteers

Many of the larger charities have their own shops in high streets around the country. These shops sell second-hand items that are donated by the public, and they are mainly run by volunteers, although they are usually managed by a paid employee of the charity.

Charity fundraising

Thousands of volunteers carry out fundraising events for their chosen charities every single day. Charitable organisations rely on voluntary donations as their main source of funding. Fundraising can take many forms – ranging from standing in a street collecting with a tin, to jumping out of a plane with a parachute! Sponsored events, such as marathons, swimming, walking, and even waxing legs or chests are good ways of raising quite a lot of money. You could volunteer to organise such an event yourself, or you could help out at an organised event, acting as a steward, running a stall, selling raffle tickets and so on.

Activity

Make a list of all the different ways you can think of to raise money for charity.

Grading Tip!

To achieve P3 you should write about several different types of voluntary work and explain a little about the work and what would be involved.

To achieve the M2 grade you should look at the different types of voluntary work. You should explain what the work would involve and then compare the different volunteering activities by looking at what commitment of time will be involved, what skills may be required, and anything else you would need to consider before undertaking the activity.

For the D2 grade you should assess the different volunteering opportunities and evaluate the skills and qualities required to carry these out. Carry out some self-evaluation to see what types of work you would enjoy, what skills you already possess and what you may be good at doing.

33.3 The skills and qualities required for voluntary work

Different kinds of voluntary work will require certain skills and qualities. There are generic skills, which may be needed for a wide range of voluntary work, and then there are specific skills, which would only be required for certain kinds of volunteering. In this section we will look at these skills in some detail.

When you apply to the Uniformed Public Services you will be asked to give examples of when and how you have demonstrated certain skills and qualities. Having carried out voluntary work, you should be able to relate to this work and give the necessary examples.

Qualities

Some of the qualities for voluntary work are general qualities, which would be needed for any type of volunteering. These include honesty, commitment, reliability, cheerfulness and empathy.

- Honesty – this is an obvious requirement for any volunteering activity. Many volunteers are trusted to be allowed into people's homes. Also, if you have organised a fundraising event you would be responsible for making sure that all the money raised is collected and passed to the relevant charity.
- Commitment – this is one of the most important qualities required by volunteers. Being committed means doing what you say you will do, not giving up on a task until you've completed it, and not letting people down.
- Reliability – this goes along with commitment. People need to know that they can rely on you to carry out your part of the task.
- Empathy – being able to show empathy means being able to show some understanding of another person's problems. Being empathetic can mean listening to someone, being sympathetic and understanding, but not patronising or condescending.

Skills

As with qualities, some of the skills required for voluntary work are general skills, which would be needed for any type of volunteering.

Communication skills

Good communication skills will be essential for anyone who is considering volunteering in any situation. There are many reasons for this. If working with children or the elderly, or people with special needs, the way you communicate with them is extremely important, and will need to be adapted in order to suit the particular situation.

Some of the time spent volunteering, particularly with elderly people, may simply involve sitting listening to them talk. Many elderly people love to reminisce about their youth, and young people may be surprised to hear about the lives they have led and the things they have done. This can be a two-way process where both people benefit and gain something from the experience.

If collecting for charity, volunteers need to be polite and friendly at all times when communicating with members of the public, otherwise they will just walk away and you'll be left with an empty tin!

Teamwork

Most volunteering activities will involve teamwork. Teamwork is extremely important in most situations, but especially where people are giving up their free time without being paid. All members rely on one another and everyone needs to contribute and pull their weight to share the workload. Often, volunteers need to encourage and support each other or they will soon become discouraged and disillusioned, and will give up on the volunteering.

Leadership

Leadership skills are required by many employers, particularly the uniformed public services. Volunteering is a really good way to acquire some leadership skills. Good leaders usually have a number of qualities, and these are often the same qualities that can be found in people who volunteer successfully:

- charisma
- embracing responsibility
- altruism
- enthusiasm
- assertiveness
- consistency
- sense of humour
- experience.

Organisational skills

Many volunteering activities require some form of organising. When planning and arranging your volunteering activity, you may need to apply and go through a particular process. This will mean you will need to be fairly organised. When you start to carry out volunteering work, you may be working to a rota, along with other volunteers. You will definitely need to be organised so that you turn up for volunteering at the agreed time. If you fail to turn up, you could be letting down not only the rest of your team, but if working with vulnerable people, they could also be seriously affected.

Time management

Skills in time management are necessary in any type of employment. Punctuality is an essential requirement in any uniformed public service. Volunteering could help you to develop your time-management skills

Problem-solving skills

It would be very easy to develop your problem-solving skills by doing some voluntary work. If you choose to organise a charity event, you may come across all sorts of problems that need to be overcome. You may need to find ways to obtain prizes for a raffle or tombola, or you may need to think of ways to obtain sponsorship for an event. You may find yourself having to think 'out of the box' to solve some of your problems.

Administration skills

Many voluntary activities will require some administration work of some kind. You may need to send out letters to local businesses to ask for sponsorship, or produce posters, leaflets or tickets. You may need to keep records, use a database or produce a spreadsheet. All of these tasks would help you to develop your administration skills which could come in very useful in later employment.

Specific skills

Certain types of voluntary work may demand particular skills. For example, any of the following skills could be required for different kinds of work or activity: driving, cooking, computer skills, sign language, physical fitness, first aid.

How can you demonstrate these skills?

For the P4 grade you will need to prove that you have demonstrated a number of the above skills. How can you do this? Think of all the things you do in your life, such as studying at college, working part-time, looking after younger brothers or sisters or relatives, socialising. How many of the above skills or qualities do you think you have already demonstrated when doing these things? Think about the activities you do on your course when taking part in units such as Outdoor Activities, Team Development or Team Leadership. Which skills do you use?

> **Ask Yourself!**
>
> **Which skills or qualities do you think you have already demonstrated?**

> **g** **Grading Tip!**
>
> To achieve P4 you should identify areas of your life where you have used different skills. Keep a log or diary to record these.
>
> To achieve the M4 grade you should not only demonstrate the skills which you would need for volunteering, but you should also write some notes to explain in detail which skills are needed for certain types of voluntary work, and why.

33.4 Carrying out voluntary work

 P5

Once you have decided what volunteering work you would like to do, you need to find out how to go about it!

If you are considering working locally you could contact your local Volunteer Centre, which will try to organise this for you (see below). Or, if you want to do your voluntary work at a particular hospital or home for the elderly, for example, you could write a letter to the manager stating your interest. You may be asked to go for an interview, in which case you should treat this like any job interview. Any volunteer work provider will need to be sure that the volunteers they appoint will be honest and trustworthy individuals. The way you present yourself at the interview is therefore very important.

Visit your nearest volunteer centre. Volunteer centres coordinate and advertise volunteering opportunities in your area. You can find your nearest volunteering centre on the www.do-it.org website. You can also search thousands of opportunities and apply online using the www.do-it.org database. You select the type of volunteering you are interested in and enter your postcode for a list of opportunities in your area.

Find out about community projects being run by your local council – contacting your local council may be a useful way to find out about community projects in your area. You can also visit your local library, which will have information about local groups, charities and any seasonal opportunities.

The direct.gov website gives details of lots of different ways to volunteer, including how to volunteer for the 2012 Olympic Games. The website also gives lots of other useful information and advice for anyone looking for volunteer work.

Grading Tip!

In order to achieve P5 you need to undertake some type of voluntary work of your choice. There is no set length of time for this period of voluntary work, but you should discuss this with your tutor who will advise what would be appropriate. You should keep a record, i.e. log or diary of the work you do, and also, for grade P4 remember that you need to note which skills you use while carrying out the work.

End-of-unit knowledge check

1. Why do BTEC Level 3 National Public Services students need to do some voluntary work?
2. Name some of the benefits a volunteer can gain from doing voluntary work.
3. Identify five different volunteer roles.
4. Name three skills required for volunteering.
5. Give three examples of how the Uniformed Public Services use volunteer roles.

Grading criteria

In order to pass this unit, the evidence you present for assessment needs to demonstrate that you can meet all the learning outcomes for the unit. The criteria for a pass grade describe the level of achievement required to pass this unit.

To achieve a pass grade the evidence must show that you are able to:	To achieve a merit grade the evidence must show that, in addition to the pass criteria, you are able to:	To achieve a distinction grade the evidence must show that, in addition to the pass and merit criteria, you are able to:
P1 Explain why volunteering is important in the public services [IE, CT]	**M1** Analyse the importance of volunteering in the public service sector	**D1** Evaluate the importance of volunteering in the public service sector
P2 Discuss the benefits to be gained from volunteering [IE, RL]		
P3 Identify the different types of voluntary work available [CT]	**M2** Compare and contrast the different types of voluntary work available	**D2** Appraise the different types of voluntary work available
P4 Demonstrate skills required for voluntary work [CT, RL, EP]	**M3** Explain in detail the skills required for voluntary work	
P5 Carry out voluntary work [EP, SM, TW]		

Unit 36
Employment in the uniformed public services

Introduction

We've all seen the TV programmes showing our uniformed public service workers in action, often involving spectacular car chases, emergency rescues, daring military actions etc. – but does this show the real picture? If you are considering a career in the uniformed public services you will need to find out as much as you can about this service so that you can then decide if this is what you want to do as a career. You could also find out about other uniformed services which you were previously not aware of.

This unit is a Level 2 unit, but if you have not studied this at Level 2 it is recommended that you study the unit at Level 3.

The unit aims to give you an overview of several different uniformed services in order to help you to make your career choice, and you can then carry out your own research to study some of these in more detail. You will learn about the different jobs that exist within the services, what would be expected of you if you were to join, and what you would receive in return.

Figure 36.1 Royal Marines in action

Learning outcomes:

1. Know the main roles of different uniformed public services.

2. Understand the main responsibilities of different uniformed public services.

3. Understand the different employment opportunities available in the uniformed public services.

4. Know the conditions of service for different public service jobs.

36.1 Purpose, roles and responsibilities of different uniformed public services

What is a public service?

> **Key term**
>
> Statutory – required by law

A public service is a non-profit-making organisation which has been set up to protect or help people. Most public services are funded by the government, using money paid in tax by members of the public. These public services are classed as '**statutory**' services, which means they are required to exist by law. Non-statutory services are those services which are not required by law and which are usually self-funded, such as charities. Both statutory and non-statutory services can either be uniformed or non-uniformed, which can be confusing!

The main uniformed public services are:

- Police Service
- Ambulance Service
- Fire Service
- British Army
- Royal Air Force
- Royal Navy
- Royal Marines
- UK Border Agency
- HM Revenue & Customs
- Mountain/Cave Rescue
- Coastguard
- Prison Service
- National Health Service.

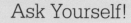

> **Ask Yourself!**
>
> **Which of the services listed above are statutory and which are non-statutory?**

Every uniformed public service has a main purpose, and several roles and responsibilities.

Purpose

The **purpose of a public service** is the overall aim of the service. For statutory public services, this is laid down in law. All public services will have a main aim or purpose, which is often laid down as a '**mission statement**' or 'vision'.

Roles

The **role of a public service** is what it actually does. Most of the public services perform more than one role. For instance, you may think the main role of the fire service is to put out fires, but there are many other roles within the fire service. These include the prevention of fires, educating people about how to avoid fires, visiting schools and colleges to talk about fire safety, inspecting premises, gathering evidence for court. Similarly, the armed forces are trained to fight when necessary, but they also provide an important peace-keeping role, and can also be called on to perform other duties such as refuse collection and fire fighting in the event of industrial disputes.

> **Key terms**
>
> Mission statement – a statement that sets out the overall aims of a service
> Purpose of a public service – the overall aim of the service, which is laid down by law
> Role of a public service – what it actually does

Responsibilities

The **responsibilities of a public service** are to carry out its duties fairly, effectively and efficiently. Public services are mainly paid for by the public, through taxation, including income tax, VAT and local council taxes. This gives certain responsibilities and makes the services **accountable to** others, who need to know that they are getting good value for their money. This means that they need to keep written records of everything they do, for other people to inspect. The uniformed public services have to show accountability in three ways:

- Legally, which means strictly following the laws which govern them.
- Professionally, which means doing the job in a fair, efficient and conscientious manner.
- Politically, which means they should abide by policies set by national or local government or local government, whichever political party is in power.

Key terms

Accountable to – answerable to, responsible to

Responsibilities of a public service – to carry out their duties fairly, effectively and efficiently

Public services are governed by councils or committees that will monitor their performance to ensure that they are giving good value for money. There are other groups who also keep an eye on the services and how they are performing. These include the Commission for Racial Equality, Members of Parliament and pressure groups such as Greenpeace. It is important to remember, however, that the public services are responsible to society, generally, and are monitored closely by central government and local government, who set performance targets and ensure that the services meet their responsibilities and spend public money wisely.

Performance indicators

The government requires all uniformed public services to set and achieve targets. Statutory Performance Indicators are a measure of how a service is performing against these targets. Policing targets could be set to reduce crime; Fire Service targets could be to measure emergency response times. There are also statistics for each service which measure sickness and absenteeism.

Activity

In 2003 the House of Commons Public Administration Select Committee called on the Government to move quickly to rationalise the number of performance targets in health, education and other public services.

Go online to www.parliament.uk/ parliamentary_committees/public_ administration_select_committee/pasc_ pn_16.cfm and look at the document.

What does it say about performance targets?

Table 36.1 Example of performance indicator data

Crimes	Previous year	Current year	Local change	Constabulary change
Total reported crimes	7761	6624	Down by 14.7%	Down by 10.5%
Public disorder and assaults	1732	1797	Up by 3.8%	Up by 0%
Criminal damage	1881	1325	Down by 29.6%	Down by 22.1%
Vehicle crime	647	501	Down by 23%	Down by 16.2%
House burglary	255	206	Down by 19.2%	Down by 5%
Incidents				
Rowdy and inconsiderate	3240	2099	Down by 35.2%	Down by 23.7%

Detection detail	Local detection rate	Constabulary detection rate
Total reported crimes	27.01%	26.38%
Public disorder and assaults	41.68%	37.71%
Criminal damage	13.81%	13.59%
Vehicle crime	9.18%	6.82%
House burglary	18.93%	18.69%

Source: www.hampshire.police.uk © Crown copyright material is reproduced with the permission of the Controller of HMSO and the Queen's Printer for Scotland

Emergency services

Fire and Rescue Services

Table 36.2 Firefighters at work

Purpose

The Fire and Rescue Services Act 2004 is the Act that governs the Fire and Rescue Services, formerly known as Fire Services. There are 45 Fire and Rescue Services in England and they all have similar aims and purposes, as follows:

● fire fighting
● fire safety
● protecting life and property
● attending road traffic accidents
● other rescues.

Most Fire and Rescue Services will have a mission statement or vision. The London Fire Service is the largest fire service in the UK, and the vision is to be 'an increasingly efficient, effective and flexible fire and rescue service in London – which is ever responsive to the increasing wide range of emergencies we need to respond to' (www.london-fire.gov.uk).

Activity

Find three other mission statements from the Fire and Rescue Services and compare them.

Roles

The Fire and Rescue Services carry out the following roles:

- putting out fires
- rescuing people from road traffic accidents
- preventing fires
- flood rescue
- investigating fires
- decontamination training

Assignment tip

Uniformed services can be split into emergency services (Fire, Police, Ambulance) and armed services (British Army, Royal Navy/Royal Marines, RAF) and other services such as the Prison Service and the UK Border Agency. Sometimes your assignment task will ask you to describe 'contrasting services'. This means choosing two services from different categories.

NB: When using the internet for research, remember to add 'UK' to your search to make sure you find services in the UK.

- inspecting premises for fire regulations
- attending court to give evidence
- fire safety education
- protecting the environment
- animal rescue
- disaster management
- fitting smoke detectors in homes.

Responsibilities

All Fire and Rescue Services have a *professional* responsibility to provide an efficient and effective service to the public. They should ensure that they recruit fairly and that their workforce is as diverse as possible. They are accountable to the taxpayers who help to pay for these services and they should keep records to show that taxpayers' money is being spent wisely and efficiently. They are also accountable to the local authority and central government, which also provide funding and monitor their overall performance.

They also have a *political* responsibility in that they have to abide by the policies of whichever government is in power. Unlike the Police Service, the Fire and Rescue Services can take industrial action, including going on strike. When this happens, the Armed Forces have to be called in to take over their fire-fighting role.

All 45 services also have *legal* responsibilities and have to abide by the laws that govern them. The main piece of law is the Fire and Rescue Services Act 2004.

Ask Yourself!

Do you think that the Fire and Rescue Services should be allowed to go on strike?

Key term

Priorities – most urgent, main concerns

Activity

In groups of three, examine the following article taken from the *Oldham Chronicle* and discuss this. What are your opinions regarding this incident?

Yobs attack fire crews with concrete slab

FIREFIGHTERS came under attack on Sunday night after hoax callers ambushed two crews.

Officers from Chadderton Fire Station were called to the Ancora Pub, Broadway, at 11.10pm. Reports of a fire in the kitchen were false but the crews came under attack from youths. Rocks and stones were launched and one youth threw a concrete slab. Watch manager Paul Brunt said: 'The hoax call was made from a phone box and was quite specific. 'Two appliances turned out and came under attack as we were heading back to the station. 'One of the youths picked up a parasol weight and launched it at the first vehicle. He then ran out into the road, picked up the weight again and threw it again. 'The other four youths were shouting abuse.' None of the nine crew members was injured. Officers used CCTV cameras to zoom in on the offenders' faces and the footage has been passed to Greater Manchester Police. Watch Commander Brunt said: 'This was malicious and premeditated. Although only the ladders were hit, the intent to cause damage was still there and

we were under attack. 'All the youths were aged 17 to 18, about 5ft 10in and wearing black clothes with hoods up. 'It highlights the danger we face from areas you don't expect. Hopefully, CCTV cameras on the appliance will be fruitful in getting a conviction.'

Source : www.oldham-chronicle.co.uk

g Grading Tip!

Grading tips if your chosen service is the Fire Service

To upgrade to M1, when talking about the responsibilities of the fire service you could search on the internet and find the performance reports of two different Fire and Rescue Services. You will find facts and figures for each service. You can then compare and contrast the two services.

When talking about the roles, you should explain in detail the different roles of the service and give examples. For instance, instead of just saying that one of the roles is educating the community about fire safety, you should explain how they do this, i.e. by going into schools and colleges, old people's homes, hospitals etc.

Fire inspections of public premises involve annual visits from the service to check that all fire procedures and equipment are adequate in case of a fire. If systems or equipment are not satisfactory, the building can be closed down by the service.

- protect, help and reassure the community
- be seen to do all this with integrity, commonsense and sound judgement.

Most police services have a mission statement which sets out how they will do the above and what that particular service sees as its own priorities, which may differ from area to area. The vision of the Greater Manchester Police service is shown in Figure 36.3 on page 300.

Police

Purpose

The Police and Criminal Evidence Act 1984 is a law that governs police powers; the Police Reform Act 2002 was brought in to make the police more efficient and cost-effective and to give powers to community support officers. In recent years the police, along with other public services, have become more accountable and answerable to the public who provide funding to pay for such services.

There are 43 police services in England and Wales, and the purpose of all of them is to:

- uphold the law fairly and firmly
- prevent crime
- pursue and bring to justice those who break the law
- keep the Queen's Peace

Roles

When we talk about the roles of the police we are talking about the work that they do and services that they provide. Listed below are just some of the roles – there are others:

- responding to emergencies
- reducing the fear of crime
- crime prevention
- improving community relations
- crime investigation
- escorting abnormal loads
- paperwork
- licensing of pubs and clubs
- anti-terrorism
- providing government statistics
- giving evidence in court
- missing persons
- visiting schools
- community safety
- drug raids
- firearms licensing.

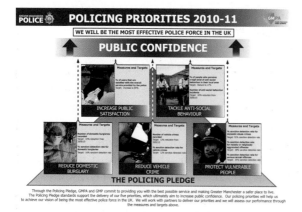

Figure 36.3 The policing priorities of the Greater Manchester Police Service

which investigates complaints against the police. The police are banned, by an Act of Parliament, from striking or taking other industrial action.

The government has now introduced a new national 'Policing Pledge', which demonstrates how the police are accountable to the public. It's a new set of promises from the police on the service they should provide, and every force has committed to keeping those promises. The police promise to listen to your concerns, act on these concerns, and then keep you informed of the progress they've made. Each neighbourhood will have locally agreed priorities, as agreed by the community.

Every police service is judged on its performance by the government (Home Office) and by local police authorities. Each service is assessed on seven areas of performance which are set by the government. These seven areas are:

1. Tackling crime
2. Serious crime and public protection
3. Protecting vulnerable people
4. Satisfaction and fairness

Case Study

A recent complaint against the police involved a serial sex attacker who remained free to continue preying on women because police officers made serious mistakes during their investigations and failed to take victims seriously. An inquiry into the Metropolitan Police found that John Worboys, a black-cab driver, remained at large to drug, rape and sexually assault at least 85 victims, despite numerous women reporting attacks over many years. The Commission upheld complaints against five Metropolitan Police officers, ranked constable, sergeant and inspector, recommending two should be given written warnings and three should receive words of advice. But there were no disciplinary hearings or dismissals.

1. Do you think the police officers should have been dismissed?

5. Implementation of neighbourhood policing
6. Local priorities
7. Resources and efficiency.

Targets are set for each area. You will find the performance targets statistics for each service on its website and you can also view these targets and the statistics for each service in a publication called *Police Performance Assessments* – you will find a copy of this at www.police.homeoffice.gov.uk/publications/performance-and-measurement.

Case Study

G20 Summit, April 2009

The case of Ian Tomlinson has brought not only the issue of police brutality into the spotlight, but also the way the police handle the publicity in its immediate aftermath. In the case of Mr Tomlinson, when briefed, police reported bottle-throwing protestors hindering attempts to save him, but made no reference to the fact that one of their own had shoved Mr Tomlinson to the ground 10 minutes before.

There have been a number of high-profile cases where negative information or rumours have been quickly spread about a victim of heavy-handed police behaviour – often by the police themselves.

Source: www.telegraph.co.uk/finance/financetopics/g20-summit/5126375/G20-death-of-Ian-Tomlinson-brings-police-brutality-into-spotlight.html © Telegraph Media Group Limited

Figure 36.4 Riot police

ⓖ Grading Tip!

For P1 you need to choose *two* contrasting services and describe their main roles and purpose as shown above.

For P2 you should talk about the responsibilities and accountabilities of these *two* services.

For M1 this grade requires a more detailed explanation of the above *two* services, i.e. how and why the services do what they do.

For D1 you need to evaluate the rules, purpose and responsibilities of *one* service. This means looking at how well the service performs its role and responsibilities. You could find statistics to help with this.

Activity

Is your local police service giving good value for money? Go to the Home Office website mentioned above and find out how the service performed last year. Have crime rates in your area fallen? What were the performance rates?

ⓖ Grading Tip!

Grading tips if your chosen service is the Police Service

When upgrading to M1 you could explain in detail the main purpose and roles of the police. What methods do the police use to prevent crime? What things do they do to make communities safer? How do they improve public confidence? How much time do police officers spend on completing paperwork. Look on the different police websites and find out what the priorities and objectives of each constabulary are. How do they compare? Do they give good value for money? Find statistics on performance targets and compare these. Refer to case studies such as the G20 Summit and the Jean Charles de Menezes case.

To achieve the D1 grade you should focus on *one* service and provide some evaluation on it. When writing about the police you could look at the Macpherson Report into the Stephen Lawrence case and discuss the implications of this. Explain if and how the police have changed their policies and practices since publication of the report. When examining performance targets, you could discuss the implications of police having targets to meet. Should there be more police officers on the beat? Should their time be spent completing paperwork? What do you think about the role of Police Community Support Officers?

Armed services

The Ministry of Defence (MOD) is the headquarters of the British Armed Forces, i.e. the British Army, the Royal Navy (including the Royal Marines) and the Royal Air Force.

Purpose

The MOD has an overall vision which applies to all the armed forces, and each service will usually have its own mission statement which says how they will carry out the MOD vision. The MOD vision is achieved over land (the Army), in the air (the Royal Air Force) and on the sea (the Royal Navy), but all three services frequently work together to achieve their aims.

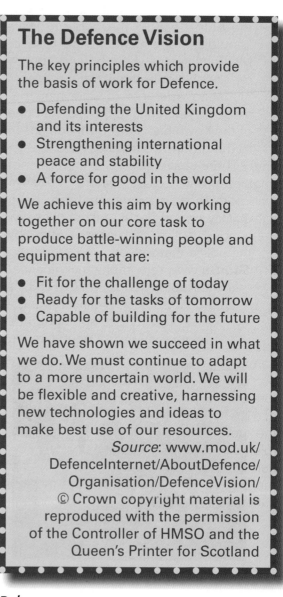

The Defence Vision

The key principles which provide the basis of work for Defence.

- Defending the United Kingdom and its interests
- Strengthening international peace and stability
- A force for good in the world

We achieve this aim by working together on our core task to produce battle-winning people and equipment that are:

- Fit for the challenge of today
- Ready for the tasks of tomorrow
- Capable of building for the future

We have shown we succeed in what we do. We must continue to adapt to a more uncertain world. We will be flexible and creative, harnessing new technologies and ideas to make best use of our resources.

Source: www.mod.uk/ DefenceInternet/AboutDefence/ Organisation/DefenceVision/ © Crown copyright material is reproduced with the permission of the Controller of HMSO and the Queen's Printer for Scotland

Roles

The main roles of the armed forces are to defend our country. This could be by acting as a deterrent because other countries can see that we have a strong army, navy and airforce. It could also mean fighting for our country, if necessary. Under systems of joint command, where all the armed services are involved together in an operation, the roles of each service are very similar.

Currently, our services are fighting a group called the Taliban in Afghanistan. They also carry out peace-keeping activities to prevent fighting in certain countries where there is a risk of unrest.

The British armed forces carry out humanitarian work after major disasters such as earthquakes or floods. British forces carried out relief and reconstruction work after the 2004 tsunami and the 2010 earthquake in Haiti.

The British Royal Electrical and Mechanical Engineers were also involved in building a road bridge and a temporary train station after floods cut off the area of Ambleside in the Lake District in 2009.

British Army

You will be aware that British soldiers are currently fighting the Taliban in Helmand Province in southern Afghanistan. Groups such as the Taliban are known as 'insurgents', as these are not foreign governments but are groups who are fighting friendly foreign governments. British troops are part of a NATO-led multinational force supporting the government of Hamid Karzai. Other roles also include peace-keeping, providing humanitarian aid, enforcing anti-terrorism measures and helping to combat the international drugs trade.

Purpose

The main purposes of the Army are the same as those of other armed services:

- To defend the UK and its interests.
- To strengthen international peace and stability.
- To be a force for good in the world.

Roles

There are many different regiments and divisions in the Army and they all carry out different roles in order to achieve the main purposes of the service, as shown above. Table 36.1 lists some of the main divisions and their roles.

Responsibilities

The Army has a legal responsibility to comply with the laws which govern the service. These are the Army Act 1955 and the Armed Forces Act 2001. They also have the same professional and political responsibilities as other uniformed services, described earlier.

Activity

There have been many discussions recently about whether our Armed Forces have been provided with adequate equipment to enable them to carry out their duties. Find and read a recent newspaper article about this.

Table 36.1 Army divisions and their roles

Army division	Role
Royal Regiment of Artillery	Defence of troops, target acquisition and surveillance using weaponry
Royal Corps of Engineers	Construction of camps, building bridges, clearing mines, laying mines
Royal Logistics Corps	Distribution of all equipment and provisions
Royal Electrical and Mechanical Engineers	Equipment maintenance
Royal Army Medical Corps	Medical care of soldiers and families
Army Air Corps	Airborne combat
Household Cavalry	Ceremonial duties and reconnaissance

Royal Navy

The Royal Navy is the oldest of our armed forces and has played a crucial part in times of conflict, both as a fighting force, and also as a means of providing provisions and equipment to the other armed services. Current roles include seizing illegal drugs, disaster relief, supporting British troops in Afghanistan and helping in the fight against world terrorism. The Royal Marines are part of the Royal Navy.

Figure 36.5 A Royal Navy crew

Roles

The main roles of the Royal Navy are:

- Maintenance of the UK Nuclear Deterrent.
- Delivery of the UK Commando force.
- Supplying assets to other forces.
- Patrolling areas which the UK is responsible for.
- Removal of mines.
- Sea exploration, weather research and other science projects.
- Protection of UK and EU fishing sites.

Responsibilities

The Royal Navy has the same professional, legal and political responsibilities as the other armed services. The navy must ensure that it provides an efficient and effective service in a way which is fair and honourable.

Royal Marines

The Royal Marines Commandos are the amphibious infantry of the Royal Navy. This means that they are trained and equipped to operate on land, sea and air. They are recognised as one of the world's most elite fighting forces.

Activity

Carry out research to find out all you can about the Royal Marines.

Purpose

Table 36.2 The eight defence missions of the Royal Navy

Contribute to the security of the UK and its citizens worldwide in peacetime, including providing military aid to civil authorities.	Contribute to the internal and external security of the UK's Overseas Territories, e.g. Bermuda, Gibraltar and the Falklands.
Participate in the Defence Diplomacy initiative through the building of international trust.	Support British interests, influence and standing abroad extending to the support of defence exports.
Participate in Peace Support and Humanitarian Operations.	Provide forces required to counter a strategic attack on NATO.
Maintain capability to mount a response to a regional conflict outside NATO which could adversely affect European Security or UK interests.	Provide forces needed to respond to a regional conflict inside NATO where an ally calls for assistance under Article 5 of the Washington Treaty.

Source: www.royalnavy.mod.uk/role-of-the-royal-navy © Crown copyright material is reproduced with the permission of the Controller of HMSO and the Queen's Printer for Scotland

Grading Tip!

Grading tips if your chosen service is one of the armed services

When upgrading to M1 and writing about any of the armed services, you could talk about the roles which each service is carrying out at the moment. If you are writing about the Army, you could explain the current deployment in Afghanistan and carry out research to find out where else they are currently deployed. You should explain what main role they are carrying out in each deployment. If choosing to write about any of the other armed services, you should carry out similar research to discover what their current deployments and roles are. You will probably find that all the services are involved in the same operations, as they support one another.

To achieve the D1 grade you should evaluate the performance of *one* service. You could carry out research and examine news articles about the war in Afghanistan and discuss the roles of the British Army or the Royal Marines. You could discuss the topic of whether our armed services are properly equipped for such a war. Should the government be spending more money on our armed services?

Other/specialist uniformed services

HM Prison Service

Her Majesty's Prison Service serves the public by keeping in custody those committed to prison by the courts.

Purpose

All 138 prisons in the UK are under the control of central government. The vision of Her Majesty's Prison Service is as follows:

- 'To provide the very best prison services so that we are the provider of choice.
- To work towards this vision by securing the following key objectives:'

Roles/objectives

The main roles or objectives of the Prison Service are:

- Holding prisoners securely.
- Reducing the risk of prisoners re-offending.
- Providing safe and well ordered establishments in which we treat prisoners humanely, decently and lawfully.

Responsibilities

Prisons are regulated to ensure that they are run securely and safely, with the welfare of both prisoners and staff a prime concern. The Prison Service is responsible to central government. Her Majesty's Inspectorate of Prisons is an independent body that inspects prisons and makes recommendations to the Home Secretary. The Prison Service also carries professional and financial responsibilities to ensure that resources are being used effectively and the taxpayer is getting value for money.

 Grading Tip!

Grading tips if your chosen service is the Prison Service

For the M1 grade you should discuss the purpose and main roles of the Prison Service. Are our prisons adequate? Are they achieving their main aims and objectives? How well do they perform? You could carry out research and find case studies to support your discussions.

To upgrade to D1, you could evaluate the use and effectiveness of our prisons. How many offenders re-offend after leaving prison?

Ask Yourself!

The Prison Governors' Association is calling for sentences of less than one year to be scrapped to help the prison overcrowding situation. What is your opinion on this?

The UK Border Agency

This agency is a fairly new agency which was formed when parts of the Border and

Figure 36.6 UK Border Agency Officer

Immigration Agency and parts of the HM Revenue and Customs Agency merged together.

Purpose

'We work to ensure independent scrutiny of the work of the UK Border Agency, delivering confidence and assurance that it is effective and efficient.'

OUR VISION
Our vision is 'to see that the United Kingdom Border Agency delivers fair, consistent and respectful services, continuously driving improvement, so that their operation is thorough and effective'.
Source: www.ukba.homeoffice.gov. uk/ © Crown copyright material is reproduced with the permission of the Controller of HMSO and the Queen's Printer for Scotland

Roles

'The UK Border Agency is responsible for securing the United Kingdom borders and controlling migration in the United Kingdom. We manage border control for the United Kingdom, enforcing immigration and customs regulations. We also consider applications for permission to enter or stay in the United Kingdom, citizenship and asylum.'
Source: www.ukba.homeoffice.gov. uk/ © Crown copyright material is reproduced with the permission of the Controller of HMSO and the Queen's Printer for Scotland

The Agency is responsible for the issuing of visas for entry to this country. It is also responsible for border control, including the checking of passports and customs checks.

The Agency also deals with immigration, including the processing of applications from people seeking asylum in this country.

Responsibilities
The UK Border Agency has a responsibility to be:

- high quality, rigorous and respected
- fair and transparent
- delivery focused
- frank and straightforward
- impartial and objective.

(g) Grading Tip!

Grading tips if your chosen service is the UK Border Agency

To achieve the M1 grade you could explain in detail how the UK Border Agency carries out its main roles. What is involved in border control, immigration control and customs control? You should explain how the Agency deals with applications for citizenship and asylum.

You will find lots of information in recent news articles to help you to upgrade to D1. You could look at government targets for immigration and how these are implemented. You could also look at recent developments and the change to the laws for UK citizenship. You could also refer to case studies on the UK Border Agency website.

36.2 The different employment opportunities available in the uniformed public services

It would not be practical to describe in this book all the individual jobs available in the uniformed public services. You should carry out your own independent research to find out more about the particular jobs which you are interested in. You should:

- Have questions ready to ask of visiting speakers.
- Go on any group visits to a public service.
- Visit your local police/fire/ambulance station and pick up any literature/ information.
- Find out if there are volunteer opportunities available in the service you are interested in.

Below is a small selection of job roles.

Job roles in the British Army

Everyone who joins the Army trains to be a soldier first, but then may train in another specialist area. So, for instance, after completing your initial soldier training you can then choose to train for the career of your choice, as an engineer, a tank driver, chef, electrician, dentist etc.

Listed below are some of the job roles available in the Army. There are many others.

- Chef
- Gunner
- Tank driver
- Musician
- Dentist
- Postal courier

- Clerk
- Logistic specialist
- Mechanic
- Ammunition technician
- Doctor
- Communication systems operator
- Nurse
- Chaplain
- Engineer
- Human resource specialist
- Electrician
- Lawyer
- Plumber
- Medical scientist
- Fire fighter
- Physiotherapist
- Military police
- Optician
- Infantry soldier
- Dental nurse
- Mounted cavalry
- Pharmacist
- Vet.

Activity

Choose three of the job roles listed above, then log on to the Army website and find out as much as you can about these jobs.

Job description

Anyone who is applying for a particular job needs to see the job description for that job. A job description describes the job role and lists the duties that an employee will be required to do.

Job roles in the Police Service

New police recruits will be required to work a probationary two-year period on the beat, after their initial training. After this period they can continue to work as a beat officer or they can choose to specialise – and carry out further training to work in a choice of jobs. These could include working in the Criminal Investigation Department (CID) as a detective, or working in the Road Traffic Department as a traffic officer, or as a dog handler.

There are also many civilian roles in the uniformed services, and the police in particular. Many roles, such as Control-Room Operators and Scenes of Crime Officers, are now carried out by civilian staff. Civilian staff are mainly support staff who are not regular police officers.

Police Constable

A Police Constable may carry out the following tasks in their day-to-day routine:

- foot patrol
- crime prevention
- assisting in emergency incidents
- attending court
- information gathering
- paper work
- visiting schools.

Police Community Support Officer

These officers wear a similar uniform to regular police officers but they are civilian employees and do not have the same powers as regular police officers. They do not have the power to arrest. They carry out similar duties as those above for a police constable.

Police Specials

Specials are police volunteers. Although they are not paid, they wear a similar uniform to regular officers and they do have the same powers as regular police officers, including the power to arrest.

Ask Yourself!

Should Police Community Support Officers have powers to arrest people?

Job roles in the Prison Service

Prison officer

Job description

- To carry out security duties as required, contributing effectively to the safe and secure custody of Prisoners.
- Ensure that all incidents are reported and dealt with effectively, including bullying, assaults, substance misuse and self harm.
- Prepare reports as required in a timely manner.
- Follow set procedures for dealing with Prisoner applications.
- Encourage Prisoners to deal with personal challenges through offending behaviour programmes.
- Complete searching in adherence to local and national policy.
- Encourage Prisoners to follow regime activities.
- Comply with audit requirements.
- Upholding respect for Prisoners, their property, rights and dignity.
- Apply authorised control and restraint procedures where appropriate.
- Ensure Control and Restraint training (C & R) is completed each year as required.
- Complete observation book entries.
- Monitor vulnerable Prisoners appropriately.
- Act as Personal Officer to a group of Prisoners.
- Ensure standards of hygiene and cleanliness are maintained.
- Ensure Suicide and Self Harm processes are complied with.
- Ensure information system for Prisoners is effective.

- Contribute to own development through the Staff Performance & Development Record.
- Ensure all work is carried out to a high professional standard.

Source: http://www.hmprisonservice.gov.uk/careersandjobs/becomingaprisonofficer/prisonofficerjobdescription/ © Crown copyright material is reproduced with the permission of the Controller of HMSO and the Queen's Printer for Scotland

Case Study

Name: John Ward

Job: Prison Officer

People join for different reasons. Some because a family member, relative or close friend was, or is, in the Service. The opportunity of job security, financial and pension entitlements are an influencing additional factor, as is the uniqueness of the work and the obvious challenge that it brings with it. Working as part of a team is another plus.

The challenges are far too many to outline here. A prison is unique in that it holds persons of a highly violent nature; many with serious drug dependency problems, and psychiatric/psychological conditions – all of whom are deemed unruly and unsafe to be left within the general community. The gang culture and organised crime that has so evidently manifested itself in the Ireland of today has to be managed and contained 24 hours a day, every day. The challenge in that is enormous. Working in a prison gives one a unique insight into a life that is completely unknown to most others in society.

Undoubtedly the main and essential attributes are: commonsense; inter-personal skills; observation skills; firm but fair approach to inmates, one's duties and obligations. A level of physical fitness is also essential.

Most officers work from 8am to 8pm. They supervise all aspects of the daily routine: unlocking of cells; provision of all meals; supervision of the allocation and attendance of inmates to their workplaces; court appearances; hospital or other medical treatment; monitoring of gangs; responding to, and dealing with, the many daily acts of violence; transferring of inmates to and from other prisons; and the supervision of visits. This is to name but a few of the tasks involved. Any inmate has a statutory entitlement to meet with the Governor, doctor, chaplain, or Probation Service. In essence our job is to comply with the order of the court: 'to safely keep the person in custody and to cause the order of the court to be carried out'.

Source: www.daycourses.com/careers/g_to_z/careers/public_services/careers.html

Activity

Write down six questions that you would like to ask a visiting speaker, either from the Army or the Police Service. The questions should be related to their job role, and *not* about salary, holidays or pensions, which are part of their conditions of service, and are covered in the next section.

Grading Tip!

For P3, you need to carry out relevant research and provide an outline of the different job opportunities within a selection of uniformed services.

For the P4 grade, you should describe the conditions of service for *two* jobs in contrasting public services.

To upgrade to M2, you need to explain in detail the work of a chosen job in the uniformed services. Talk to visiting speakers or anyone you know who is a member of the uniformed public services and ask them about their daily routine.

36.3 Conditions of service

P4

When we talk about conditions of service, we are talking about things like salary, pensions, security, holidays, sickness benefits, etc. These conditions should always be set out at the very start of employment and are legally binding on both the employee and the employer.

Salary

Salaries vary between the different uniformed public services, and usually rise according to the length of service of an employee. In Table 36.3 you will see the starting salaries of some of the uniformed services. Salaries in the armed forces are often paid in addition to free or low-cost accommodation and include all meals.

Annual leave (or holiday entitlement)

Holiday entitlement varies from service to service and can also rise in accordance with length of service. Members of the armed forces are entitled to 30 days holiday per year. Members of the police and prison services usually receive between 22 and 30 days annual leave, depending on length of service. Members of the armed forces also have other kinds of leave in addition to holidays. For example, if they are being posted abroad they are given ten days' relocation leave to spend at home to make the necessary arrangements.

Sick pay

Members of the armed forces receive normal pay when they are on sick leave. Other uniformed public service workers receive statutory sick pay, as in the private sector.

Retirement age

Members of the public services can retire at an earlier age than workers in the private sector, but some services have raised their retirement age. For example, the retirement age for Fire and Rescue Service workers has risen from 50 years of age with 30 years' service to 60 years of age with 40 years' service.

Table 36.3 Starting salaries of some of the uniformed services

Fire and Rescue	Royal Navy	British Army	Prison Service	Police Service	Paramedic	RAF
£20,896	£16,227	£13,337.24	£17,744	£23,259	£19,683	£16,266

Pension arrangements

Most uniformed public service workers will be entitled to a pension when they retire from the service. Uniformed public service workers can usually retire and draw their pension at a younger age than private sector workers. Public service pensions have always traditionally been considered to be more generous than those in the private sector, but recent changes mean that these may not be as generous as they used to be.

Working hours

Conditions of service should include details of the working hours of employees. Uniformed public services employees usually need to work unsocial hours and shifts in order to provide a 24-hour service, 7 days a week.

Accommodation

Some uniformed public services, i.e. the armed services, provide free or low-cost accommodation for their members. Sometimes an allowance is given to help to pay for accommodation.

Training

All uniformed public services will require new recruits to undergo a period of initial training. The length of training varies from service to service. After completing the initial training period, recruits will often then complete a probationary period, and further training is usually ongoing throughout the length of service.

All new prison officers must complete an eight-week training course at the beginning of an appointment. The course aims to equip you with the necessary knowledge, skills and values needed to become a confident, safe and accountable prison officer.

The course

Week 1

You will complete a formal induction programme at your home establishment.

Weeks 2, 3 and 4

This period combines classroom-based learning, practical training and team-building exercises. Students are assessed throughout to identify progress and development needs, with a written exam to confirm learning at the end of this phase.

Week 5

This important element gives you the opportunity to get to know your colleagues and workplace. Supported by your training manager, you will meet set objectives, some of which are detailed below:

- Meet Healthcare staff to discuss local healthcare issues.
- Under supervision, take part in rub down and full searching.
- Meet the Diversity Officer to discuss local roles and procedures.
- Under supervision, take part in cell searching and Accommodation Fabric Checks.
- Observe the adjudication process.
- Lock and unlock cell doors under supervision.

Weeks 6, 7 and 8

This period consolidates earlier learning and provides new skills and knowledge through realistic prison-based scenarios. Classroom work continues, with more practical assessments including C&R (control and restraint), with a second exam to pass. A graduation ceremony is held on the last Friday morning.

Activity

Carry out research to find the training programme for the service you are interested in. How would you cope with the training?

g) Grading Tip!

For P4 describe the salary, pension, holidays, working hours and other conditions of service for *one* service. This is a straightforward description.

End-of-unit knowledge check

1. Identify three roles of the Police Service.
2. What does 'accountability' mean?
3. What is a mission statement?
4. What is the main role of the Royal Air Force?
5. What are 'conditions of service'?

Grading criteria

In order to pass this unit, the evidence you present for assessment needs to demonstrate that you can meet all the learning outcomes for the unit. The criteria for a pass grade describe the level of achievement required to pass this unit.

To achieve a pass grade the evidence must show that you are able to:	To achieve a merit grade the evidence must show that, in addition to the pass criteria, you are able to:	To achieve a distinction grade the evidence must show that, in addition to the pass and merit criteria, you are able to:
P1 Outline the main purpose and roles of two contrasting uniformed public services [IE2, IE4]		
P2 Discuss the main responsibilities of two contrasting uniformed public services [IE2, IE4]	**M1** Explain the role, purpose and responsibilities of two contrasting uniformed public services	**D1** Evaluate the role, purpose and responsibilities of a chosen uniformed public service
P3 Outline the different employment opportunities available in the uniformed public services	**M2** Explain the work of a chosen job in the uniformed services	
P4 Describe the current conditions of service for two contrasting jobs within uniformed public services		
P5 Carry out voluntary work [EP, SM, TW]		

GLOSSARY

Absolute discharge – means that no further action is taken

Accountable to – answerable to, responsible to

Aerobic fitness – this refers to endurance, or the ability to sustain work for prolonged periods

Aims – the aims of participants in adventurous activities might include recreation, skill development, team development, personal development – personal reasons to improve practical skills and techniques

Anaerobic system – this is the body system that is used to increase non-endurance fitness, such as strength, speed and power

Anarchy – a situation in which there is a total lack of organisation or control

Anti-social behaviour – any aggressive, intimidating or destructive activity that damages or destroys another person's quality of life

Biological theories – relates to the role of genetics and hereditary factors

Briefing – a meeting where relevant information and instructions are given, usually by a senior officer, before any operation or mission

Brief – when a senior officer gives information and instructions to team members, usually before some type of operation

By-election – if you vote by proxy

By proxy – if you vote by proxy you appoint another person to vote on your behalf

Cabinet – the main government body that controls policy and co-ordinates the activities of governmental departments

Citizenship – the state of being a citizen of a particular social, political, or national community

Citizen – a person who lives in, has loyalty to and contributes to a community

Closed question – a question that is often accompanied by a set of answers from which the interviewee must select one

Command and control – the term used for situations where objectives are achieved by the giving and receiving of instructions

Components of fitness – aerobic endurance, strength, flexibility, muscular endurance, power, speed

Conditional discharge – the offender receives no immediate punishment, but may do at a later date

Conformity – behaviour or thought that is socially acceptable or expected

Constitutional reform – a major change to the constitution of a nation or state

Coroner – the person who presides at an inquest

Curriculum vitae – life story

Debrief – when a team gathers together after an operation to review and discuss how things went and what lessons have been learned

Delegate – to give authority, or hand over a task, to someone else

Discipline – (noun) calm, controlled behaviour; order and control; training to ensure proper behaviour

Disclosure – a process in legal proceedings, whereby parties are required to inform others of any relevant documents

Diversity – this word is often used in connection with equal opportunities – it means a variety or mixture

Double jeopardy – a legal principle which prevents someone from being tried for the same crime twice

Either-way offences – can be dealt with in either the Magistrates' or Crown Court

Employability skills – skills that future employers will find valuable

Expedition – an organised journey or voyage; for exploration; for scientific or military purpose

Extrinsic factors – factors which are not directly related to you personally, e.g. training indoors or outdoors, time of training, weather, footwear, clothes

FITT – an acronym for four of the principles of training: frequency, intensity, time and type

Function – the natural action of something; the specific role of each structure

Green paper – a consultation document, to find out if there is sufficient interest in the suggested policy

Harassment – unwanted behaviour or attention that causes harm or distress to the victim

Health-related components of fitness – aerobic endurance, muscular endurance, strength, flexibility and body composition

Hereditary peer – a title conferred on an individual and which, on their death, is passed on to the oldest son

Hierarchical structure – an organisational structure, commonly depicted as a pyramid structure, where the head of the organisation, with the most power, is shown at the top of the pyramid and those with the least power are shown at the bottom of the pyramid

Hierarchy – an organisation or group whose members are arranged in ranks, e.g. in ranks of power and seniority

Homophobic – having an irrational hatred, intolerance and fear or lesbian, gay and bisexual people

Human rights – rights set out under the United Nations Declaration of Human Rights 1948

Hypothesis – a theory or an assumption to be proved or disproved

Indictable offences – trials for this sort of offence take place only in Crown Court

Indigenous population – people originating from the country they live in

Inquest – a hearing to determine the cause of death

Institutionally racist – when there is a 'collective failure of an organisation to provide an appropriate and professional service to people because of their colour, culture of ethnic origin'

Intrinsic factors – factors which are directly related to you personally, e.g. age, diet, health, motivation, self-confidence, level of ability and previous training

Libel – a published false statement damaging to a person's reputation

Life peer – a title conferred on an individual but which is not passed on, and ends with the death of the holder what a political party will do, if they get into power

Lifestyle factors – these include stress, smoking, alcohol, family history, sleep and rest, physical exercise, drugs, diet, personal hygiene, environment

Local authority – local council

Major incident – any emergency that requires special arrangements by one or all of the emergency services

Manifesto – a document that sets out what a political party will do, if they get into power

Mentor – somebody, usually older and more experienced, who advises and guides a younger, less experienced person

Mission statement – a statement that sets out the overall aims of a service

Morality – concerned with the goodness or badness of human behaviour (knowing right from wrong)

Networking – the practice of building up or maintaining informal relationships, especially with people whose friendship could bring business or job opportunities

Norms – standard patterns of behaviour that are considered normal in a society

Obedience – the act or practice of following instructions, complying with rules or regulations, or submitting to somebody's authority

Objectives – the aims of participants in adventurous activities might be environmental, discovery, educational, a journey – the extrinsic factors that will develop and enhance the participant's ability in the activities

Objective – looking at the facts, remaining free from bias

Open question – a question that allows varied responses rather than simply answering 'yes' or 'no'

Operational – this is the part of the operation where the plan is actually implemented

Opinion poll – an examination of the popularity of the major parties at any time, based upon the responses given by a portion of the electorate

Prejudice – an attitude (usually negative) about a group of people

Primary research – original research; information is collected personally by the person undertaking research

Priorities – most urgent, main concerns

Privatisation – changing something from state ownership to private ownership or control

Psychological theories – look at the reasons why people adopt criminal behaviour

Public sector – a part of the state that deals with either the production, delivery and allocation of goods and services by and for the government or its citizens

Purpose of a public service – the overall aim of the service, which is laid down by law

Racism – the theory that one group of people (one race) is superior to another

Referee – someone who is asked to provide a reference and comment on the character or qualifications of another person who is applying for a job

Regulation – an official rule, law or order stating what may or may not be done or how something must be done

Reliability – the method used to obtain information is consistent and can be repeated

Repatriated – when someone is sent back to the country where they are from

Responsibilities of a public service – to carry out their duties fairly, effectively and efficiently

Risk controls – controls that are already in place to prevent a hazard or the risk of the hazard causing harm, for example: trying a less risky option, preventing access or alternative work methods

Role of a public service – what it actually does

Royal Assent – the final stage of an Act becoming law, when it receives official approval from the monarch

Rule – a principle which has been made to guide behaviour or action

Secondary research – the use of information collected by others

Self-discipline – the ability to do what is necessary or sensible without needing to be urged by somebody else

Skill-related components of fitness – speed, power, agility, balance, reaction time and coordination

Skills – practical ability; a craft requiring skill

Skills (sport) – an action or set of actions in sport; the learned ability to perform the right techniques at the right time, effectively, efficiently and consistently.

Slander – a malicious and false statement spoken about a person

Sociological theories – focus on society as the primary cause of crime

SPORT – an acronym for five of the principles of training: specificity, progression, overload, reversibility and tedium

Statutory – required by law

Strategic – planning something in a considered, calculated and deliberate manner to take all the factors involved into account

Structure – the way in which something is constructed; the framework around which things are added

Subjective – looking at things from your own point of view; not being impartial

Summary trial – takes place only in a Magistrates' Court

SWOT analysis – an acronym for Strengths, Weaknesses, Opportunities and Threats

Tactical – the methods used to implement a formulated plan

Tactics – methods used to put strategies into practice in a sport; plan or procedure designed to gain advantage or success

Team sports – skilful physical activity in which individuals come together to take part in meeting a particular challenge

Techniques – methods of achieving a purpose; the manner of execution

Training methods – continuous, interval, circuit, Fartlek, plyometric, weight or resistance and flexibility training

Transphobic – hostile towards transsexual or transgendered people

Treasure trove – property that had been hidden and is discovered when no heirs can be traced

Validity – the method used and information gathered are relevant to the study

White paper – a proposal for the new law, follows on after initial consultation is over

Index